The Meaning of Death
Herman Feifel, Editor

McGraw-Hill Book Company

New York   London   Sydney   Toronto

First McGraw-Hill Paperback Edition, 1965

Library of Congress Catalog Card Number: 59–15049

McGraw-Hill Paperbacks

14151617 MUMU 9
ISBN 07-020347-4

Contributors

ARTHUR M. ADLERSTEIN, Ph.D.
Psychologist, The Neurological Research Center, The Children's Hospital of Philadelphia.

IRVING E. ALEXANDER, Ph.D.
Professor of Psychology, Duke University, Durham, North Carolina.

GERALD J. ARONSON, M.D.
Private practice, Beverly Hills, California; Clinical Instructor, Department of Psychiatry, University of California at Los Angeles.

NORMAN L. FARBEROW, Ph.D.
Co-Director, Suicide Prevention Center, Los Angeles; Associate Clinical Professor of Psychiatry (Psychology), University of Southern California School of Medicine, Los Angeles; Co-principal Investigator, Central Research Unit, Veterans Administration Center, Los Angeles.

HERMAN FEIFEL, Ph.D.
Chief Psychologist, Veterans Administration Outpatient Clinic, Los Angeles; Clinical Professor of Psychiatry (Psychology), University of Southern California School of Medicine, Los Angeles.

CARLA GOTTLIEB, Ph.D.
Professor of Art, Sarah Lawrence College, Bronxville, New York; The New School, New York.

FREDERICK J. HOFFMAN, Ph.D.
Chairman and Professor, Department of English, University of California at Riverside.

ARNOLD A. HUTSCHNECKER, M.D.
Private practice, Internal and Psychosomatic Medicine, New York.

REV. EDGAR N. JACKSON, Ph.D.
Pastor, Mamaroneck Methodist Church, Mamaroneck, New York; Chairman, Advisory Board, Guidance Center of New Rochelle, New York.

CARL G. JUNG, M.D.
Late Professor, Jung Institute for Analytical Psychology, Zürich, Switzerland.

AUGUST M. KASPER, M.D.
Private practice, Beverly Hills, California; Assistant Clinical Professor of Psychiatry, University of Southern California School of Medicine, Los Angeles.

ROBERT KASTENBAUM, Ph.D.
Director of Psychological Research, Cushing Hospital, Framingham, Massachusetts.

WALTER KAUFMANN, Ph.D.
Associate Professor of Philosophy, Princeton University, Princeton, New Jersey.

DAVID G. MANDELBAUM, Ph.D.
Professor of Anthropology, University of California, Berkeley.

HERBERT MARCUSE, Ph.D.
Professor of Politics and Philosophy, Brandeis University, Waltham, Massachusetts.

GARDNER MURPHY, Ph.D.
Director of Research, The Menninger Foundation, Topeka, Kansas.

MARIA H. NAGY, Ph.D.
Clinical Psychologist, Neurological Institute, Columbia Presbyterian Medical Center, New York.

CURT P. RICHTER, Ph.D.
Professor of Psychobiology, Phipps Psychiatric Clinic, Johns Hopkins Medical School, Baltimore.

EDWIN S. SHNEIDMAN, Ph.D.
Chief, Center for Studies of Suicide Prevention, National Institute of Mental Health, Chevy Chase, Maryland.

PAUL TILLICH, D.D.
Late Professor of Religion, The Divinity School, University of Chicago.

CHARLES W. WAHL, M.D.
Associate Professor of Psychiatry, University of California School of Medicine, Los Angeles; attending psychiatrist, Sepulveda Veterans Administration Hospital, Sepulveda.

Preface

Even after looking hard in the literature, it is surprising how slim is the systematized knowledge about death. Far too little heed has been given to assessing thoroughly the implications of the meaning of death. There is no book on the American scene which offers a multi-faceted approach to its problems. The purpose of this volume is a first attempt to narrow that gap by coming to grips with the problem of death as seen by philosophers, religionists, and scientists from varying bases.

It is not an organized text but rather a series of spotlights beamed on a common area. The contributors encompass the specific fields of anthropology, art, literature, medicine, philosophy, physiology, psychoanalysis, psychiatry, psychology, and religion. Those who seek an integration of the available information are likely to be disappointed. There is no pretense of providing definitive answers. We do perceive the book, however, as providing a groundwork of reflection and information that will illuminate issues and stimulate fresh insights, suggest therapeutic and practical possibilities, and direct the way toward future research requirements.

This book should prove of value to those concerned with persons facing the prospect of death, engaged in coping with grief and bereavement, interested in aspects of human personality making for adaptive and maladaptive reactions to stress and disaster situations, and persons studying the social scene. Its usefulness may extend beyond the professional worker, since few individuals are likely to escape the experience of losing loved ones by death during their lifetimes.

I want to thank Rascher und Cie A. G. of Switzerland for making it possible for Professor Jung's paper "Seele and Tod," from *Wirklichkeit der Seele* to be brought to the attention of the English-speaking public for the first time, and to R. F. C. Hull for his lucid and faithful translation of the paper. Mr. Hull's translation is soon to appear in volume 8 of Jung's *Collected Works,* "The Structure and Dynamics of the Psyche," Bollingen Series 20, Pantheon Books, Inc., New York.

I also wish to thank the following publishers for permission to reprint, with certain changes in some instances, the articles listed below.

Hoffman, F. J.: "Grace, violence, and self," *Virginia Quarterly Review,* **34:**439–454, 1958.

Nagy, Maria H.: "The child's theories concerning death," *Journal of Genetic Psychology,* **73:**3–27, 1948.

Richter, Curt P.: "The phenomenon of unexplained sudden death in animals and man," in *Physiological Bases of Psychiatry,* W. H. Gantt (ed.), Charles C Thomas, Publisher, Springfield, Ill., 1958.

Wahl, C. W.: "The fear of death," *Bulletin of the Menninger Clinic,* **22:**214–223, 1958.

In addition, permission to use quotations has been gratefully received from the publishers of the following books and journal articles:

Camus, A.: *The Myth of Sisyphus and Other Essays,* J. O'Brien (tr.), Alfred A. Knopf, Inc., New York, 1955.

Cather, Willa: *Death Comes for the Archbishop,* Alfred A. Knopf, Inc., New York, 1950.

Frankl, V. E.: *The Doctor and the Soul,* Alfred A. Knopf, Inc., New York, 1955.

Geertz, C.: "Ritual and social change. A Javanese example," *American Anthropologist,* **59:**32–54, 1957.

Heidegger, M.: *Sein und Zeit: Erste Hälfte,* Max Niemeyer Verlage, Halle, 1927. An English translation is scheduled for publication next year by the Student Christian Movement Press, Ltd., London.

Hocking, W. E.: *The Meaning of Immortality in Human Experience,* Harper & Brothers, New York, 1957.

Inoguchi, R., T. Nakajima, with R. Pineau: *The Divine Wind,* copyright 1958 by the United States Naval Institute, Annapolis, Md.

Kelly, W.: "Cocopa attitudes and practices with respect to death and mourning," *Southwestern Journal of Anthropology,* **5:**151–164, 1949.

Malinowski, B.: *Magic, Science, and Religion and Other Essays,* Free Press, Glencoe, Illinois, 1948.

Menninger, K.: "Dr. Karl's reading notes," *The Menninger Library Journal,* **1:**15, 1956.

Rilke, M. R.: *The Notebooks of Malte Laurids Brigge,* M. D. Herter (tr.), W. W. Norton & Company, Inc., New York, 1949.

Sartre, J. P.: *Being and Nothingness,* Hazel Barnes (tr.), Philosophical Library, Inc., New York, 1956.

Stevens, W.: "Peter Quince at the Clavier," in *The Collected Poems of Wallace Stevens,* Alfred A. Knopf, Inc., New York, 1954.

Tolstoi, L. N.: "The Death of Ivan Ilyitch," in *The Works of Lyof N. Tolstoi,* Charles Scribner's Sons, New York, 1904, vol. 14.

Vallee, F. G.: "Burial and mourning customs in a Hebridian Community," *Journal Royal Anthropological Institute,* **85:**119–130, 1955.

Van Gogh, V.: *The Complete Letters of Vincent Van Gogh,* New York Graphic Society, Greenwich, Connecticut, 1958, vol. 3.

Volkart, E.: "Bereavement and Mental Health," in *Explorations in Social Psychiatry,* A. H. Leighton, J. A. Clausen, and R. N. Wilson (eds.), Basic Books, New York, 1957.

Wertenbaker, Lael T.: *Death of a Man,* Random House, Inc.,
   1957.

Yourcenar, Marguerite, E.: *Memoirs of Hadrian,* Farrar, Straus
   and Cudahy, Inc., New York, 1954.

Finally, I wish to indicate my deep gratitude to the contributors
who, with understanding of the book's true import, labored so
willingly.

Herman Feifel

Contents

Introduction

מי גבר יחיה, ולא יראה מות

"What man shall live and not see death?"

PSALMS 89:49

Dying and death are events that happen to each one of us. We can postpone, gain reprieves, but ultimately we all must die, *hora incerta, mors certa.* And with world events being what they are, life's temporality tends to move even further into the foreground. There is a sardonic Viennese saying, "So many people now die who never died before." Many people react to this state of affairs with the feeling that there is something morbid in paying attention to death. They comment, "I'm interested in life, not death." The seventeenth century French writer and moralist, La Rochefoucauld, epitomized this viewpoint in his remark, "One can no more look steadily at death than at the sun." But, at the same time, we must not overlook the knowledge we have gained about our planet and man by studying that sun. Is it not a form of ostrich adjustment to neglect one of the essential realities of life, a kind of fraud perpetrated on ourselves?

The critical question is not the sham dichotomy of life and death but rather how each one of us relates to the knowledge that death is certain. Throughout man's history, the idea of death has posed the eternal mystery which is the core of our religious and philosophical systems of thought. And it is quite possible that this idea is also the prototype of human anxiety. Insecurity may well be a symbol of death. Any loss may represent total loss. One of man's most distinguishing characteristics, in contrast to other species, is his capacity to grasp the concept of a future—and inevitable death. In chemistry and physics, a "fact" is always determined by events which have preceded it; in human beings, present behavior is dependent not only on the past but even more potently, perhaps, by orientation toward *future* events. When we stop to consider the matter, the notion of the uniqueness and individuality of each one of us gathers full meaning only in realizing that we are finite. And it is in this same encounter with death that each of us discovers his hunger for immortality.

In the presence of death, Western culture, by and large, has tended to run, hide, and seek refuge in group norms and actuarial statistics. The individual face of death has become blurred by embarrassed incuriosity and institutionalization. The shadows have begun to dwarf the substance. Concern about death has been relegated to the tabooed territory heretofore occupied by diseases like tuberculosis and cancer and the topic of sex. We have been compelled, in unhealthy measure, to internalize our thoughts and feelings, fears, and even hopes concerning death. As some of the book's contributors indicate, profound contradictions exist in our thinking about the problem of death. Our tradition assumes that "man is both terminated by death and capable of continuing in some other sense beyond death." Death is viewed on the one hand as a "wall," the ultimate personal disaster, and suicide as the act of a sick mind; on the other, death is regarded as a "doorway," a point in time on the way to eternity.

Part 1, Theoretical Outlooks on Death, deals with the meaning of death and the role it plays in man's life from the positions of psychiatry, religion, and philosophy. Jung stresses the point that the rationalistic view of death tends to isolate man from his psychological self and underlines the need for psychology to digest certain parapsychological findings. Wahl notes the predominantly magical defenses and irrational means we use to cope with the idea of death. He feels that many neurotic symptoms are genetically related to the fear of death. Tillich poses the vital question: "If one is not able to die, is he really able to live?" He then makes a distinction between eternity and an endless future. Kaufmann critically evaluates the existentialist position concerning death and contrasts the attitudes toward death of people like Heidegger, Freud, Tolstoi, Sartre, and Camus. He contends that the individual who has made something of his life can meet death without anxiety. Finally, Marcuse offers the suggestion that if death is regarded as an existential category then life tends to become a means rather than an end. He sees man as not being free as long as death is not brought under his autonomy.

Part 2, Developmental Orientation Toward Death, analyzes the changes in conceptualizing death that develop with age and the varying attitudes held toward death by different segments of the population. Nagy delineates the alterations that occur in the ideas about death found in children aged from three through ten. Kastenbaum reports his investigations on the meaning of time and death for adolescents. He suggests that the way a person integrates the prospect of death into his personality while he is still a youth may have far-reaching implications for that person's mastery of the problems of later life. Feifel describes the attitudes toward death of various groups; among these are the older person, emotionally disturbed individual, and the dying patient. He offers the finding that the dying person wants very much to talk about his feelings and thoughts concerning death but feels that we, the living, close off the avenues for his accomplishing this.

Part 3, Death Concept in Cultural and Religious Fields, illustrates the influence of the death theme in modern literature and art, social implications of the funeral rite, and the management of grief in a religious framework. Hoffmann indicates that the disposition toward death in twentieth century literature is different than in any other. He points out the impact that personal outlook on death has on the writer's choice of image and metaphor and analyzes this utilizing the concepts of grace, violence, and self.

The changing ways in which the artist pictures the idea of death are delineated by Gottlieb. She feels that even though modern art has introduced new motifs in its portrayal, it has tended to minimize the role of death as compared with art of other periods. Mandelbaum states that although the funeral ceremony is personal in focus it is societal in its consequences, and that the rites performed for the dead generally have important effects on the living. He suggests that American culture, in certain respects, has become deritualized with a concomitant lessening of help toward personal reorganization for the mourner. Jackson throws light on the way certain religious practices meet mourning situations and needs at many levels, conscious and unconscious. He also wonders about the sufficiency of existing scientific space-time ideas in measuring experiences related to dying and death.

Part 4, Clinical and Experimental Studies, presents the clinical experiences of a physician and a psychiatrist in treating dying persons, a psychiatrist examining the attitudes toward death of the physician himself, experimental and empirical findings of psychologists working in the fields of religion and suicide, and the data of a physiologist investigating the phenomenon of sudden death. Hutschnecker discusses the diverse personality syndromes seen in patients dying from different diseases, particularly heart disease and cancer. He advances the thought that fear of death may be more present with the living than with the dying. In addition, he points out the importance of a dynamic psychological frame of reference for the physician who is called upon to handle the death threat in his patient. Aronson illustrates how often we can rob the dying person of his sense of individuality and identity because of unenlightened attitudes toward death. He underscores the responsibility that physicians and others have in helping humanize "dehumanizing illness" and offers some suggestions in this respect. Kasper deals with the personal and cultural factors that influence the physician's choice of occupation and his own attitudes toward death. He indicates that the physician's outlook on death is significantly related to the way in which he treats his patients. Alexander and Adlerstein report the finding that death is seemingly a negatively toned affective concept for the religious as well as nonreligious individual. They feel, nevertheless, that taking a definite position in viewing death tends to reduce anxiety and to be therapeutic. Suicide, an increasing social development, is examined by Shneidman and Farberow who attempt a systematic approach to some of its psychological problems. And finally, Richter focuses our attention on the phenomenon of unexplained sudden death in animals and man. His observations suggest, on the physiological level, that excessive stimulation of the vagal system and to a lesser extent of the sympathicoadrenal system plays a major role; on the psychological level, hopelessness, where the future holds no expectation, appears as the dominating factor.

Murphy, our discussant, comments on the papers in the book and highlights his own view about dying and death. He emphasizes the deep contradictions that exist in our culture concerning attitudes toward death, elucidates the nonhomogeneous psychological quality of "fear of death," and asks the challenging question as to whether we properly command all the necessary variables to meaningfully investigate death.

Despite the diversity of disciplines and approaches, and occasional diametrical stands evidenced in the book, three dominant leitmotivs emerge:

1. Denial and avoidance of the countenance of death characterize much of the American outlook. Life is not comprehended truly or lived fully unless the idea of death is grappled with honestly. This has implications not only for the individual but for society as well.

2. It is conceivable that our science-conscious culture, which tends to measure all experience within the bounds of space and time, does not furnish us with all the necessary parameters for investigating and understanding death.

3. There is a pressing need for more reliable information and

systematic, controlled study in the field. This is an area where theoretical formulations have not been lagging behind an accumulating body of descriptive and empirical data. Research on the meaning of death and dying can enhance our understanding of the individual's behavior and yield an additional entryway to an analysis of cultures.

Of course, it is quite possible that the overlapping of certain ideas in the book may emphasize not only the extent and degree of mutual understanding but those of ignorance as well. We will have fulfilled a major aim of the book if it opens up interest and catalyzes organized examination of the field.

Herman Feifel

| CARL G. JUNG

The Soul and Death*

I have often been asked what I believe about death, that unproblematical ending of individual existence. Death is known to us simply as the end. It is the period, often placed before the close of the sentence and followed only by memories or aftereffects in others. For the person concerned, however, the sand has run out of the glass; the rolling stone has come to rest. When death confronts us, life always seems like a downward flow or like a clock that has been wound up and whose eventual "running down" is taken for granted. We are never more convinced of this "running down" than when a human life comes to its end before our eyes, and the question of the meaning and worth of life never becomes more urgent or more agonizing than when we see the final breath leave a body which a moment before was living. How different does the meaning of life seem to us when we see a young person striving for distant goals and shaping the future, and compare this with an incurable invalid, or with an old man who is sinking reluctantly and without strength to resist into the grave! Youth—we should like to think—has purpose, future, meaning, and value, whereas the coming to an end is only a meaningless cessation. If a young man is afraid of the world, of life and the future, then everyone

---

* Translated by R. F. C. Hull from *Wirklichkeit der Seele,* 1934, with permission from Rascher und Cie.A.G., Zürich, Switzerland.

finds it regrettable, senseless, neurotic; he is considered a cowardly shirker. But when an aging person secretly shudders and is even mortally afraid at the thought that his reasonable expectation of life now amounts to only so many years, then we are painfully reminded of certain feelings within our own breast; we look away and turn the conversation to some other topic. The optimism with which we judge the young man fails us here. Naturally we have on hand for every eventuality one or two suitable banalities about life which we occasionally hand out to the other fellow, such as "everyone must die sometime," "one doesn't live forever," etc. But when one is alone and it is night and so dark and still that one hears nothing and sees nothing but the thoughts which add and subtract the years, and the long row of disagreeable facts which remorselessly indicate how far the hand of the clock has moved forward, and the slow, irresistible approach of the wall of darkness which will eventually engulf everything you love, possess, wish, strive, and hope for—then all our profundities about life slink off to some undiscoverable hiding place, and fear envelops the sleepless one like a smothering blanket.

Many young people have at bottom a panic-fear of life (though at the same time they intensely desire it), and an even greater number of the aging have the same fear of death. Yes, I have known those people who most feared life when they were young to suffer later just as much from the fear of death. When they are young, one says they have infantile resistances against the normal demands of life; one should really say the same thing when they are old, for they are likewise afraid of one of life's normal demands. We are so convinced that death is simply the end of a process that it does not ordinarily occur to us to conceive of death as a goal and a fulfillment, as we do without hesitation the aims and purposes of youthful life in its ascendance.

Life is an energy process. Like every energy process, it is in principle irreversible and is therefore unequivocally directed towards a goal. That goal is a state of rest. In the long run everything that happens is, as it were, nothing more than the initial disturbance of a perpetual state of rest which forever attempts to reestablish itself. Life is teleology par excellence; it is the intrinsic striving towards a goal, and the living organism is a system of directed aims which seek to fulfill themselves. The end of every process is its goal. All energy flow is like a runner who strives with the greatest effort and the utmost expenditure of strength to reach his goal. Youthful longing for the world and for life, for the attainment of high hopes and distant goals, is life's obvious teleological urge which at once changes into fear of life, neurotic resistances, depressions and phobias if at some point it remains caught in the past, or shrinks from risks without which the unseen goal cannot be achieved. With the attainment of maturity and at the zenith of biological existence, life's drive towards a goal in no wise halts. With the same intensity and irresistibility with which it strove upward before middle age, life now descends; for the goal no longer lies on the summit, but in the valley where the ascent began. The curve of life is like the parabola of a projectile which, disturbed from its initial state of rest, rises and then returns to a state of repose.

The psychological curve of life, however, refuses to conform to this law of nature. Sometimes the lack of accord begins early in the ascent. The projectile ascends biologically, but psychologically it lags behind. We straggle behind our years, hugging our childhood as if we could not tear ourselves away. We stop the hands of the clock and imagine that time will stand still. When after some delay we finally reach the summit, there again, psychologically, we settle down to rest, and although we can see ourselves sliding down the other side, we cling, if only with longing backward glances, to the peak once attained. Just as, earlier, fear was a deterrent to life, so now it stands in the way of death. We may even admit that fear of life held us back on the upward slope, but just because of this delay we claim all the more right to hold fast to the summit we have now reached. Though it may be obvious

that in spite of all our resistances (now so deeply regretted) life
has reasserted itself, yet we pay no attention and keep on trying
to make it stand still. Our psychology then loses its natural basis.
Consciousness stays up in the air, while the curve of the parabola
sinks downward with ever increasing speed.

Natural life is the nourishing soil of the soul. Anyone who fails
to go along with life remains suspended, stiff and rigid in mid-air.
That is why so many people get wooden in old age; they look
back and cling to the past with a secret fear of death in their
hearts. They withdraw from the life process, at least psychologically, and consequently remain fixed like nostalgic pillars of
salt, with vivid recollections of youth but no living relation to the
present. From the middle of life onward, only he remains vitally
alive who is ready to *die with life*. For in the secret hour of life's
midday the parabola is reversed, death is born. The second half of
life does not signify ascent, unfolding, increase, exuberance, but
death, since the end is its goal. The negation of life's fulfillment
is synonymous with the refusal to accept its ending. Both mean
not wanting to live; not wanting to live is identical with not wanting
to die. Waxing and waning make one curve.

Whenever possible our consciousness refuses to accommodate
itself to this undeniable truth. Ordinarily we cling to our past and
remain stuck in the illusion of youthfulness. Being old is highly
unpopular. Nobody seems to consider that not being able to grow
old is precisely as absurd as not being able to outgrow child-sized
shoes. A still infantile man of thirty is surely to be deplored, but
a youthful septuagenarian—isn't that delightful? And yet both
are perverse, lacking in style, psychological monstrosities. A
young man who does not fight and conquer has missed the best
part of his youth, and an old man who does not know how to
listen to the secrets of the brooks as they tumble down from the
peaks to the valleys makes no sense; he is a spiritual mummy who
is nothing but a rigid relic of the past. He stands apart from life,
mechanically repeating himself to the last triviality.

Our relative longevity, substantiated by present-day statistics, is a product of civilization. It is quite exceptional for primitive people to reach old age. For instance, when I visited the primitive tribes of East Africa I saw very few men with white hair who might have been over sixty. But they were really old, they seemed to have always been old, so fully had they assimilated their age. They were exactly what they were in every respect. We are forever only more or less than we actually are. It is as if our consciousness had somehow slippèd from its natural foundations and no longer quite knew how to get along on nature's timing. It seems as though we are suffering from a *hubris* of consciousness which fools us into believing that one's time of life is a mere illusion which can be altered according to one's desire. (One asks oneself where our consciousness gets its ability to be so contrary to nature and what such arbitrariness might signify.)

Like a projectile flying to its goal, life ends in death. Even its ascent and its zenith are only steps and means to this goal. This paradoxical formula is no more than a logical deduction from the fact that life strives towards a goal and is determined by an aim. I do not believe that I am guilty here of playing with syllogisms. We grant goal and purpose to the ascent of life, why not to the descent? The birth of a human being is pregnant with meaning, why not death? For twenty years and more the growing man is being prepared for the complete unfolding of his individual nature, why should not the older man prepare himself twenty years and more for his death? Of course, with the zenith one has obviously reached something, one is it and has it. But what is attained with death?

At this point, just when it might be expected, I do not want suddenly to pull a belief out of my pocket and invite my reader to do what nobody can do, that is, believe something. I must confess that I myself could never do it either. Therefore I shall certainly not assert now that one must believe death to be a second birth leading to a survival beyond the grave. But I can at

least mention that the *consensus gentium* has decided views about
death, unmistakably expressed in all the great religions of the
world. One might even say that the majority of these religions are
complicated systems of preparation for death, so much so that life,
in agreement with my paradoxical formula, actually has no significance except as a preparation for the ultimate goal of death.
In both the greatest living religions, Christianity and Buddhism,
the meaning of existence is consummated in its end.

Since the age of enlightenment a viewpoint has developed concerning the nature of religion which, although it is a typically
rationalistic misconception, deserves mention because it is so
widely disseminated. According to this view, all religions are
something like philosophical systems, and like them are con-
cocted out of the head. At some time someone is supposed to have
invented a God and sundry dogmas and to have led humanity
around by the nose with this "wish-fulfilling" fantasy. But this
opinion is contradicted by the psychological fact that the head is
a particularly inadequate organ when it comes to thinking up
religious symbols. They do not come from the head at all, but
from some other place, perhaps the heart; certainly from a deep
psychic level very little resembling consciousness, which is always
only the top layer. That is why religious symbols have a distinctly
"revelatory" character; they are usually spontaneous products of
unconscious psychic activity. They are anything rather than
thought up; on the contrary, in the course of the millennia, they
have developed, plant-like, as natural manifestations of the human
psyche. Even today we can see in individuals the spontaneous
genesis of genuine and valid religious symbols, springing from
the unconscious—like flowers of a strange species, while consciousness stands aside perplexed, not knowing what to make of
such creations. It can be ascertained without too much difficulty
that in form and content these individual symbols arise from the
same unconscious mind or "spirit" (or whatever it may be called)
as the great religions of mankind. At all events, experience shows

that religions are in no sense conscious constructions but arise from the natural life of the unconscious psyche and somehow give adequate expression to it. This explains their universal distribution and their enormous influence on humanity throughout a history which would be incomprehensible if religious symbols were not at the very least truths of man's psychological nature.

I know that very many people have difficulties with the word "psychological." To put these critics at ease I should like to add that no one knows what "psyche" is, and one knows just as little how far into nature "psyche" extends. A psychological truth is therefore just as good and respectable a thing as a physical truth, which limits itself to matter as the former does to the psyche.

The *consensus gentium* that expresses itself through religion is, as we saw, in sympathy with my paradoxical formula. Hence it would seem to be more in accord with the collective psyche of humanity to regard death as the fulfillment of life's meaning and as its goal in the truest sense, instead of a mere meaningless cessation. Anyone who cherishes a rationalistic opinion on this score has isolated himself psychologically and stands opposed to his own basic human nature.

This last sentence contains the fundamental truth about all neuroses, for nervous disorders consist primarily in an alienation from one's instincts, a splitting off of consciousness from certain basic facts of the psyche. Hence rationalistic opinions come unexpectedly close to neurotic symptoms. Like these, they consist of distorted thinking which takes the place of psychologically correct thinking. The latter kind of thinking always retains its connection with the heart, with the depths of the psyche, the taproot. For, enlightenment or no enlightenment, consciousness or no consciousness, nature prepares itself for death. If we could observe and register the thoughts of a young person when he has time and leisure for daydreaming, we would discover tha´, aside from a few memory images, his fantasies are mainly concerned with the future. As a matter of fact, most fantasies consist of anticipations.

They are for the most part preparatory acts, or even psychic exercises for dealing with certain future realities. If we could make the same experiment with an aging person—without his knowledge, of course—we would naturally find, owing to his tendency to look backwards, a greater number of memory images than with a younger person, but we would also find a surprisingly large number of anticipations, including those of death. Thoughts of death pile up to an astonishing degree as the years increase. Willy-nilly, the aging person prepares himself for death. That is why I think that nature herself is already preparing for the end. Objectively, it is a matter of indifference what the individual consciousness may think about it. But subjectively it makes an enormous difference whether consciousness keeps step with the psyche, or whether it clings to opinions of which the heart knows nothing. It is just as neurotic in old age not to focus upon the goal of death as it is in youth to repress fantasies which have to do with the future.

In my rather long psychological experience I have observed a great many people whose unconscious psychic activity I was able to follow into the immediate presence of death. As a rule the approaching end was indicated by those symbols which, in normal life also, proclaim changes of psychological condition—rebirth symbols such as changes of locality, journeys, and the like. I have frequently been able to trace back for over a year, in a dream series, the indications of approaching death, even in cases where such thoughts were not prompted by the outward situation. Dying, therefore, has its onset long before actual death. Moreover, this often shows itself in peculiar changes of personality which may precede death by quite a long time. On the whole, I was astonished to see how little ado the unconscious psyche makes of death. It would seem as though death were something relatively unimportant, or perhaps our psyche does bother about what happens to the individual. But it seems that the unconscious is all the more interested in *how* one does; that is, whether the attitude of consciousness is adjusted to dying or not. For example, I once had to treat a woman of sixty-two. She was still hearty, and moderately intelligent. It was not for want of brains that she was unable to understand her dreams. It was unfortunately only too clear that she did not *want* to understand them. Her dreams were very plain, but also very disagreeable. She had got it fixed in her head that she was a faultless mother to her children, but the children did not share this view at all, and the dreams too displayed a conviction very much to the contrary. I was obliged to break off the treatment after some weeks· of fruitless effort because I had to leave for military service (it was during the First World War). In the meantime the patient was smitten with an incurable disease, which after a few months led to a moribund condition which might bring about the end at any moment. Most of the time she was in a sort of delirious or somnambulistic state, in which curious mental condition she spontaneously resumed analytical work. She spoke of her dreams again and acknowledged to herself everything that she had previously denied to me with the greatest vehemence, and a lot more besides. This self-analytic work continued daily for several hours, for about six weeks. At the end of this period she had calmed herself, just like a patient during normal treatment, and then she died.

From this and numerous other experiences of the kind I must conclude that our psyche is at least not indifferent to the dying of the individual. The urge, so often seen in those who are dying, to set to rights whatever is still wrong might point in the same direction.

How these experiments are ultimately to be interpreted is a problem that exceeds the competence of empirical science and goes beyond our intellectual capacities, for in order to reach an ultimate conclusion one must necessarily have had the actual experience of death. This event unfortunately puts the observer in a position that makes it impossible for him to give an objective account of his experiences and of the conclusions resulting from them. Consciousness moves within narrow confines, the brief span of time between its beginning and its end, shortened by about a third by periods of sleep. The life of the body lasts somewhat longer; it always begins earlier, and, very often, it ceases later than consciousness. Beginning and end are unavoidable aspects of all processes. Yet on closer examination it is extremely difficult to see where one process ends and another begins, since events and processes, beginnings and endings, merge into each other and form, strictly speaking, an indivisible continuum. We divide the processes from one another for the sake of discrimination and understanding, knowing full well that at the bottom every division is arbitrary and conventional. This procedure in no way infringes the continuum of the world process, for "beginning" and "end" are primarily necessities of conscious cognition. We may establish with reasonable certainty that an individual consciousness as it relates to ourselves has come to an end. But whether this means that the continuity of the psychic process is interrupted too remains doubtful, since the psyche's attachment to the brain can be affirmed with far less certitude today than it could fifty years ago. Psychology must first digest certain parapsychological facts, which it has hardly begun to do as yet.

The unconscious psyche appears to possess qualities which throw a most peculiar light on its relation to space and time. I am thinking of those spatial and temporal telepathic phenomena which as we know are much easier to ignore than to explain. In this regard science, with a few praiseworthy exceptions, has so far taken the easier path of ignoring them. I must confess, however, that the so-called telepathic faculties of the psyche have caused me considerable headaches, for the catchword "telepathy" is very far from explaining anything. The limitation of consciousness in space and time is such an overwhelming reality that every occasion when this fundamental truth breaks through must rank as an event of the highest theoretical significance, for it would prove that the space-time limitation can be annulled. The annulling factor would then be the psyche, since space-time would attach to it at most as a relative and conditioned quality. Under certain conditions it could even break through the limitations of space and time precisely because of a quality essential to it, that is, its relatively transspatial and transtemporal nature. This possible transcendence of space-time, which it seems to me lies very close at hand, is of such incalculable import that it should spur the spirit of research to the greatest effort. Our present development of consciousness is, however, so backward that in general we still lack the scientific and intellectual equipment for adequately evaluating the facts of telepathy so far as they have bearing on the nature of the psyche. I have referred to this group of phenomena merely in order to point out that the psyche's attachment to the brain, i.e., its space-time limitation, is no longer as self-evident and incontrovertible as we have hitherto been led to believe.

Anyone who has the least knowledge of the parapsychological material which already exists and has been thoroughly verified will know that so-called telepathic phenomena are undeniable facts. An objective and critical survey of the available data would establish that perceptions occur as if in part there were no space, in part no time. Naturally one cannot draw from this the metaphysical conclusion that in the world of things as they are "in themselves" there is neither space nor time, and that the space-time category is therefore a web into which the human mind has woven itself as into a nebulous illusion. Space and time are not only the most immediate and naïvest certainty for us, but are also empirically obvious, since everything observable happens as though it occurred in space and time. In the face of this overwhelming certainty it is understandable that reason has the greatest difficulty in granting validity to the peculiar nature of telepathic phenomena. But anyone who does justice to the facts cannot but admit that their apparent space-timelessness is their most essential quality. In the last analysis our naïve perception and immediate certainty are strictly speaking no more than evidence of a psychological a priori form of perception which simply rules out any other form. The fact that we are totally unable to imagine a form of existence without space and time by no means proves that such an existence is in itself impossible. And therefore, just as we cannot draw, from an appearance of space-timelessness, any absolute conclusion about a space-timeless form of existence, so we are not entitled to conclude from the apparent space-time quality of our perception that there is no form of existence *without* space and time. It is not only permissible to doubt the absolute validity of space-time perception; it is, in view of the available facts, even imperative to do so. The hypothetical possibility that the psyche impinges on a form of existence outside space and time presents a scientific question mark that deserves serious consideration for a long time to come. The ideas and doubts of theoretical physicists in our own day should prompt a cautious mood in psychologists too; for, philosophically considered, what do we mean by the "limitation of space" if not a relativization of the space category? Something similar might easily happen to the category of time (and to that of causality as well).[1] Doubts about these matters are more warranted today than ever before.

The nature of the psyche reaches into obscurities far beyond the scope of our understanding. It contains as many riddles as the universe with its galactic systems, before whose majestic configurations only a mind lacking in imagination is unable to admit its own insufficiency. This extreme uncertainty of human comprehension makes the intellectualistic hubbub not only ridiculous, but also deplorably dull. If, therefore, from the needs of his own heart, or in accordance with the ancient lessons of human wisdom, or out of respect for the psychological fact that "telepathic" perceptions occur, anyone should draw the conclusion that the psyche, in its deepest reaches, participates in a form of existence beyond space

---

[1] Cf. "Synchronicity: An Acausal Connecting Principle," in C. J. Jung and W. Pauli, *The Interpretation of Nature and the Psyche,* Bollingen Series XLVIII, Pantheon Books, Inc., New York, 1955.

and time, and thus partakes of what is inadequately and symbolically described as "eternity"—then critical reason could counter
with no other argument than the *non liquet* of science. Furthermore, he would have the inestimable advantage of agreeing with
a trend of the human psyche which has existed from time im-
memorial and is universal in incidence. Anyone who does not draw
this conclusion, whether from skepticism or rebellion against
tradition, from lack of courage or inadequate psychological experience or thoughtless ignorance, stands very little chance,
statistically, of becoming a pioneer of the mind, but has instead
the indubitable certainty of coming into conflict with the truths of
his blood. Now whether these are in the last resort absolute truths
or not we shall never be able to determine. It suffices that they
are present in us as a "trend," and we know to our cost what it
means to come into unthinking conflict with these truths. It means
the same thing as the conscious denial of the instincts, namely
uprootedness, disorientation, meaninglessness, and whatever else
these symptoms of inferiority may be called. It is one of the most
fatal of those sociological and psychological errors in which our
time is so fruitful that one so often supposes that something
could become entirely different all in a moment; for instance,
that a man can change himself from the ground up, or that some
formula or truth might be found which would represent an entirely new beginning. Any essential change, or even a slight improvement, has always been a miracle. Deviation from the truths
of the blood begets neurotic restlessness, and we have had about
enough of that these days. Restlessness begets meaninglessness,
and the lack of meaning in life is a soul-sickness whose full extent
and full import our age has not as yet begun to comprehend.

2 C. W. WAHL

The Fear of Death*

Physical man, silhouetted against the backdrop of the passing centuries, is largely a static figure. Paleoanthropologists tell us that the physical bodies of our remote ancestors functioned very much like our own, with most of the advantages, defects, and deficiencies which we share today. Social and thinking man, however, is a very different creature from his Cro-Magnon brother. For he has learned with his cleverness to pit his brain rather than his brute strength against the opposing forces of nature, and so it has been by the application of his mental rather than his physical strength that he has made his gradual way from cave to penthouse.

In all this complex progression, no attribute more clearly differentiates present from past man than does this steadily increasing ability of his to alter and control his physical environment. This is truly the hallmark of modern man, and today, more than ever in his history, man is the undisputed master of his physical world. Even miracles in this sphere have become commonplace. In less than a century he has learned not only to move himself rapidly and conveniently from place to place but to move mountains and rivers with equal casualness. He has forced the very atom to his purpose to make for himself

---

* Reprinted (with additions by the author) with permission from *Bulletin of the Menninger Clinic,* **22:** 214–223, 1958.

the means of a more comfortable and easy life. And he has been equally masterful with himself. Physical pain, man's curse for generations, has been largely banished by new and better drugs. Through his knowledge of medicine man has succeeded in wresting for himself an average 36.7 years of extra life. Millions now go from birth to death without ever once experiencing what it is like to endure even so elemental a thing as intense hunger, a state that was a daily torment to our forebears.

This is the age of man and his triumphs, and we have come to accept as a certain and established thing that man can surmount any obstacle and is equal to the solution of any problem which may confront him. Success has become a habit of the species. It is therefore not surprising that we should be so strongly and universally impelled to the belief that there can be no problem that can remain unyielding to our concerted and determined efforts. Understandably this belief is a beguiling one when we have so manifestly succeeded in subverting the very lineaments of nature and of geography, when our successes have been so numerous and our failures so few.

But there is a glaring exception to this paean of man's conquests, one problem where all his assurance, ingenuity, and wit avail him nothing; an area which stands in bold contrast to the rest of nature which is so malleable to his will. I refer, of course, to the phenomenon of death. Here man, with all his cleverness, is powerless. He may postpone death, he may assuage its physical pains, he may rationalize it away or deny its very existence, but escape it he cannot.

Hence, we have the remarkable paradox of an almost universal recourse to magic and irrationality in the handling of this anxiety, in an age and among people who have an otherwise invincible belief in Science and the scientific method.

The extent to which we do this is often not clear to us without deliberate reflection. Consider the lengths to which we go. Firstly, we do not even refer to death as death, but instead employ cumbersome and elaborate euphemisms such as "passed away" or "passed on" or "departed." This has been true at all times and in all cultures. The word "perish" has its origin in the Latin "to pass through," i.e., a denial even in those days of life as terminative and finite. We, ourselves, at immense expense maintain an entire industry whose sole purpose is to shield us from the crasser realities of its presence. We attempt to preserve and prettify the corpse and endeavor to create the illusion in it of momentary sleep. Moreover, the vast majority of us identify ourselves with religious and philosophical systems of belief which asseverate that death is not death at all, but is rather a fictive experience, a brief transition between one more important existence and another. Most of these purport to guarantee the existence of an immortal state and propose to supply in return for credence and adherence to their system a means of avoidance of death and its supposed sequelae. We flee from the reality of our eventual deaths with such purpose and persistence and we employ defenses so patently magical and regressive that these would be ludicrously obvious to us if we should employ them to this degree in any other area of human conflict.

It must be kept in mind, however, that it is not my purpose here either to discourage or condemn these practices and beliefs, but only to describe them; for by their very ubiquity and massive acceptance we are prone not to see their defensive purpose and paradoxical character.

It is clear, however, that in this respect modern man has not advanced very far beyond his primitive ancestors. He shares with his skin-clad forebear the belief that death is a fictive experience and does not truly exist. Furthermore, he maintains this in the face of the absence of any slightest shred of evidence of a type which he prefers to collect for the solution of his other problems. Here he remains obdurately immune to reality testing. But this pell-mell dash of mankind from the central and inescapable fact of existence, viz., its finitude, is not the matter to which it is my intention to address myself here. Rather it is to point out that any heavy reliance upon magical thinking and delusion formation, even when collectively shared, raises problems of emotional sickness and health, for both the individual and society, which are directly germane to the field of psychiatry.

Psychiatry, by the very nature of its field, has always been concerned with the investigation and elucidation of those aspects of human character and symptom formation which the average man is prone to shun. And yet it is a surprising and significant fact that the phenomenon of the fear of death, or anxiety about it (*thanatophobia* as it is called), while certainly no clinical rarity, has almost no description in the psychiatric or psychoanalytic literature. It is conspicuous by its absence. Could this suggest that psychiatrists, no less than other mortal men, have a reluctance to consider or study a problem which is so closely and personally indicative of the contingency of the human estate? Perhaps they, no less than their patients, would seem to confirm de La Rochefoucauld's observation that "One cannot look directly at either the sun or death." It is interesting also to note that anxiety about death, when it is noted in the psychiatric literature, is usually described solely as a derivative and secondary phenomenon, often as a more easily endurable form of "castration fear." There is good clinical evidence that this kind of displacement occurs, as we shall see subsequently. But it also is important to consider if this formulation also subserves in part a defensive need on the part of psychiatrists themselves.

Study of the fear of death and the predominantly magical defenses against it are extremely important. For it is the consistent experience of psychiatry that any defense which enables us to *persistently* escape the perception of any fundamental internal or external reality is psychologically costly. To employ a physical model, this concealment or displacement uses up energy which must be drawn from other sources, leaving us less for the business of living in an unhampered, free, and creative way. There is a merit and an advantage in seeing ourselves, as well as life, clearly and wholly, and the greater economy with which we can employ dereism, delusion, magical thinking, or defense formation in the solution of our problems or the formulation of our beliefs, in general the happier and richer will be our lives. We have yet to determine if the fear of death, because of the realistic and uncontrollable nature of its referent, must remain a solitary exception to this axiom. As yet we do not know because this phenomenon has not been sufficiently studied in order to give us relatively certain answers. But indicative answers, if not certain ones, are available, and it is evident that the fear of death and the irrational methods of its reduction present a paradox which can be investigated by the same methods which the behavioral sciences employ in the study of any other paradoxical aspect of human function or adaptation.

The psychiatrist, when presented with an irrational paradox in human life, turns to many sources for its elucidation. The first of these is in the person of himself and takes the form of a detailed personal psychoanalysis. A second major avenue of exploration is the field of psychopathology, the study of persons evincing neurotic or psychotic behavior. One might wonder how the study of an aberrant mental process can teach us anything of the "normal." Such, however, is indeed the case. For in each instance of mental and emotional illness different aspects of the human psyche are magnified and hypertrophied. Just as the microscopist and histologist use the microscope to magnify cell structure and from many such views piece together a composite picture of the total physical structure, so each psychotherapeutic case throws into bold and magnified relief some different aspect of psychic function. This enables the experienced psychotherapist in time to piece together an accurate composite of the normal psychical structure. He sees the normal man thereby "writ bold," a picture which could not be obtained from the normal person for the very good reason of the proper functioning of his psychical apparatus.

Study of dreams is another avenue into the recondite land of the unconscious mind, and one to which the psychiatrist constantly has recourse. Studies of primitive races and of the "fossil thought" condensed in pictographic languages, such as used by the ancient Egyptians or the Chinese, are still other ways.

But the *via magna* to the study of the unconscious is the study of children. Here in the child we are able to look upon our primordial selves naked of the overburden of years and of the thick layers of repression and acculturation which make us all strangers to the arcane, lost land of our own childhoods. It is the child who holds the secrets, if we can but look, to this ancient riddle of death and of our methods of handling and coping with this fearful eventuality.

It is only recently, however, that we have been able to learn from this source. It was formerly thought that children had little concern with, or fear of, death. Freud, himself, said that to the child death means little more than a departure or journey, and he felt that there was no unconscious correlate to be found for the conscious concept of death. If a fear of death was evidenced, it was expected to appear subsequent to the oedipal period, and was to be explained as a symbolic product of the fear of castration attendant upon the improper resolution of the Oedipus complex. Present-day experience does not altogether support these views. Thanatophobia is a frequently encountered fear in children. One may see it in evidence as early as the third year. Its appearance seems to be contiguous to the development of concept formation and the formation of guilt, both of which greatly antedate the Oedipus complex. It is found to be associated with many different types of intrafamilial stress. The only factors which these seem to have in common is that they all may act as inducers of intense frustration, rage, or anxiety, or may threaten in some way parental loss. Still, many children go through this entire early development with no apparent fear of death. How may we account for this seeming paradox?

To understand the conflict in the child's mind at such a time we must take into consideration two aspects of his developing sense of causality. The first is the innate incapacity of the child of one to four years of age to perceive cause and effect sequences in any complete fashion. He initially is even unable to realize that the fulfillment of his bodily needs are related to and dependent upon the ministration of outsiders. For since the needed satisfactions usually follow his wishes for them, he concludes that there is a causal nexus between the two events and that he omnipotently controls his outside environment by his powerful wishes. He makes, as we would say with an adult, a *post hoc* fallacy. This omnipotence is not invincible but is rather quickly modified as he finds that gratification does not invariably succeed wishes. Nevertheless, a precipitate of this propensity for narcissistic omnipotence appears to persist throughout life in all persons, and, if governed and subdued, has many useful subsequent by-products. One of these is its role in the development of individual feelings of security and adequacy. For by this mechanism and by the mechanism of parental identification the child is able to conceive of himself as a confident and adequate person in the facing of new situations in which he has had no prior experience of successful solution. In other words, part of this confidence is "borrowed" magically from his parents by identification with their adequacy and strength, and another moiety is formed from the residue of his feelings of omnipotence. This development occurs, however, in this form only in the *loved* child. The feeling of benignant omnipotence is almost completely extinguished if the child has been prematurely or excessively exposed to a nonsuccorent environment or when parents have been absent, unloving, or nonnurturent to him.

Hence, the well-loved and nonrejected, nondeprived child is more likely to retain in his unconscious throughout life a quintessence of this infantile omnipotence. It is this proclivity which the average person is able to put to use in the handling of the death anxiety. It enables us to effectively isolate the possibility of eventual death from ourselves. We can then look upon death as did the psalmist David, who said, "A thousand shall fall at thy right hand and ten thousand at thy left, but it shall not come nigh thee." This persistent feeling of personal invulnerability is puissant enough to enable the majority of mankind to remain relatively untroubled in the face of the vast array of facts which should convince them that death is the inevitable end of all men, even themselves.

If, however, our magical feelings of omnipotence are our main defense against death anxiety, it is an ironic paradox to note that it is also this very same factor which is most responsible for its presence. For the characteristic feature of the thought of the child, viz., that his wishes have magical power to influence events, is a double-edged sword. It lends, as we have just seen, a comforting illusion of credence to our wishes for invincibility and immortality, but it also forces the child to take responsibility for his hating, annihilating, and destructive thoughts, which he also regards as magically fulfillable wishes. Not only does he consider his benevolent wishes to be magically fulfilled, but the malevolent ones as well. The child, no less than the savage, is alien to the concept of chance. All motivation is to him personified. And any unseen or unwanted eventuality is conceived of as having been the result of the malignancy of some person or agency. The child reifies or hypostasizes thought. He equates the symbol with the thing symbolized and does not differentiate between objective causation and wishful causation. No child can avoid experiencing in the course of his maturation a considerable amount of frustration, often of a peculiarly severe and painful kind. Of course, this is by no means an undesirable thing. All education is, in effect, frustration-based. It is true, however, that the child's characteristic pristine response to frustration or annoyance is a banishment wish of the frustrating agent or person, or a reversal wish of the frustrating act. Early in his life these wishes become equated with "death wishes" toward frustrating objects. This equation of banishment with death is easily accomplished, since death is not at that

time conceived of as an infinite or permanent state, as the games
of children clearly show us.

In the game "Cowboy and Indians" each side kills the other
off, and then all resurrect to play another game. Death seems to
mean little more than banishment at this time. It is interesting,
also, to note that this theme, violent death and its magical undoing
and reversibility, runs like a leitmotiv through the folk tales and
fairy stories of all generations and cultures. This deep and ubiquitous wish is a classic theme in the literature of children and
should suggest to us the importance and cogency of this matter
to the child. Only later, when the time sense becomes more fully
developed, does the child begin to learn that death is neither
casual nor reversible, and he then becomes frightened and concerned about his death wishes toward his ambivalently loved,
significant persons. He attempts then to suppress these or to undo
them by the use of words, using these much as the primitive does
in the formation of rite and spell. Reflect that the most ancient
and popular of children's prayers, the origin of which is lost in
antiquity, contains a plea against the fear of death ("If I should
die before I wake"). And one of the earliest symptoms manifested
by the thanatophobic child is his obsessive blessing of persons at
the end of this prayer. He will often clearly show his fear that
these persons would surely die if he forgot to mention their names
in benison or failed to repeat this blessing the proper number of
times. These destructive, hating thoughts are doubly frightening,
since the child not only fears the loss of his parents through the
operation of his death wishes, but also, since he reasons by the
Law of Talion (to think a thing is to do that thing: to do a thing
is to ensure an equal and similar punishment to the self), he becomes fearful of his own death. It must be remembered that the
socialization processes for all children are painful and frustrating,
and hence no child escapes forming hostile death wishes towards
his socializers. Therefore, none escape the fear of personal death
in either direct or symbolic form. Repression is usually so immedi-

ate and effective that we rarely see this process in its pristine form. This process is greatly accentuated, however, if the frustrations naturally implicit in socialization are magnified by external circumstances which operate to increase the frequency or intensity of the frustration which the child has had to endure. These circumstances are usually punitive rejection of the child by unloving, vacillating, or capricious parents, strong sibling rivalry, or the actual experience of parental loss by separation or death. The first two strongly induce the formation of death wishes toward the frustrating figures (and Talion-law death fears for the self), and the latter is perceived by the child as proof positive via the *post hoc ergo propter hoc* principle that his thoughts have magical power which can kill and destroy. The individual, therefore, lives in expectation that the same Talion punishment will be visited upon him by a malignant or wrathful divinity or fate. In addition, the child conceives of parental death or separation as a deliberate abandonment of him by the absent parents, a hostile act on their part for which he is, again, responsible, and for which he will have to pay.

In summary, we see that the child's concept of death is not a single thing, but is rather a composite of mutually contradictory paradoxes. Firstly, death is not conceived of as a possibility in relationship to the self; but conversely, if strong adults die, how can the weaker child survive? Secondly, death is never conceived of as resulting from chance or a natural happening. Causation is personified and the child feels guilt subsequent to a death, as though he were the secret slayer. Yet, paradoxically, he simultaneously experiences rage toward the decedent, as though he had been deliberately abandoned by that person. Consciously these contradictory views would be mutually exclusive, but we must remember that in the unconscious these types of paradoxes can endure in juxtaposition without contradiction.

We see, therefore, that death is itself not only a state, but a complex symbol, the significance of which will vary from one person to another and from one culture to another, and is also profoundly dependent upon the nature and the vicissitudes of the developmental process. We also see that death, as a cessation of being, involves aspects of reality inadmissible to the omnipotent and narcissistic self, and for this reason strong defenses are developed against its recognition.

There is a third aspect of the child's interest in causality which serves often to intensify his fear of death. This is concerned with his inability to obtain direct factual data about this problem. Sigmund Freud once described the child's curiosity about the nature of the universe as "the riddle of the Sphinx." He centered his attention upon the child's need to gain meaningful answers to the age-old question "Whence came I?" or in the form in which the child grapples with it, "Where do babies come from?" And he described at great length the extensive personality deformations which result from the repression of the sexual curiosity which ensues as the child discovers from his parents and from his culture the forbidden nature of this tabooed area.

Modern parents, thanks to Freud and to the generation of educators sparked by his genius, are now able, for the most part, to approach the problem of the child's sexuality in a rational and sensible manner, and as a result there has been a steady diminution during the last fifty years of neurotic symptom formations such as conversion hysteria, whose main etiology is massive sexual repression.

I suggest, however, that there is a second half to the riddle of the Sphinx to which we have not addressed ourselves. I refer to the complement of "Whence came I?" viz., "Whither go I?," or in the child's language, "What is it to be dead?" Again, clinical experience abundantly proves that children have insatiable curiosity not only about "where people come from" but also about "where people go to." In his efforts to find an answer to this conundrum he is met today as his questions about sexuality would have been met in the 1890s with evasion and subterfuge. He encounters the same embarrassed prudery and frightened withdrawal which he would have encountered fifty years ago in his efforts to find out about sex. Due to our own gnawing anxieties about death (which the child empathically perceives, just as he perceives parental embarrassment about sex), the average parent is of little help to the child in his search for answers to these pressing and exigent questions. And the answers which are supplied are as straining to his credulity and faith in his parents as were the "stork" and "baby-in-the-basket" stories which were proffered to him three decades ago in response to his sexual questions. We have seen quite clearly the consequences of parental inability to accept or handle the sexual curiosity of children. It has become clear that this curiosity is a complex thing, subsuming not only an interest in the nature and function of the genitals and the purpose and mechanics of the sexual act, but also a deep wonder and concern about the origin of our species and of the self. Contained within this broad area of curiosity is the nuclear question of "Whence came I?" to which the individual addresses himself in an ever-increasing complexity during the whole of his life. This should make us seriously consider if there may not be an equal risk to the rendering taboo of that opposite end of the question posed by the child, viz., the nature and the end of man. The classic adult defense against coping with these anxieties in our children is the assertion, maintained even by professional persons, that children cannot conceive in *any* form of death, and, hence, do not need to be reassured about it. One is reminded again of the certainty of a generation ago that the child *has* no sexual feelings, and hence there cannot be a problem about childhood sexuality. Some excellent research by Sylvia Anthony [1], as well as a wealth of clinical experience, belies this view. My own psychotherapeutic work with children and adults suggests that many of their anxieties, obsessions, and other neurotic symptom formations are genetically related to the fear of death or its symbolic equivalents and that these symptoms are, just as in the sexual repressions, symbolic substitutive attempts to bind this death anxiety. These relationships are particularly clear in the study of the phenomenon of suicide [3].

Are we then justified in relegating this phenomenon of death to the area of tabooed mysticism, as we do with no other phenomenon in modern life?

In parenthesis, let me again cite the earlier analogy of sexual repression, particularly the form in which it appeared fifty years ago. Reflect on the general incredulity and distrust which would have met any statement which advised imparting to children sexual knowledge as a basic part of their learning of the scheme of things. These critics would have been certain that lust and depravity would have inevitably resulted. Experience has belied that fear.

The fear of death, like the fear of sexuality, when deeply repressed is heavily and expensively symbolized. When we fear death intensely and unremittingly, we fear instead, often, some of the unconscious irrational symbolic equivalences of death. Hence, the fear of death is in reality two things: a realistic concern that some day we shall cease to be and, secondly, a variety of other anxieties which parade under the panoply of the death fear, and these are varied in character and scope. Some of these symbolic equivalents are the fear of abandonment and the fear of Talion punishment, but by a very complex mechanism this fear may also be equated with pleasure, with revenge, with immortality, with power, etc. While the state of our knowledge is not such as to allow us to say what death *is* with absolute certainty, it is a great help to know what it is *not*. The child who is strongly dependent upon his significant adults for his security and his conception of himself as a worthy and adequate person is capable, if they meet these needs, of integrating the concept of "not-being" if his parents can do so, and he is solaced by the thought that his demise (and theirs) is yet far away. Spinoza has said that the adult who sees death as a completion of a pattern and who has spent his time, unfettered by fear, in living richly and productively can integrate and accept the thought that his self will one day cease to be.

And in this resolve we have no better example than that given us by the Olympian of our profession, Sigmund Freud. Exploration of the phenomenon of death is not usually done by dying men. Its very propinquity to the old prevents them from forming the necessary detachment which makes scientific investigation possible. Freud is one of the few exceptions to this rule. This old man, who was to live for sixteen years with the daily reality of a malignant cancer, pointed out, while his own sons faced death on the battlefield, in his essay entitled *Thoughts for the Times on War and Death* [2], that it might be well for us to realize more fully the true nature of our attitude toward death, an attitude which we are all too willing to distort and suppress. He said, "To deal frankly with the psychology of death has the merit of taking more into account the true state of affairs and in making life more endurable for us." This may be an austere and Spartan hope, but it is on just such a hope, rather than on the promises of the mystics, that the progress of mankind depends.

REFERENCES

1. Anthony, S.: *The Child's Discovery of Death,* Harcourt, Brace and Company, Inc., New York, 1940.
2. Freud, S.: "Thoughts for the Times on War and Death," *Collected Papers,* Hogarth Press, London, 1925, vol. 4, pp. 288–317.
3. Wahl, C. W.: "Suicide as a Magical Act," *Bull. Menninger Clin.,* **21:** 91–98, 1957.

3 PAUL TILLICH

The Eternal Now

It is our destiny and the destiny of everything in our world that we must come to an end. Every end that we experience in nature and mankind says to us in a loud voice, "You also will come to an end!" It may reveal itself in the farewell to a place where we have lived for a long time, the separation from the fellowship of intimate associates, the death of someone near to us. Or it may become apparent to us in the breakdown of a work which gave meaning to us, the ending of a whole period of life, the approach of old age, or even in the melancholy side of nature visible in the autumn. All this tells us, "You also will come to an end."

Whenever we are shaken by this voice reminding us of our end, we ask anxiously what it means that we have a beginning and an end, that we come from the darkness of the "not yet" and rush ahead towards the darkness of the "no more"? When Augustine asked this question, he began his attempt to answer it with a prayer. And it is right to do so because praying means elevating oneself to the eternal. In fact, there is no other way of judging time than to see it in the light of the eternal. In order to judge something, one must be partly within it, partly out of it. If we were totally within time, we would not be able to elevate ourselves in prayer, meditation, and thought to the eternal. We would be children of time like all other creatures and could not ask the question of the meaning of time. But as men we are aware of the eternal to which we belong and from which we are estranged by the bondage of time.

1

We speak of time in three ways or modes: the past, present, and future. Every child is aware of them, but no wise man has ever penetrated their mystery. We become aware of them when we hear a voice telling us, "You also will come to an end." It is the future which awakens us to the mystery of time. Time runs from the beginning to the end, but our awareness of time goes in the opposite direction. It starts with the anxious anticipation of the end. In the light of the future we see the past and present. So let us first think about our going into the future and toward the end which is the last point that we can anticipate in our future.

The image of the future produces contrasting feelings in man. The expectation of the future gives one a feeling of joy. It is a great thing to have a future in which one can actualize one's possibilities, in which one can experience the abundance of life, in which one can create something new, be it new work, a new living being, a new way of life, or the regeneration of one's own being. Courageously, one goes ahead toward the new, especially in the earlier part of one's life. But this feeling struggles with others: the anxiety about what is hidden in the future, the ambiguity of everything it will bring us, the brevity of its duration which decreases with every year of our lives and becomes less the nearer we come to the unavoidable end, and finally the end itself, with its impenetrable darkness and the threat that one's whole existence in time will be judged as a failure.

How do men react to this image of the future with its hope and threat and inescapable end? Probably most of us react by looking at the immediate future, anticipating it, working for it, hoping for it, and being anxious about it, while cutting off from our awareness the future which is farther away, and above all, by cutting off from our consciousness the end, the last moment of our future. Perhaps we could not live without doing so most of our time. But perhaps we will not be able to die if we *always* do so. And if one is not able to die, is he really able to live?

How do we react if we become aware of the inescapable end contained in our future? Are we able to take it, to take its anxiety into a courage that faces ultimate darkness? Or are we thrown into utter hopelessness? Do we hope against hope, or do we repress our awareness of the end because we cannot stand it? Repressing the consciousness of our end expresses itself in several ways.

Many try to do so by putting the expectation of a long life between now and the end. For them it is decisive that the end be delayed. Even old people who are near the end take this attitude, for they cannot face the fact that the end can no longer be delayed.

Many people realize that this is deception and hope for a continuation of this life after death. They expect an endless future in which they may achieve or possess what has been denied them in this life. This is a prevalent attitude about the future, and also a very simple one. It denies that there *is* an end. It refuses to accept that we are creatures, that we come from the eternal ground of time and return to the eternal ground of time and have received a limited span of time as *our* time. It replaces eternity by endless future.

But endless future is without a final aim, it repeats itself and could well be described as an image of hell. This is not the Christian way of dealing with the end. The Christian message says that the eternal stands above past and future. "I am the alpha and the omega, the beginning and the end."

The Christian message acknowledges that time runs toward an end, and that we move toward the end of that time which is our time. Many people—but not the Bible—speak loosely of the "hereafter" or of the "life after death." Even in our liturgies, eternity is translated by "world without end." But the world, by its very nature, is that which comes to an end. If we want to speak in truth without foolish, wishful thinking, we should speak about the eternal which is neither timelessness nor endless time. The mystery of the future is answered in the eternal of which we may speak in images taken from time. But if we forget that the images are images, we fall into absurdities and self-deceptions. There is no time after time, but there is eternity *above* time.

2

We go toward something that is not yet, and we come from something that is no more. We are what we are by what we come from. We have a beginning as we have an end. There was a time which was not our time. We hear of it from those who are older than we; we read about it in history books; we try to envision the unimaginable billions of years in which we did not exist, nor did anyone who could tell us of them. It is hard for us to imagine our "being-no-more." It is equally difficult to imagine our "being-not-yet." But we usually don't care about our not yet being, about the indefinite time before our birth in which we were not. We think, "*Now* we are; this is *our* time"—and we do not want to lose it. But we are not concerned about what lies before our beginning. We ask about life after death, yet seldom do we ask about our being before birth. But is it possible to do one without the other? The writer of the fourth Gospel does not think so. When he speaks of the eternity of the Christ, he does not only point to His return to eternity, but also to His coming *from* eternity. "Truly, truly, I say to you, before Abraham was, I *am*." The Christ comes from another dimension than that in which the past lies. Those to whom He speaks misunderstand Him because they think of the historical past. They believe that He makes Himself hundreds of years old and they rightly take offense at this absurdity. Yet He does not say "I *was*" before Abraham; but He says "I *am*" before Abraham was. He speaks of his beginning out of eternity. And this is the beginning of everything that is—not the uncounted billions of years but the eternal is the ultimate point in our past.

The mystery of the past from which we come is that it is and is not in every moment of our lives. It is, insofar as we are what the past has made of us. In every cell of our bodies, in every trait of our faces, in every movement of our souls, our past is in the present.

In few periods has there been more knowledge about the continuous working of the past in the present than in ours. We know about the influence of childhood experiences on our characters. We know about the scars left by events in early years. We have rediscovered what the Greek tragedians and the Jewish prophets knew, that the past is present in us, both as a curse and as a blessing. For "past" always means both a curse and a blessing not only for individuals, but for nations and even continents.

History lives from the past, from its heritage. The glory of the European nations is their long, inexhaustibly rich tradition. But the blessings of this tradition are mixed with curses resulting from early splits into separate nations whose bloody struggles filled century after century and brought Europe again and again to the edge of self-destruction. Great are the blessings *this* nation has received in the course of its short history. But from earliest days on, elements have been at work which have been and will remain a curse for many years to come. I could refer, for instance, to racial consciousness, not only within the nation itself, but also in its dealings with races and nations outside its own boundaries. "The American way of life" is a blessing coming from the past; but it is also a curse, threatening the future.

Is there a way of getting rid of these curses which threaten the life of nations and continents, and more and more, of mankind as a whole? Can we banish elements of our past so that they lose their power over the present? In man's individual life this is certainly possible. It has been rightly said that the strength of a person's character is dependent on the quantity of things that he has thrown into the past. In spite of the power his past holds over him, a man can separate himself from it, throw it out of the present into the past in which it is condemned to remain ineffective —at least for a time. It may return and conquer the present and destroy the person, but this is not necessarily so. We are not inescapably victims of our past. We can make the past remain nothing but *past*. The act in which we do this has been called "repentance." Genuine repentance is not the feeling of sorrow about wrong actions, but it is the act of the whole person in which he separates himself from certain elements of his being, discarding them into the past as something that no longer has any power over the present.

Can a nation do the same thing? Can a nation or any other social group have genuine repentance? Can it separate itself from curses of the past? On this possibility rests the hope of a nation. The history of Israel and the history of the Church show that it is possible, and they also show that it is rare and extremely painful. Nobody knows whether it will happen to *this* nation. But we know that its future depends on the way it will deal with its past and whether it can discard into the past elements which are a curse!

In each human life a struggle is going on with the past. Blessings fight with curses. Often we do not recognize what are blessings and what are curses. Today, in the light of the discovery of our unconscious strivings, we are more inclined to see curses than blessings in our individual pasts. The remembrance of our parents, which in the Old Testament is so inseparably connected with their blessings, is now much more connected with the curses they have unconsciously and against their will brought upon us. Many of those who suffer from mental afflictions see their pasts, especially their childhoods, only as sources of curses. We know how often this is true. But we should not forget that we would not be able to live and to face the future if there were not blessings which support us and which come from the same sources as the curses. A pathetic struggle with their past is going on almost without interruption in many men and women in our time. No medical healing can solve *this* conflict, because no medical healing can change the past. Only a blessing which lies above the conflict of blessing and curse can heal; it is the blessing which changes what seems to be unchangeable—the past. It cannot change the facts: what has happened has happened and remains so in all eternity! But the *meaning* of the facts can be changed by the eternal, and the name of this change is the experience of "forgiveness." If the meaning of the past is changed by forgiveness, its influence on the future is also changed. The character of curse is taken away from it. It has become a blessing by the transforming power of forgiveness.

There are not always blessings and curses in the past. There is also emptiness in it. We remember experiences which in the time they happened were filled with a seemingly abundant content. Now we remember them and their abundance has vanished, their ecstasy is gone, their fullness has turned into a void. Pleasures, successes, and vanities have this character. We don't feel them as curses; we don't feel them as blessings. They have been swallowed by the past. They did not contribute to the eternal. Let us ask ourselves how much in our lives does *not* fall under this judgment.

3

The mystery of the future and the mystery of the past are united in the mystery of the present. Our time, the time we have, is the time in which we have "presence." But how can we have "presence"? Is not the present moment gone when we think of it? Is not the present the ever-moving boundary line between past and future? But a moving boundary is not a place to stand upon. If nothing were given to us except the "no more" of the past and the "not yet" of the future, we would not have anything. We

could not speak of the time which is our *time;* we would not have
"presence."

The mystery is that we *have* a present; and even more, that we
have *our* future also because we anticipate it in the present; and
that we have *our* past also because we remember it in the present.
In the present our future and our past are *ours.* But there is no
"present" if we think of the never-ending flux of time. The riddle
of the present is the deepest of all the riddles of time. Again,
there is no answer except from that which comprises all time and
lies beyond it—the eternal. Whenever we say "now" or "today,"
we stop the flux of time for ourselves. We accept the present and
do not care that it is gone in the moment that we accept it. We
live in it and it is renewed for us in every new "present." This is
possible because every moment of time reaches into the eternal.
It is the eternal which stops the flux of time. It is the eternal "now"
which provides for us a temporal "now." But sometimes it breaks
powerfully into our consciousness and gives us the certainty of
the eternal, of a dimension of time which cuts into time and gives
us *our* time.

People who are never aware of this dimension lose the possibility of resting in the present. As the letter to the Hebrews describes it, they never enter into the divine rest. They are held by
the past and cannot separate themselves from it, or they escape
towards the future unable to rest in the present. They have not
entered the eternal rest which stops the flux of time and gives us
the blessing of the present. Perhaps this is the most conspicuous
characteristic of our period, especially in the Western world and
particularly in this country. It lacks the courage to accept "presence" because it has lost the dimension of the eternal.

"I am the beginning and the end." This is said to us who live
in the bondage of time, who have to face the end, who cannot
escape the past, who need a present to stand upon. Each of the
modes of time has its peculiar mystery, each of them gives its
peculiar anxiety. Each of them drives us to an ultimate question.

There is *one* answer to these questions—the eternal. There is *one* power which surpasses the all-consuming power of time—the eternal: He who was and is and is to come, the beginning and the end. He gives us forgiveness for what has passed; He gives us courage for what is to come. He gives us rest in His eternal presence.

4 WALTER KAUFMANN

Existentialism and Death

Existentialism is not a doctrine but a label widely used to lump together the works of several philosophers and writers who are more or less opposed to doctrines but consider a few extreme experiences the best starting point for philosophic thinking. Spearheading the movement, Kierkegaard derided Hegel's system and wrote the books *Fear and Trembling* (1843), *The Concept of Anxiety* (1844), and *The Sickness unto Death,* which is despair (1849). Three-quarters of a century later, Jaspers devoted a central section of his *Psychology of Weltanschauungen* (1919) to extreme situations (*Grenzsituationen*), among which he included guilt and death. But if existentialism is widely associated not merely with extreme experiences in general but above all with death, this is due primarily to Heidegger who discussed death in a crucial 32-page chapter of his influential *Being and Time* (1927). Later, Sartre included a section on death in his *Being and Nothingness* (1943) and criticized Heidegger; and Camus devoted his two would-be philosophic books to suicide (*The Myth of Sisyphus,* 1942) and murder (*The Rebel,* 1951).

It was Heidegger who moved death into the center of discussion. But owing in part to the eccentricity of his approach, the discussion influenced by him has revolved rather more around his terminology than around the

39

phenomena which are frequently referred to but rarely illuminated. A discussion of existentialism and death should therefore begin with Heidegger, and by first giving some attention to his *approach* it may throw critical light on much of existentialism.

1

Heidegger's major work, *Being and Time* [6], begins with a 40-page Introduction that ends with "The Outline of the Treatise." We are told that the projected work has two parts, each of which consists of three long sections. The published work, subtitled "First Half," contains only the first two sections of Part One. The "Second Half" has never appeared.

Of the two sections published, the first bears the title, "The preparatory fundamental analysis of Being-there." "Being-there" (Dasein) is Heidegger's term for human existence, as opposed to that of things and animals. Heidegger's central concern is with "the meaning of Being"; but he finds that this concern itself is "a mode of the Being of some beings" (page 7), namely human beings, and he tries to show in his Introduction that "the meaning of Being" must be explored by way of an analysis of "Being-there." This, he argues, is the only way to break the deadlock in the discussion of Being begun by the Greek philosophers—a deadlock due to the fact that philosophers, at least since Aristotle, have always discussed beings rather than Being.[1] To gain an approach to Being, we must study not things but a mode of Being; and the mode of Being most open to us is our own Being: Being-there. Of this Heidegger proposes to offer a *phenomenological* analysis, and he expressly states his indebtedness to Husserl, the founder of the

---

[1] My suggestion that the distinction between *das Sein* and *das Seiende* be rendered in English by using Being for the former and beings for the latter has Heidegger's enthusiastic approval. His distinction was suggested to him by the Greek philosophers, and he actually found the English "beings" superior to the German *Seiendes* because the English recaptures the Greek plural, *ta onta*. (Cf. my *Existentialism from Dostoevsky to Sartre*, p. 206.)

phenomenological school (especially on page 38). Indeed, *Being and Time* first appeared in Husserl's *Jahrbuch für Philosophie und phänomenologische Forschung*.

It is entirely typical of Heidegger's essentially unphenomenological procedure that he explains "The phenomenological method of inquiry" (paragraph 7) by devoting one subsection to "the concept of the phenomenon" and another to "the concept of the *logos*," each time offering dubious discussions of the etymologies of the Greek words, before he finally comes to the conclusion that the meaning of phenomenology can be formulated: "to allow to see from itself that which shows itself, as it shows itself from itself. (*Das was sich zeigt, so wie es sich von ihm selbst her zeigt, von ihm selbst her sehen lassen*)." And he himself adds: "But this is not saying anything different at all from the maxim cited above: 'To the things themselves!' " This had been Husserl's maxim. Heidegger takes seven pages of dubious arguments, questionable etymologies, and extremely arbitrary and obscure coinages and formulations to say in a bizarre way what not only could be said, but what others before him actually had said, in four words.

In *Being and Time* coinages are the crux of his technique. He calls ". . . the characteristics of Being-there *existentials* (Existenzialien). They must be distinguished sharply from the determinations of the Being of those beings whose Being is not Being-there, the latter being categories" (page 44). "Existentials and categories are the two basic possibilities of characteristics of Being. The beings that correspond to them demand different modes of asking primary questions: beings are either *Who* (existence) or *Which* (Being-at-hand in the widest sense)" (page 45).

It has not been generally noted, if it has been noted at all, that without these quaint locutions the book would not only be much less obscure, and therefore much less fitted for endless discussions in European and South American graduate seminars, but also a fraction of its length—considerably under 100 pages instead of 438. For Heidegger does not introduce coinages to say briefly what would otherwise require lengthy repetitions. On the contrary.

While Kierkegaard had derided professorial manners and concentrated on the most extreme experiences, and Nietzsche wrote of guilt, conscience, and death as if he did not even know of academic airs, Heidegger housebreaks Kierkegaard's and Nietzsche's problems by discussing them in such a style that Hegel and Aquinas seem unacademic by comparison. The following footnote is entirely characteristic: "The auth. may remark that he has repeatedly communicated the analysis of the about-world (*Umwelt*) and, altogether, the 'hermeneutics of the facticity' of Being-there, in his lectures since the wint. semest. 1919/20" (page 72). Husserl is always cited as "E. Husserl" and Kant as "I. Kant" —and his own minions dutifully cite the master as "M. Heidegger."

How Kierkegaard would have loved to comment on Heidegger's occasional "The detailed reasons for the following consideration will be given only in . . . Part II, Section 2"—which never saw the light of day (page 89)! Eleven pages later we read: ". . . only now the here accomplished critique of the Cartesian, and fundamentally still presently accepted, world-ontology can be assured of its philosophic rights. To that end the following must be shown (cf. Part I, Sect. 3)." Alas, this, too, was never published; but after reading the four questions that follow one does not feel any keen regret. Witness the second: "Why is it that inworldly beings take the place of the leaped-over phenomenon by leaping into the picture as the ontological topic?" (That is, why have beings been discussed instead of Being?) Though Heidegger is hardly a poet, his terminology recalls one of Nietzsche's aphorisms [14]: "The poet presents his thoughts festively, on the carriage of rhythm: usually because they could not walk" (page 54).

If all the sentences quoted so far are readily translatable into less baroque language, the following italicized explanation of understanding (page 144) may serve as an example of the many, more opaque pronouncements. (No other well-known philosophic work contains nearly so many italics—or rather their German

equivalent which takes up twice as much space as ordinary type.)
"Understanding is the existential Being of the own Being-able-to-be
of Being-there itself, but such that this Being in itself opens up
the Where-at of Being with itself. (*Verstehen ist das existenziale
Sein des eigenen Seinkönnens des Daseins selbst, so zwar, dass
dieses Sein an ihm selbst das Woran des mit ihm selbst Seins
erschliesst.*)" The sentence following this one reads in full: "The
structure of this existential must now be grasped and expressed
still more sharply." Still more?

Heidegger's discussion of death comes near the beginning of
the second of the two sections he published. To understand it, two
key concepts of the first section should be mentioned briefly: The
first is *Das Man,* one of Heidegger's happier coinages. The German word *man* is the equivalent of the English *one* in such locutions as "one does not do that" or "of course, one must die."
However the German *man* does not have any of the other meanings
of the English word *one.* It is therefore understandable why *Das
Man* has been translated sometimes as "the public" or "the anonymous They," but since Heidegger also makes much of the phrase
Man selbst, which means "oneself," it is preferable to translate
Das Man as "the One." The One is the despot that rules over the
inauthentic Being-there of our everyday lives.

The other notion in the first section of *Being and Time* which
requires mention is the concept of *Angst* to which Kierkegaard had
already devoted a major work. It is sharply distinguished from
fear, which is said to be focused on objects. Kierkegaard's book
has been translated as *The Concept of Dread* [12], but probably
the only way to crystallize the crucial contrast in English is to use
"anxiety." In anxiety we are said not to be afraid of any thing
or object. *"The of-what of anxiety is Being-in-the-world as such."*
"The of-what of anxiety is no in-worldly being." "That that which
is threatening is *nowhere,* is characteristic of the of-what of
anxiety." "In the of-what of anxiety the 'it is nothing and nowhere' stands revealed" (page 186). And on the next page Heideg-

ger repeats, again in italics: *"The of-what of which anxiety feels
anxiety is Being-in-the-world itself."*

This is surely dubious. It is true that human beings occasionally
experience anxiety without being able to say of what they are
afraid, but Heidegger has not shown at all that either in many
or in any of these cases people are afraid of "Being-in-the-world"
—either *"itself"* or *"as such."* Nor has he shown or given reasons
to believe that investigation might not show a man who feels
anxiety without knowing of what he is afraid that he was in fact
afraid of this or that. The fact that some of us sometimes feel a
desperate sense of loneliness and abandonment does not settle such
questions.

There might be different types of anxiety, and one might find
that a sense of guilt and intimations of possibilities that we
associate with guilt play a crucial role in some types. This was
suggested by Kierkegaard, whom Heidegger merely paraphrases
when he says: "Anxiety reveals in Being-there the *Being* for
ownmost Being-able-to-be, i.e., the *Being-free* for the freedom
to choose and grasp our selves. Anxiety confronts Being-there
with its *Being-free* for—(*propensio in*)—the ownmost authenticity
of its Being as a possibility, which it always is already. . . . Anxiety makes single and thus opens up Being-there as *'solus ipse.'* "
(page 188).

"Fear is," according to Heidegger, "inauthentic anxiety which
conceals anxiety from itself" (page 189). "The physiological trig-
gering of anxiety becomes possible only because Being-there feels
anxiety in the ground of its Being" (page 190). A footnote on the
same page begins with the false assertion that "The phenomena
of anxiety and fear . . . have, without exception, never been differentiated" and then ends with the startling understatement: "In
the analysis of the phenomena of anxiety S. Kierkegaard has penetrated relatively farthest. . . ."

In fact, Kierkegaard, for better or for worse, anticipated
Heidegger's distinction and linked anxiety with the concept of

"nothing" [12, page 38]: "What effect does Nothing produce? It begets anxiety. . . . One almost never sees the concept of anxiety dealt with in psychology, and I must therefore call attention to the fact that it is different from fear and similar concepts which refer to something definite, whereas anxiety is the reality of freedom as possibility anterior to possibility." On page 39 Kierkegaard reveals that the linking of anxiety with Nothing was suggested to him at least in part by a Danish idiom. Later (page 53) he mentions that Schelling "often talks about anxiety," and then (page 55) he offers us the epigram: "Anxiety is the dizziness of freedom."

A distinction between fear and anxiety was also made by Freud [5] in his lecture on "Anxiety" in *General Introduction to Psychoanalysis* (1917): "Anxiety refers to the state and ignores the object, while fear directs attention precisely to the object." Freud's distinction, unlike Heidegger's, leaves open the question whether in the case of anxiety, too, there may not be an object after all, even though not, as it were, in focus. The object, of course, need not be a *thing* any more than in fear. It could be an event, for example, or a situation.

Heidegger's discussion of anxiety ends with the claim that anxiety, by making man feel single or, as we might say, completely alone, tears him out of the everyday world, dominated by the anonymous One, "and reveals to him authenticity and inauthenticity as possibilities of his Being. These basic possibilities of Being-there, which is always mine, show themselves in anxiety as in themselves, without being obstructed by any in-worldly beings to which Being-there at first and for the most part clings" (page 191).

2

The second of the six chapters that constitute the second and last section of *Being and Time* bears the title: "The possible Being-whole of Being-there and Being-toward-death (*Das mögliche Ganzsein des Daseins und das Sein zum Tode*)." On page 235 where it begins we find a footnote referring to the preceding, introductory discussion in which we are told about Kierkegaard that "from his 'edifying' discourses one can learn more philosophically than from his theoretical works—excepting his treatise on the concept of anxiety."

At great length, Heidegger argues to establish this conclusion (pages 239 and 253): "Death does reveal itself as a loss, but rather as a loss experienced by the survivors. The suffering of this loss, however, does not furnish an approach to the loss of Being as such which is 'suffered' by the person who died. We do not experience in a genuine sense the dying of the others but are at most always only 'present.' " . . . "The public interpretation of Being-there says, 'one dies,' because in this way everybody else as well as oneself can be deceived into thinking: not, to be sure, just I myself; for this One is *Nobody.* . . . In this way the One brings about a *continual putting at ease about death.*" A footnote on page 254 adds: "L. N. Tolstoi, in his story, *The Death of Ivan Ilyitch,* has presented the phenomenon of the shattering and the collapse of this 'one dies.' "

No doubt, Tolstoi's story was one of the central inspirations of Heidegger's discussion. *The Death of Ivan Ilyitch* [16] is a superb book—with an emphatic moral. It is a sustained attack on society in the form of a story about a member of society whose life is utterly empty, futile, and pointless—but no more so than the lives of all the other members of society who surround him, notably his colleagues and his wife. They all live to no point and tell themselves and each other "one dies" without ever seriously confronting the certainty that they themselves must die. The only appealing person in the book is a poor muzhik who, realizing that he, too, will have to die one day, patiently and lovingly does all he can to help Ivan. In the final pages of the book Ivan becomes aware of the futility of his own life and overcomes it, realizing that his malady is not merely a matter of a diseased kidney or appendix but of leaving behind a pointless life to die. He ceases pretending, and "From that moment began that shriek that did not cease for three days"; but during these three days he learns to care for others, feels sorry for his wife, and, for the first time, loves. Now, "In place of death was light! . . . 'What joy!' " Death had lost its terror.

Heidegger on death is for the most part an unacknowledged commentary on *The Death of Ivan Ilyitch*. "Even 'thinking of death' is publicly considered cowardly fear . . . *The One does not allow the courage for anxiety of death to rise*." Propriety does not permit Ivan to shriek. He must always pretend that he will soon get better. It would be offensive for him to admit that he is dying. But in the end he has the courage to defy propriety and shriek. "The development of such a 'superior' indifference alienates Being-there from its ownmost, unrelated Being-able-to-be" [6, page 254]. It is only when he casts aside his self-deceiving indifference that Ivan returns to himself, to his capacity for love, and leaves behind the self-betrayal of his alienated inauthentic life. "Being-toward-death is essentially anxiety" [6, page 266]— in Tolstoi's story if not elsewhere.

It is no criticism of Tolstoi to note that not all men are like Ivan Ilyitch. I might suppose that I myself am possibly exceptional in frankly living with the vivid certainty that I must die, were it not for the fact that in a recent World War my whole generation— millions of young men—lived with this thought. Many got married, saying to themselves, "I do not have much time left, but I want to live just once, if only for one week or possibly a few months." And Heidegger's generation (he was born in 1889) had the same experience in the First World War. Tolstoi's indictment of an un-Christian, unloving, hypocritical world cannot simply be read as a fair characterization of humanity. Nor is it true that "Being-toward-death is essentially anxiety," and that all illustrations to the contrary can be explained as instances of self-deception and the lack of "courage for anxiety of death."

At this point one begins to wonder whether, under the influence of the First World War, some other thinker did not possibly consider death a little earlier than Heidegger, without basing himself so largely on a single story. Indeed, in 1915, Freud [5] published two essays under the title, *Timely Thoughts on War and Death*. I shall quote from the first two pages of the second essay, which he called "Our Relation to Death." Heidegger did not refer to Freud and did not even list Freud's later discussions of conscience in his footnote bibliography on conscience [6, page 272]. But while Heidegger's discussion of conscience is the worse for ignoring Freud's analyses, Heidegger's pages upon pages about death are in large part long-winded repetitions of what Freud had said briefly at the beginning of his paper [5, pages 332–333]:

. . . The war has disturbed our previous relation to death. This relation was not sincere. If one listened to us, we were, of course, ready to declare that death is the necessary end of all life, that every one of us owed nature his own death and must be prepared to pay this debt— in short, that death is natural, undeniable, and unavoidable. In reality, however, we used to behave as if it were different. We have shown the unmistakable tendency to push death aside, to eliminate it from life. We have tried to keep a deadly silence about death: after all, we even have a proverb to the effect that one thinks about something as one thinks about death. One's own, of course. After all, one's own death is beyond imagining, and whenever we try to imagine it we can see that we really survive as spectators. Thus the dictum could be dared in the psychoanalytic school: At bottom, nobody believes in his own death. Or, and this is the same: In his unconscious, every one of us is convinced of his immortality. As for the death of others, a cultured man will carefully avoid speaking of this possibility if the person fated to die can hear him. Only children ignore this rule. . . . We regularly emphasize the accidental cause of death, the mishap, the disease, the infection, the advanced age, and thus betray our eagerness to demote death from a necessity to a mere accident. Toward the deceased himself we behave in a special way, almost as if we were full of admiration for someone who has accomplished something very difficult. We suspend criticism of him, forgive him any injustice, pronounce the motto, *de mortuis nil nisi bene,* and consider it justified that in the funeral sermon and on the gravestone the most advantageous things are said about him. Consideration for the dead, who no longer need it, we place higher than truth—and, most of us, certainly also higher than consideration for the living.[2]

The simple, unpretentious clarity of these remarks, their un-oracular humanity and humor, and their straight appeal to experience could hardly furnish a more striking contrast to Heidegger's verbiage. It is said sometimes that Heidegger more than anyone else has provoked discussion of phenomena which, in spite of Kierkegaard and Nietzsche, were ignored by the professors and their students. But, in the wake of Heidegger, discussion concentrated not on these phenomena but on his terms and weird locutions. Death, anxiety, conscience, and care became part of the jargon tossed about by thousands, along with Being-there, to-hand-ness, thrown-ness, Being-with, and all the rest. But he did not present definite claims for discussion, not to speak of hypotheses.

His remarks about death culminate in the italicized assertation [6, page 266]: "The running-ahead reveals to Being-there the lost-ness into Oneself and brings it before the possibility . . . of Being itself—itself, however, in the passionate *freedom for death* which has rid itself of the illusions of the One, become factual, certain of itself, and full of anxiety." (The words italicized here are printed in boldface type in the original.) Unquestionably, the acceptance of the fact that I must die (my running-ahead to my death in thought) may forcibly remind me of the limited amount of time at my disposal, of the waste involved in spending it in awe of the anonymous One, and thus become a powerful incentive to make the most of my own Being here and now. But Heidegger's habits of gluing his thoughts to words, or of squeezing thoughts out of words, or of piling up such weird locutions that, as he himself insists, not one of his disciples of the days when he wrote, taught, and talked *Being and Time* seems to have got the point, have not encouraged questions like this one: Is it necessary that the resolute

---

[2] Author's translation.

acceptance of my own death must still be accompanied by a feeling of anxiety, as Heidegger insists?

At this point Heidegger relies too heavily on the Christian writers who have influenced him most: above all, in this case, Kierkegaard and Tolstoi, and perhaps also Jacob Böhme (*Of the Incarnation of Jesus Christ,* part II, chapter 4, section 1, and *Six Theosophic Points,* part I) and Schelling, who claimed in *Die Weltalter* that anxiety is "the basic feeling of every living creature." In Heidegger, Schelling's *Grundempfindung* becomes *Grundbefindlichkeit.*

Consider the letter which President Vargas of Brazil wrote to his people before committing suicide. It ends:

. . . I fought against the looting of Brazil. I fought against the looting of the people. I have fought barebreasted. The hatred, infamy, and calumny did not beat down my spirit. I gave you my life. Now I offer my death. Nothing remains. Serenely I take the first step on the road to eternity and I leave life to enter history.[3]

Or consider this letter, included in *The Divine Wind* [8], which Isao Matsuo, a Japanese flier trained for a suicide mission, wrote to his parents:

. . . Please congratulate me. I have been given a splendid opportunity to die . . . I shall fall like a blossom from a radiant cherry tree . . . How I appreciate this chance to die like a man! . . . Thank you, my parents, for the 23 years during which you have cared for me and inspired me. I hope that my present deed will in some small way repay what you have done for me.

Or consider David Hume's complete lack of anxiety which so annoyed his Christian "friends" who hoped for a deathbed conversion. Or Socrates' calm in the face of death. Or the Stoic sages who, admiring Socrates, committed tranquil suicide when in their nineties. Or the ancient Romans.

Heidegger's talk about anxiety should be read as a document of the German 1920s, when it suddenly became fashionable to

---

[3] *New York Herald Tribune,* August 25, 1955.

admit one was afraid. In Remarque's *All Quiet on the Western Front* (1929) it was obvious that this new honesty was aimed against militarism and of a piece with Arnold Zweig's noting that when ". . . Sergeant Grischa" at the end of Zweig's great novel (1928) is shot, "his bowels discharged excrement." But while it took some courage to disregard propriety and to admit that some men, when confronting death, are scared and that some, when shot, will fill their pants, it remained for Heidegger to blow up observations of this sort into general truths about Being.

He was not quickly refuted with a list of fatal counterinstances because he put things into such outrageous language that reactions to his prose have in the main been of one of four types:

1. One did not read him at all and ignored him, as the majority of mankind did.

2. One read him a little, found him extremely difficult, and took it for granted that the fault was one's own and that, of course, there must be more to his assertions than they seemed to say—especially since he himself says frequently that they are not anthropological but ontological—truths not about man but about Being.

3. One read him, found him difficult, persevered, spent years studying him, and—what else could one do after years of study of that sort?—one became a teacher of philosophy, protecting one's investment by "explaining" Heidegger to students, warding off objections by some such remark as: "There is much that I, too, don't understand as yet, but I shall give my life to trying to understand a little more."

4. This type, now gaining ground among American intellectuals, has not read Heidegger at all but has heard about him and his influence and therefore assumes that there must be a great deal to him.

If there are a few who know his work and don't respect it, this is because most critical readers soon discover that it is not worth their while to go on reading.

3

Sartre has offered one crucial criticism of Heidegger in his own discussion of death in *Being and Nothingness* [15]. Heidegger argues that only the running-ahead to my own death can lead me to my ownmost, authentic Being because *"Dying is something which nobody can do for another. . . .* Dying shows that death is constituted ontologically by always-mineness and existence."* And more in the same vein [6, page 240]. As Sartre points out rightly, this in no way distinguishes dying [15, pages 533 and following]. Nobody can love for me or sleep for me or breathe for me. Every experience, taken as *my* experience, is "something which nobody can do for" me. I can live a lot of my life in the mode of inauthenticity in which it makes no decisive difference that it is I who am doing this or that; but in that mode it makes no difference either whether the bullet hits me or someone else, whether I die first or another. But if I adopt the attitude that it does matter, that it makes all the difference in the world to me, then I can adopt that attitude toward the experience of my loving this particular woman, toward my writing this particular book, toward my seeing, hearing, feeling, or bearing witness, no less than I can adopt it toward death. As Sartre says [15, page 535]: "In short there is no personalizing virtue which is peculiar to *my* death. Quite the contrary, it becomes *my* death only if I place myself already in the perspective of subjectivity."

Sartre goes on to criticize Heidegger's whole conception of "Being-toward-death." Although we may anticipate that we ourselves must die, we never know when we shall die; but it is the timing of one's death that makes all the difference when it comes to the meaning of one's life.

. . . We have, in fact, every chance of dying before we have accomplished our task, or, on the other hand, of outliving it. There is therefore a very slim chance that our death will be presented to us as that of Sophocles was, for example, in the manner of a resolved chord. And if it is only *chance* which decides the character of our death and therefore of our life, then even the death which most resembles the end of a melody cannot be waited for as such; luck by determining it for me removes from it any character as a harmonious end. . . . A death like that of Sophocles will therefore *resemble* a resolved chord but will not *be* one, just as the group of letters formed by the falling of alphabet blocks will perhaps resemble a word but will not be one. Thus this perpetual appearance of chance at the heart of my projects cannot be apprehended as *my* possibility but, on the contrary, as the nihilation of all my possibilities, a nihilation which *itself is no longer a part of my possibilites.* [15, page 537]

. . . Suppose that Balzac had died before *Les Chouans;* he would remain the author of some execrable novels of intrigue. But suddenly the very expectation which this young man was, this expectation of being a great man, loses any kind of meaning; it is neither an obstinate and egotistical blindness nor the true sense of his own value since nothing shall ever decide it. . . . The final value of this conduct remains forever in suspense; or if you prefer, the ensemble (particular kinds of conduct, expectations, values) falls suddenly into the absurd. Thus death is never that which gives life its meanings; it is, on the contrary, that which on principle removes all meaning from life. [15, page 539]

. . . The unique characteristic of a dead life is that it is a life of which the Other makes himself the guardian. [15, page 541]

Suicide is no way out, says Sartre. Its meaning depends on the future. "If I 'misfire,' shall I not judge later that my suicide was cowardice? Will the outcome not show me that other solutions were possible? . . . Suicide is an absurdity which causes my life to be submerged in the absurd" [15, page 540].

Finally, Sartre asks: "In renouncing Heidegger's Being-toward-death, have we abandoned forever the possibility of freely giving to our being a meaning for which we are responsible? Quite the contrary." Sartre repudiates Heidegger's "strict identification of death and finitude" and says:

. . . Human reality would remain finite even if it were immortal, because it *makes* itself finite by choosing itself as human. To be finite,

in fact, is to choose oneself—that is, to make known to oneself what
one is by projecting oneself toward one possibility to the exclusion of
others. The very act of freedom is therefore the assumption and creation of finitude. If I make myself, I make myself finite and hence my
life is unique. [15, page 545]

Sartre has also dealt with human attitudes toward death in
some of his plays and in his story *The Wall,* which is reprinted
and discussed in my *Existentialism from Dostoevsky to Sartre* [9].
But in the present chapter we cannot analyze his often admirable
plays and stories. And before proceeding to an evaluation of the
above ideas, let us first consider Camus.

4

Although Camus' politics were more acceptable to the Nobel
Prize committee and are admittedly more attractive than those of
Sartre, and although perhaps no other writer has ever equaled
Camus' charming pose of decency and honesty and a determina-
tion to be lucid, Henri Peyre is surely right when, in a review of
Camus' books and of several books about him, he charges *The
Myth of Sisyphus* and *The Rebel* with being "not only contradic-
tory, but confused and probably shallow and immature." [4]

With the utmost portentousness, Camus begins the first of his
two philosophic works, *The Myth of Sisyphus* [3, page 21]: "There
is but one truly serious philosophic problem, and that is suicide."
Soon we are told that the world is "absurd." A little later: "I said
that the world is absurd, but I was too hasty. This world in itself
is not reasonable, that is all that can be said. But what is absurd
is the confrontation of this irrational and the wild longing for
clarity whose call echoes in the human heart. The absurd depends
as much on man as on the world." This point could be put more

---

[4] H. Peyre, "Comment on Camus," *Virginia Quart. Rev.,* 34 (4): 623–
629, Autumn 1958. What Peyre says is, to be precise, that Philip Thody,
in *Albert Camus,* "is forced to confess when he comes to those two volumes
that they are not only . . . ."

idiomatically and accurately by saying that the hunger to gain clarity about and to explain all things is really absurd or, to be more precise, quixotic. But Camus prefers to rhapsodize about absurdity, although he says [3, page 40]: "I want to know whether I can live with what I know and with that alone." He speaks of "this absurd logic" (page 31), evidently meaning the special logic of talk about the absurd, as if such talk had any special logic. Then he speaks of the "absurd mind," meaning a believer in the absurdity of the world—or rather of the absurdity, or quixotism, of man's endeavors—as when he says [3, page 35]: "To Chestov reason is useless but there is something beyond reason. To an absurd mind [i.e., Camus] reason is useless and there is nothing beyond reason." The word "useless," too, is used without precision; what is meant is something like "limited" or "not omnipotent." A little later still [3, page 40]: "The absurd . . . does not lead to God. Perhaps this notion will become clearer if I risk this shocking statement: the absurd is sin without God." Without being shocked, one may note the looseness of the style and thinking: no attempt is made to explain what is meant by "sin," and Camus is evidently satisfied that his vague statement, even if it does not succeed in shocking us, is at least evocative. But from a writer who quotes Nietzsche as often as Camus does in this book—and in The Rebel, too—one might expect that he would at least raise the question whether, by not including God in our picture of the world, we don't restore to being its "innocence," as Nietzsche claimed, and leave sin behind.

As far as Kierkegaard, Jaspers, and Chestov are concerned, Camus is surely right that "The theme of the irrational, as it is conceived by the existentials [sic], is reason becoming confused and escaping by negating itself." But when he adds, "The absurd is lucid reason noting its limits," it becomes apparent that all the oracular discussions of absurdity are quite dispensable and that Camus has not added clarification but only confusion to Freud's two-sentence critique of the suggestion that the essence of religion consists in a feeling of absolute dependence: "It is not this feeling that constitutes the essence of religiousness, but only the next step, the reaction to it, which seeks a remedy against this feeling. He who goes no further, he who humbly resigns himself to the insignificant part man plays in the universe, is, on the contrary, irreligious in the truest sense of the word." (*The Future of an Illusion* [5], section 6—written in 1927, fifteen years before *The Myth of Sisyphus*.) The same thought permeates the books of Nietzsche.

Nietzsche, however, had gone on to celebrate "Free Death," especially in the penultimate chapter of Part One of *Zarathustra* [14] and in *The Twilight of the Idols* [14, pages 183 to 186 and 536 to 537]: ". . . usually it is death under the most contemptible conditions, an unfree death, death *not* at the right time, a coward's death. From love of *life,* one should desire a different death: free, conscious, without accident, without ambush." Nietzsche's thought is clear, though he collapsed, but did not die, in his boots, as it were—and his relatives then dragged out his life for another eleven years.

Camus' argument against suicide remains sketchy and unclear [3, pages 54 and following]: "Suicide, like the leap, is acceptance at its extreme. Everything is over and man returns to his essential history. . . . In its way, suicide settles the absurd. It engulfs the absurd in the same death. . . . It is essential to die unreconciled and not of one's own free will. Suicide is a repudiation." Camus wants "defiance." He is really preaching, no less than in his later work, *The Rebel* [4], in which "the rebel" replaces the editorial "we," and exhortations are presented in the form of literally false generalizations. "The rebel does *x*" means "I do *x* and wish you would." In *The Myth of Sisyphus,* Camus hides similarly behind "an absurd mind" and "an absurd logic."

Now suicide is "acceptance," now it is "repudiation." Surely, sometimes it is one and sometimes the other, and occasionally both—acceptance of defeat and repudiation of hope. Nietzsche's

"free death" was meant as an affirmation of sorts, an acceptance
of one's own life and of all the world with it, a festive realization
of fulfillment, coupled with the thought that this life, as lived up
to this point and now consummated, was so acceptable that it did
not stand in need of any further deeds or days but could be gladly
relived over and over in the course of an eternal recurrence of the
same events at gigantic intervals.

The first part of Camus' *Myth of Sisyphus* is ambiguously and
appropriately entitled "An Absurd Reasoning." Portentousness
thickens toward the end: "The absurd enlightens me on this point:
there is no future," [3, page 58]. "Knowing whether or not one
can live *without appeal* is all that interests me" (page 60). "Now,
the conditions of modern life impose on the majority of men the
same quantity of experiences and consequently the same profound
experiences. To be sure, there must also be taken into consideration the individual's spontaneous contribution, the 'given' element
in him. But I cannot judge of that, and let me repeat that my rule
here is to get along with the immediate evidence" (page 61). In
sum: men don't, of course, have the same quantity of experiences,
and least of all the same profound experiences, but in the name
of simple honesty we must pretend they do.

This paraphrase may seem excessively unsympathetic; but consider what Camus himself says on the next page:

. . . Here we have to be over-simple. To two men living the same
number of years, the world always provides the same sum of experiences. It is up to us to be conscious of them. Being aware of one's
life, one's revolt, one's freedom, and to the maximum, is living, and
to the maximum [sic]. Where lucidity dominates, the scale of values
becomes useless. Let's be even more simple. [3, page 62]

Why in heaven's name must we be so "over-simple" and then
"even more simple"? Two men who live the same number of years
do *not* always have the same number of experiences, with the sole
difference that one is more aware of them, while the other is partly
blind. Life is not like a film that rolls by while we either watch or

sleep. Some suffer sicknesses, have visions, love, despair, work, and experience failures and successes; others toil in the unbroken twilight of mute misery, their minds uneducated, chained to deadening routine. Also, Camus overlooks that a man can to some extent involve himself in experiences, that he can seek security or elect to live dangerously, to use Nietzsche's phrase. And finally Camus writes as if experiences were like drops that fall into the bucket of the mind at a steady rate—say, one per second—and as if the sequence made no difference at all; as if seeing *Lear* at the age of one, ten, or thirty were the same.

Let us resume our quotation where we broke off:

. . . Let us say that the sole obstacle, the sole deficiency to be made good, is constituted by premature death. Thus it is that no depth, no emotion, no passion, and no sacrifice could render equal in the eyes of the absurd man (even if he wished it so) a conscious life of forty years and a lucidity spread over sixty years. Madness and death are his irreparables. . . . There will never be any substitute for twenty years of life and experience. . . . The present and the succession of presents before a constantly conscious soul is the ideal of the absurd man. [3, pages 63–64]

Camus is welcome to his absurd man, who is indeed absurd, wishing to imbibe, collect, and hoard experiences, any experiences, as long as they add up to some huge quantity—the more the better. If only he did not deceive himself so utterly about the quality of his own thinking—as when he concludes the second essay of the book by counting himself among those "who think clearly and have ceased to hope." For all that, Camus' *The Stranger* is admirable, and *The Fall,* too, is superior to *The Rebel* and the arguments discussed here. Camus is a fine writer, but not a philosopher.

5

Camus' confusions bring to mind a poem by Hölderlin [7]: *"Nur einen Sommer . . ."* Heidegger has devoted essay after essay to this poet and eventually collected the lot in a book, but has not written about this poem, which is both clearer and better than the ones Heidegger likes—to read his own thoughts into.

> A single summer grant me, great powers, and
> A single autumn for fully ripened song
> That, sated with the sweetness of my
> Playing, my heart may more willingly die.
> The soul that, living, did not attain its divine
> Right cannot repose in the nether world.
> But once what I am bent on, what is
> Holy, my poetry, is accomplished,
> Be welcome then, stillness of the shadows' world!
> I shall be satisfied though my lyre will not
> Accompany me down there. Once I
> Lived like the gods, and more is not needed.[5]

Of the "absurd man" Camus says, as we have seen: "Madness and death are his irreparables." Hölderlin did become mad soon after writing this poem, but the point of the poem is that still he should not have preferred to be Camus, not to speak of lesser men. There is not only a "substitute" for twenty years of life but something more desirable by far: "Once I lived like the gods, and more is not needed."

This is overlooked by Sartre, too. Rightly, he recognizes that death can cut off a man before he has had a chance to give his life a meaning, that death may be—but he falsely thinks it always is—"the nihilation of all my possibilities." Not only in childhood but long after that one may retain the feeling that one is in this sense still at the mercy of death. "But once what I am bent on, what is Holy, my poetry, is accomplished," once I have succeeded in achieving—in the face of death, in a race with death—a project that is truly mine and not something that anybody else might have done as well, if not better, then the picture changes: I have won the race and in a sense have triumphed over death. Death and madness come too late.

We see the poet's later madness in the light of his own poem;

---

[5] Author's translation.

nor does it greatly matter that Nietzsche, like Hölderlin, vegetated for a few years before death took him: his work was done. To be sure, others make themselves the guardians of the dead life and interpret it according to their lights; but we have no defense if they begin to do the same while we are still alive. Nor can we say that this is the price of finitude, of finite works no less than finite lives. Men say that God is infinite but can hardly deny that theologians and believers make themselves the guardians of the infinite and offer their interpretations, if not behind His back then in His face.

And Heidegger? Does he not say little indeed? He reminds us of the commonplace—much better, more succinctly and humanely, put to us by Freud and, still earlier at greater length, but much more vividly, by Tolstoi—that most men would rather not face up to the certainty that they themselves must die. Before the end of World War I it may even have taken courage to be openly afraid of death—or of anything else, for that matter; but since the 1920s it has been fashionable to admit to *Angst*. That the man who accepts his death may find in this experience a strong spur to making something of his life and may succeed in some accomplishment that robs him of the fear of death and permits him to say "welcome then" was better said by Hölderlin in sixteen lines than by Heidegger in sixteen books.

Kierkegaard and Nietzsche challenged their age and were, to use two Nietzschean phrases "untimely" and "born posthumously." Heidegger's reputation, on the contrary, depends on his great timeliness: long before most other philosophers of his generation he took up the concerns of his age. In view of the exceeding difficulty of his prose, the reader who penetrates to the point of recognizing that the author is alluding to a genuine experience—say, the recognition of one's utter loneliness in this world—feels that there is more to Heidegger than those who shrug him off as "all nonsense" admit. But the question remains whether Heidegger has illuminated the phenomena of which he speaks and which others had described better before he did. The answer is that he is invariably less enlightening than the best among his predecessors.

To give a final example, both Georg Büchner (1813–1837), the author of the two plays, *Danton's Death* [1] and *Woyzeck* [2], and Heinrich von Kleist (1777–1811), whose *Prince Friedrich von Homburg* [13] is one of the most popular German plays, not only anticipated Heidegger but far surpassed him in insight. Kleist, who had been a Prussian officer over a hundred years before World War I, had the courage to describe and bring to life upon the stage the prince's dread of death—the prince being a general sentenced to death—but then went on to depict in the same drama the prince's conquest of anxiety, to the point where in the final scene he is ready to be shot without the slightest remnant of anxiety. He is blindfolded but—one thinks of Dostoevsky and of the end of Sartre's story *The Wall*—pardoned.

Those who want a better understanding of human attitudes toward death may learn more from Hölderlin, Kleist, and Büchner, and from Sartre's and Camus' fiction and plays than from existentialist exercises in philosophy. Indeed, the awesome terminology of Heidegger and others who have followed in his wake has distracted attention from many important distinctions. I shall mention four:

First, the world's major religions have encouraged different attitudes toward death. Although some early Christian martyrs died fearlessly, in eager anticipation of eternal bliss, Christianity has on the whole used its vast influence to make men dread death. The Buddha's attitude was very different: after his enlightenment experience he transcended all anxiety, and the stories of his death represent an outright antithesis to the stories of Christ's dread-full death.

Second, we should ask to what extent vitality influences attitudes toward death; but existentialists have not considered differences between patients and soldiers or the influence of weariness. From this point of view, Malraux's novel *La Condition Humaine,* translated as *Man's Fate,* is much more interesting than Heidegger. The last part is nothing less than a study of different attitudes toward death.

Third, one should ask to what extent attitudes toward death would be changed by the assurance that the world would end for all when we die—that there is absolutely nothing we shall miss.

Finally, not one of the existentialists has grasped the most crucial distinction that makes all the difference in facing death. Nietzsche stated it in *The Gay Science,* section 290 [14, pages 98 and following]: "For one thing is needful: that a human being attain his satisfaction with himself—whether it be by this or by that poetry and art; only then is a human being at all tolerable to behold. Whoever is dissatisfied with himself is always ready to revenge himself therefor; we others will be his victims, if only by always having to stand his ugly sight. For the sight of the ugly makes men bad and gloomy." Or, as Hölderlin says: "The soul that, living, did not attain its divine Right cannot repose in the nether world." But he that has made something of his life can face death without anxiety: "Once I Lived like the gods, and more is not needed."

REFERENCES

1. Büchner, G.: "Danton's Death," J. Holmstrom (tr.), E. Bentley (ed.), *The Modern Theatre,* Doubleday & Company, Inc., Anchor Books, New York, 1957, vol. 5.
2. Büchner, G.: "Woyzeck," T. Hoffman (tr.), E. Bentley (ed.), *The Modern Theatre,* Doubleday & Company, Inc., Anchor Books, New York, 1955, vol. 1.
3. Camus, A.: *The Myth of Sisyphus and Other Essays,* J. O'Brien (tr.), Alfred A. Knopf, Inc., New York, 1955.
4. Camus, A.: *The Rebel: An Essay on Man in Revolt,* A. Bower (tr.), Alfred A. Knopf, Inc., Vintage Books, New York, 1956.
5. Freud, S.: *Gesammelte Schriften* (12 vol.), Internationaler Psychoanalytischer Verlag, Leipzig, 1924.

6. Heidegger, M.: *Sein und Zeit: Erste Hälfte,* Max Niemeyer Verlag, Halle, 1927.

7. Hölderlin, F.: *An Die Parzen* (To the Fates). 1798.

8. Inoguchi, R., T. Nakajima, with R. Pineau: *The Divine Wind: Japan's Kamikaze Force in World War II.* Copyright 1958 by the United States Naval Institute, Annapolis, Md.

9. Kaufmann, W. (ed.): *Existentialism from Dostoevsky to Sartre,* Meridian Books, Inc., New York, 1956.

10. Kaufmann, W.: *Critique of Religion and Philosophy,* Harper & Brothers, New York, 1958.

11. Kaufmann, W.: *From Shakespeare to Existentialism: Studies in Poetry, Religion, and Philosophy,* The Beacon Press, Boston, 1959.

12. Kierkegaard, S.: *The Concept of Dread,* W. Lowrie (tr.), Princeton University Press, Princeton, N. J., 1940.

13. Kleist, H. von: *The Prince of Homburg,* J. Kirkup (tr.), E. Bentley (ed.), *The Classic Theatre,* Anchor Books, New York, 1959, vol. 2.

14. Nietzsche, F.: *The Portable Nietzsche,* W. Kaufmann (tr.), The Viking Press, Inc., New York, 1954.

15. Sartre, J. P.: *Being and Nothingness,* Hazel Barnes (tr.), Philosophical Library, Inc., New York, 1956.

16. Tolstoi, L. N.: "The Death of Ivan Ilyitch," *The Works of Lyof N. Tolstoi,* Charles Scribner's Sons, New York, 1904, vol. 14.

5 HERBERT MARCUSE

The Ideology of Death

*Der Mensch stirbt auch aus Ge-
wohnheit . . .*

HEGEL

*Il regardait la souffrance et la mort
comme les effets heureux de sa
toute-puissance et de sa souveraine
bonté.*

ANATOLE FRANCE

In the history of Western thought, the interpretation
of death has run the whole gamut from the notion of a
mere natural fact, pertaining to man as organic matter,
to the idea of death as the *telos* of life, the distinguishing
feature of human existence. From these two opposite poles,
two contrasting ethics may be derived: On the one hand,
the attitude toward death is the stoic or skeptic acceptance
of the inevitable, or even the repression of the thought of
death by life; on the other hand the idealistic glorification of
death is that which gives "meaning" to life, or is the precondition for the "true" life of man. If death is considered as an *essentially* external though *biologically* internal event in human existence, the affirmation of life tends
to be final and, as it were, unconditional: life is not and

cannot be redeemed by anything other than life. But if death appears as an essential as well as biological fact, ontological as well as empirical, life is transcended even though the transcendence may not assume any religious form. Man's empirical existence, his material and contingent life, is then defined in terms of and redeemed by something other than itself: he is said to live in two fundamentally different and even conflicting dimensions, and his "true" existence involves a series of sacrifices in his empirical existence which culminate in the supreme sacrifice—death. It is this idea of death to which the following notes refer.

It is remarkable to what extent the notion of death as not only biological but ontological necessity has permeated Western philosophy—remarkable because the overcoming and mastery of mere natural necessity has otherwise been regarded as the distinction of human existence and endeavor. Such an elevation of a biological fact to the dignity of an ontological essence seems to run counter to a philosophy which sees one of its foremost tasks in the distinction and discrimination between natural and essential facts and in teaching man to transcend the former. To be sure, the death which is presented as an ontological category is not simply the natural end of organic life—it is rather the comprehended, "appropriated" end that has become an integral part of man's own existence. However, this process of comprehension and appropriation neither changes nor transcends the natural fact of death but remains in a brute sense hopeless submission to it.

Now all philosophical thinking presupposes acceptance of facts —but then, the intellectual effort consists in dissolving their immediate facticity, by placing them into the context of relationships in which they become comprehensible. Thus they emerge as the product of factors, as something that has become what it is or has been made what it is, as elements in a process. Time is constitutive of facts. In this sense, all facts are historical. Once comprehended in their historical dynamic, they become transparent as nodal points of possible changes—changes which are defined and determined by the place and function of each respective fact in the respective totality within which it has coagulated. There is no necessity —there are only degrees of necessity. Necessity indicates lack of power: inability to change what is—the term is meaningful only as coterminus of freedom: the limit of freedom. Freedom implies knowledge, cognition. Insight into necessity is the first step toward the dissolution of necessity, but comprehended necessity is not yet freedom. The latter requires progress from theory to practice: actual conquest of those necessities which prevent or restrain the satisfaction of needs. In this process, freedom tends to be universal, for the servitude of those who are unfree restrains the freedom of those who depend on their servitude (as the master depends on the labor of his slave). Such universal freedom may be undesired or undesirable or impracticable—but then freedom is not yet real—there is still a realm of incomprehensible and unconquerable necessity.

What are the criteria for determining whether the limits of human freedom are empirical (i.e., ultimately historical) or ontological (i.e., essential and unsurpassable)? The attempt to answer this question has been one of the major efforts of philosophy. However, it has often been characterized by a tendency to present the empirical as ontological necessity. This "ontological inversion" also operates in the philosophical interpretation of death. It manifests itself in the tendency to accept death not only as fact but as necessity, and as necessity which is to be conquered not by dissolving but by accepting it. In other words, philosophy assumed that death pertained to the essence of human life, to its existential fulfillment. Moreover, the comprehended acceptance of death was considered as the prerogative of man, the very token of his freedom. Death, and only death brought the human existence into its own. Its final negation was considered as the affirmation of man's faculties and ends. In a remote sense the proposition may be true—man is free only if he has conquered his death; if he is able to determine his dying as the self-chosen end of his living; if his death is internally and externally linked with his life in the medium of freedom. As long as this is not the case, death remains mere nature, an unconquered limit to all life which is more than mere organic life, mere animal life. The poet may pray: *O Herr, gib jedem seinen eignen Tod.* The prayer is meaningless as long as man's life is not his own but a chain of preestablished and socially required performances at work and at leisure. Under these circumstances, the exhortation to make death "one's own" is hardly more than a premature reconciliation with unmastered natural forces. A brute biological fact, permeated with pain, horror, and despair, is transformed into an existential privilege. From the beginning to the end, philosophy has exhibited this strange masochism—and sadism, for the exaltation of one's own death involved the exaltation of the death of others.

The Platonic Socrates hails death as the beginning of true life —at least for the philosopher. But virtue which is knowledge makes the philosopher who heroically submits to death akin to the soldier on the battlefield, to the good citizen who obeys law and order, to every man worthy of his name; at various levels, they all share the idealistic attitude toward death. And if the authority who sentences the philosopher to death, far from annihilating him, opens to him the gates of the true life, then the executioners are absolved from the full guilt of the capital crime. The destruction of the body does not kill the "soul," the essence of life. Or have we here a terrifying ambiguity: how far does the Socratic irony go? In accepting his death, Socrates puts his judges in the wrong, but his philosophy of death acknowledges their right—the right of the polis over the individual. Does he, in accepting the verdict, even provoking it and rejecting escape, refute his philosophy? Does he suggest, in a horribly subtle and sophisticated way, that this philosophy serves to support the very forces which he fought throughout his life? Does he want to point to a deep secret—to the insoluble connection between death and unfreedom, death and domination? In any case, Plato buries the secret: the true life demands libera-

tion from the untrue life of our common existence. The transvaluation is complete; our world is a world of shadows. We are prison-
ers in the captivity of the body, chained by our appetites, cheated
by our senses. "The truth" is beyond. To be sure, this beyond is
not yet heaven. It is not yet certain whether the true life presupposes physical death, but there can be no doubt about the direction
in which the intellectual (and not only the intellectual!) effort is
guided. With the devaluation of the body, the life of the body is
no longer the real life, and the negation of this life is the beginning
rather than the end. Moreover, the mind is essentially opposed to
the body. The life of the former is domination, if not negation,
of the latter. The progress of truth is the struggle against sensuous-
ness, desire, and pleasure. This struggle not only aims at liberating
man from the tyranny of brute natural needs, it is also the separation
of the life of the body from the life of the mind—alienation of freedom from pleasure. The truth which liberates is the truth which re-
pels pleasure. Happiness is redefined a priori (i.e., without empirical foundation on the factual reasons) in terms of self-denial
and renunciation. The glorifying acceptance of death, which carries
with it the acceptance of the political order, also marks the birth of
philosophical morality.

Through all refinements and attenuations, the ontological affirmation of death continues to play its prominent role in the main
stream of philosophy. It centers on the idea of death which Hegel
described as pertaining to the romanticist concept of *Weltanschauung*. According to Hegel [1]: death has the significance of
the "negation of the negative," i.e., of an affirmation—as the
"resurrection of the spirit from the bare husk of nature and the
finiteness which it has outgrown." Pain and death are thus
perverted into the return of the subject to itself, satisfaction
(*Befriedigung*), bliss, and into that reconciled and affirmative
existence which the spirit can attain only through the mortification
of its negative existence, where it is separated from its true reality
and life (*Lebendigkeit*).

This tradition comes to a close in Heidegger's interpretation of human existence in terms of the anticipation of death—the latest and the most appropriate ideological exhortation to death, at the very time when the political ground was prepared for the corresponding reality of death—the gas chambers and concentration camps of Auschwitz, Buchenwald, Dachau, and Bergen-Belsen.

In contrast one might construct some kind of "normal" attitude toward death—normal in terms of the plain observable facts, although commonly repressed under the impact of the prevailing ideology and the institutions supported by it. This hypothetical normal attitude might be circumscribed as follows: death seems to be inevitable, but it is, in the vast majority of cases, a painful, horrible, violent, and unwelcome event. When it is welcome, life must have been even more painful than death. But the defiance of death is sadly ineffective. The scientific and technical efforts of mature civilization, which prolong life and alleviate its pains, seem to be frustrated, even counteracted on the part of society as well as of individuals. The "struggle for existence" within the nation and among nations still is a struggle for life and death, which demands the periodic shortening of life. Moreover, the fight for prolongation of life depends for its effectiveness on the response in the mind and in the instinctual structure of individuals. A positive response presupposes that their life is really "the good life"—that they have the possibility to develop and satisfy humane needs and faculties, that their life is an end-in-itself rather than a means for sustaining themselves. Should conditions obtain under which this possibility may become reality, quantity may turn into quality: the gradually increasing duration of life may change the substance and character not only of life but also of death. The latter would lose its ontological and moral sanctions; men would experience death primarily as a technical limit of human freedom whose surpassing would become the recognized goal of the individual and social endeavor. To an increasing extent, death would partake of freedom, and individuals would be impowered to determine their own deaths.

As in the case of incurable suffering, the means for painless death would be made available. Are there other than irrational arguments against such reasoning? Only one. A life with this attitude toward death would be incompatible with the established institutions and values of civilization. It would either lead to mass suicide (since for a great part of mankind life still is such a burden that the terror of death is probably an important factor in keeping it going) or to the dissolution of all law and order (since the fearful acceptance of death has become an integral element of public and private morality). The argument might be unshakable, but then the traditional notion of death is a sociopolitical concept which transforms nasty empirical facts into an ideology.

The connection between the ideology of death and the historical conditions under which it developed is indicated in Plato's interpretation of the death of Socrates: obedience to the law of the state without which there can be no orderly human society; the inadequacy of an existence which is imprisonment rather than freedom, falsehood rather than truth; knowledge of the possibility of a free and truthful life together with the conviction that this possibility cannot be realized without negating the established order of life. Death is the necessary entrance into real life because man's factual life is essentially unreal, i.e., incapable of existing in truth. But this argument is open to the question: Cannot perhaps the established order of existence be changed so that it becomes a "true" polis? In his *Republic,* Plato answers in the affirmative. The ideal state deprives death of its transcendental function, at least for the ruling philosophers; since they live in truth, they don't have to be liberated by death. As for the other citizens, those who are unfree do not have to be "reconciled" with death. It can occur and be made to occur as a natural event. The ideology of death is not yet an indispensable instrument of domination. It came to assume this function when the Christian doctrine of the freedom and equality of man as man had merged with the continuing institutions of unfreedom and injustice. The contradiction between the humanistic gospel and the inhumane reality required an effective solution. The death and resurrection of the god-hero, once the symbol of the periodic renewal of natural life and of a rational sacrifice, now directs all hope to the transnatural life hereafter. The supreme penalty must be suffered so that man may find supreme fulfillment after his natural life has ended. How can one protest against death, fight for its delay and conquest, when Christ died willingly on the cross so that mankind might be redeemed from sin? The death of the son of God bestows final sanction on the death of the son of man.

But the unreasonable insist upon reason. They continue to fear death as the supreme horror and the final end, the collapse of "being" into "nothing." "Anxiety" appears as existential category, but in view of the fact that death is not only inevitable but also incalculable, ubiquitous, and the tabooed limit of human freedom, all anxiety is fear, fear of a real, omnipresent danger, the most rational attitude and feeling. The rational force of anxiety has perhaps been one of the strongest factors of progress in the struggle with nature, in the protection and enrichment of human life. Conversely, the premature cure from anxiety without eliminating its ultimate source and resource may be the opposite: a factor of regression and repression. To live without anxiety is indeed the only uncompromising definition of freedom because it includes the full content of hope: material as well as spiritual happiness. But there can be (or rather there should be) no life without anxiety as long as death has not been conquered—not in the sense of a conscious anticipation and acceptance when it comes anyway, but in the sense of depriving it of its horror and incalculable power as well as of its transcendental sanctity. This means that the concerted and systematic struggle against death in all its forms would be carried beyond the socially tabooed limits. The fight against disease is not identical with the fight against death. There seems to be a point at which the former ceases to continue into the latter. Some deep-rooted mental barrier seems to arrest the

will before the technical barrier is reached. Man seems to bow
before the inevitable without really being convinced that it is inevitable. The barrier is defended by all the socially perpetuated
values that attach to the redeeming and even creative features of
death: its natural as well as essential necessity ("without death life
would not be life"). The short and incalculable duration of life en-
forces constant renunciation and toil, heroic effort, and sacrifice
for the future. The ideology of death operates in all forms of "in-
nerworldly asceticism." Destruction of the ideology of death would
involve an explosive transvaluation of social concepts: the good
conscience to be a coward, deheroization and desublimation; it
would involve a new "reality principle" which would liberate
rather than suppress the "pleasure principle."

    The mere formulation of these goals indicates why they have
been so rigidly tabooed. Their realization would be tantamount to
the collapse of the established civilization. Freud has shown the
consequences of a (hypothetical) disintegration or even essential
relaxation of the prevailing "reality principle"—the dynamic relationship between Eros and Death Instinct is such that a reduction
of the latter below the level at which it functions in a socially useful way would liberate the former beyond the "tolerable" level.
This would involve a degree of desublimation which would undo
the most precious achievements of civilization. Freud's insight was
penetrating enough to invoke against his own conception the taboo
which it violated. Psychoanalysis has all but purged itself from
these "unscientific" speculations. This is not the place to discuss
the question whether the affirmation of death is expressive of a
deep-lying "wish to die," of a primary "death instinct" in all
organic life, or whether this "instinct" has not become "second
nature" under the historical impact of civilization.[1] Society's use
of death and its attitude toward death seem to strengthen the
hypothesis concerning the historical character of the death instinct.

---

    [1] I have tried to discuss the problem in my book *Eros and Civilization*.
The Beacon Press, Boston, 1955.

Both fear of death and its repression in the acceptance of death as sanctioned necessity enter as cohesive factors into the organization of society. The natural fact of death becomes a social institution. No domination is complete without the threat of death and the recognized right to dispense death—death by legal verdict, in war, by starvation. And no domination is complete unless death, thus institutionalized, is recognized as more than natural necessity and brute fact, namely, as *justified* and as *justification*. This justification seems in the last analysis and beyond all particulars, individual guilt feeling derived from the universal guilt which is life itself, the life of the body. The early Christian notion, according to which all secular government is punishment for sin, has survived —even though it has been officially discarded. If life itself is sinful, then all rational standards for earthly justice, happiness, and freedom are merely conditional, secondary, and rightly superseded by (in terms of earthly life) irrational but higher standards. What is decisive is not whether this is still "really believed," but whether the attitude once motivated by this belief is perpetuated and reinforced by the conditions and institutions of society.

When the idea of death as justification has taken firm root in the existence of the individual, the struggle for the conquest of death is arrested in and by individuals themselves. They experience death not only as the biological limit of organic life, as the scientific-technical limit of knowledge, but also as a metaphysical limit. To struggle, to protest against the metaphysical limit of human existence is not only foolish, it is essentially impossible. What religion achieves through the notion of sin, philosophy affirms by its notion of the metaphysical finiteness of human existence. In itself, finiteness is a plain biological fact—that the organic life of individuals does not go on forever, that it ages and dissolves. But this biological condition of man does not have to be the inexhaustible source of anxiety. It may well be (and it was for many philosophical schools) the opposite, namely, the stimulus for incessant efforts to extend the limits of life, to strive for a guiltless existence, and to determine its end—to subject it to human autonomy, if not in terms of time, at least in terms of its quality, by eliminating decrepitude and suffering. Finiteness as a metaphysical structure appears in a quite different light. In it, the relationship between life and the end of life is, as it were, reversed. With death as the existential category, life becomes earning a living rather than living, a means which is an end in itself. The liberty and dignity of man is seen in the affirmation of his hopeless inadequacy, his eternal limitation. The metaphysics of finiteness thus falls in line with the taboo on unmitigated hope.

Death assumes the force of an institution which, because of its vital utility, should not be changed, even if it could perhaps be changed. The species perpetuates itself through the death of individuals; this is a natural fact. Society perpetuates itself through the death of individuals; this is no longer a natural but an historical fact. The two facts are not equivalent. In the first proposition, death is a biological event: disintegration of organic into inorganic matter. In the second proposition, death is an institution and a value: the cohesion of the social order depends to a considerable extent on the effectiveness with which individuals comply with death as more than a natural necessity; on their willingness, even urge, to die many deaths which are not natural; on their agreement to sacrifice themselves and not to fight death "too much." Life is not to be valued too highly, at least not as the supreme good. The social order demands compliance with toil and resignation, heroism, and punishment for sin. The established civilization does not function without a considerable degree of unfreedom; and death, the ultimate cause of all anxiety, sustains unfreedom. Man is not free as long as death has not become really "his own," that is, as long as it has not been brought under his autonomy. The realization of such autonomy is conceivable only if death no longer appears as the "negation of the negation," as redemption from life.

There is another sinister aspect of the exalted acceptance of

death as more than a natural fact, an aspect which becomes manifest in the ancient stories of mothers who delighted in the sacrifice
of their sons on the battlefields; in the more recent letters of
mothers who assured the killers of their sons of their forgiveness;
in the stoic indifference with which they live near atomic testing
grounds and take war for granted. To be sure, explanations are
ready at hand: defense of the nation is the prerequisite for the
existence of all its citizens, final judgment of the murderer is God's
and not man's, etc. Or, on more material grounds, the individual
has long since become powerless "to do anything about it," and
this powerlessness is rationalized as moral duty, virtue, or honor.
However, all these explanations seem to fail at one central point,
the undisguised, almost exhibitionist character of affirmation, of
instinctual consent. It seems hard indeed to reject Freud's hypothesis of an insufficiently repressed death wish. But again, the
biological drive which operates in the death wish may not be so
biological. It may have been "fed" by historical forces, the need
for sacrificing the life of the individual so that the life of the
"whole" may go on. The "whole" here is not the natural species,
mankind; it is rather the totality of the institutions and relationships which men have established in their history. Without the
instinctual affirmation of its undisputable priority, this totality
might be in danger of disintegration. When Hegel said that history
is the slaughter bench on which the happiness of individuals is
sacrificed to the progress of Reason, he did not speak of a natural
process. He identified an historical fact. The death on the slaughter
bench of history, the death which society exacts from individuals
is not mere nature—it is also Reason (with a capital R). Through
death on the field of honor, in the mines and on the highways,
from unconquered disease and poverty, by the state and its organs,
civilization advances. Is progress under such conditions throughout
the centuries conceivable without the effective agreement of individuals, an instinctual if not conscious agreement which supple-

ments and props up enforced submission by "voluntary" compliance? And if such "voluntary" agreement prevails, what are its roots and reasons?

The questions lead back to the beginning. Compliance with death is compliance with the master over death: the polis, the state, nature, or the god. Not the individual, but a higher power is the judge; the power over death is also the power over life. But this is only half the story. The other is the willingness, the wish to quit a life of untruth—a life which betrays not only the dreams of childhood but also the mature hopes and promises of man. They are referred to the beyond, the beyond of heaven or of the spirit—or of nothingness. Decisive is the element of protest— protest on the part of the powerless. Because they are powerless, they not only comply, they forgive those who mete out death. Such forgiveness may ingratiate and ensure the love of the supreme power, but it also makes a blessing out of weakness. Nietzsche's notion of the genealogy of morals also applies to the moral attitude toward death. The slaves revolt—and win—not by liberating themselves but by proclaiming their weakness as the crown of humanity. The impotence of the protest perpetuates the feared and hated power.

REFERENCES

1. Hegel, G. W. F.: *The Philosophy of Fine Art,* F. P. B. Osmaston (tr.), G. Bell & Sons, Ltd., London, 1920, vol. II.

PART 2

Developmental Orientation Toward Death

6 MARIA H. NAGY

The Child's View of Death*

The last fifty years have seen various research endeavors carried on by workers in the field of child psychology. As a result, practically all phases of the child's life have been explored and commented upon: One is struck, however, by the slim, almost neglected, attention given to the child's conception of death. This is all the more surprising since it is in childhood that the adult's outlook concerning death begins to take on basic form.

Most of the studies [2, 3, 6, 7, 8] of the child's attitudes regarding death have dealt principally with his feelings about death. None, except those of Cousinet [4] and Anthony [1], have concentrated on developmental features. This aspect will be the major focus of the paper—an investigation, from the genetic standpoint, of the ideas of children, aged 3 to 10 years, concerning the meaning of death.

METHOD

The material was assembled in three ways:

1. Compositions were written by children in the 7–10-year age range in response to the general question: "Write down everything that comes to your mind about death."

* Reprinted (with some editorial changes) with permission from the *Journal of Genetic Psychology,* **73:** 3–27, 1948.

2. Drawings about death were made by children in the 6–10-year age range. Many of the older children also wrote explanations of their creations.

3. Discussions were held with all of the children later on concerning their compositions and drawings. This was done to avoid the possibility of giving arbitrary interpretation to the child's ideas and to clarify as well as amplify his meaning and outlook about death. Since for the great proportion of three to six-year-olds there were no written compositions or drawings, the discussion had to assume a different form. The general approach was to first establish meaningful rapport with each child, then see if he understood what was being asked, and eventually get him to talking about his ideas and feelings regarding death.

The data on which the findings reported herein are based were obtained from 378 children living in Budapest and its environs. They were practically equally divided as to sex (51 per cent = boys; 49 per cent = girls). The children participating represented different religions, different schools, and varying social levels. Intelligence level ranged from dull normal to superior with most of the children belonging in the "normal" range. Loss of some of the original background material, unfortunately, does not permit further background specification.

Naturally the findings have to be considered in terms of their sampling limitations and as being tentative with respect to the broad spectrum of all children. I feel, nevertheless, that they can serve as a fruitful springboard for our thinking in the field.

RESULTS

What does death mean to the child? The replies given can be categorized into three major developmental stages: (1) The child who is less than five years of age usually does not recognize death as an irreversible fact; in death he sees life. (2) Between the ages of five and nine, death is most often personified and thought of as a contingency. (3) Only at the age of nine and later does he begin to view death as a process which happens to us according to certain laws. It should be kept in mind that neither the stages nor the above-mentioned ages at which they occur are watertight compartments as it were. Overlapping does exist. They do, however, reflect definite modal developments in the child's thinking about death.

Stage One: There Is no Definitive Death

In this first stage, the child does not know death as such. He attributes life and consciousness to the dead. There are two variations of this affirmation: (a) death is a departure, a sleep—this denies death entirely; and (b) the child recognizes the fact of physical death but cannot separate it from life—he considers death as gradual or temporary. Some concrete examples of these outlooks follow:

a. Death as departure, sleep. B. J. (3 years, 11 months): "The dead close their eyes because sand gets into them."

The child has heard something about the eyes of the dead being closed. He explains this by an exterior cause. The dead person voluntarily, defensively, closes his eyes.

S. T. (4, 8): "It can't move because it's in the coffin."

"If it weren't in the coffin, could it?"

"It can eat and drink."

Also here the immobility is the consequence of exterior circumstances. The dead person doesn't move because the coffin does not permit it. He considers the dead as still capable of taking nourishment.

S. J. (5, 0) had already seen a dead person. "Its eyes were closed, it lay there, so dead. No matter what one does to it, it doesn't say a word."

"It will be older then, it will always be older and older. When it is 100 years old it will be exactly like a piece of wood."

"How will it be like a piece of wood?"

"That I couldn't say. My little sister will be five years old now. I wasn't alive yet when she died. She will be so big by this time. She has a small coffin, but she fits in the small coffin."

"What is she doing now, do you think?"

"Lying down, always just lies there. She's still so small, she can't be like a piece of wood. Only very old people."

In the beginning she sees the matter realistically. The dead person cannot speak. The closed eyes do not necessarily mean the cessation of sight. The dead person is compared to a piece of wood. In all probability she wanted thus to express immobility. Later it comes out that young people grow in the grave. The growth is not great. She says her sister is five years old because she herself is five.

B. I. (4, 11): "What happens there under the earth?"

"He cries because he is dead."

"But why should he cry?"

"Because he is afraid for himself."

She feels that death is bad. Perhaps she has had the experience of seeing the dead mourned. She transfers this sentiment to the dead themselves.

T. P. (4, 10): "A dead person is just as if he were asleep. Sleeps in the ground, too."

"How do you know whether someone is asleep or dead?"

"I know if they go to bed at night and don't open their eyes. If somebody goes to bed and doesn't get up, he's dead or ill."

"Will he ever wake up?"

"Never. A dead person only knows if somebody goes out to the grave or something. He feels that somebody is there, or is talking."

"Are you certain? You're not mistaken?"

"I don't think so. At funerals you're not allowed to sing, just talk, because otherwise the dead person couldn't sleep peacefully. A dead person feels it if you put something on his grave."

"What is it he feels then?"

"He feels that flowers are put on his grave. The water touches the sand. Slowly, slowly, he hears everything. Auntie (the author was referred to after a while by the cheerful name of "Auntie Death"), does the dead person feel if it goes deep into the ground?" (i.e., the water).

"What do you think?"

"He would like to come out, but the coffin is nailed down."

"If he weren't in the coffin, could he come back?"

"He couldn't root up all that sand."

Death is identified with sleep, yet is supposed to be in connection with the outside world. The dead person has knowledge of what goes on in the world. It does not merely think, but also feels.

F. R. (9, 11): "I was six years old. A friend of my father's died. They didn't tell me but I heard. Then I didn't understand. I felt it was like when mother goes traveling somewhere—I don't see her any more."

He feels the same about news of death as about traveling. The dead person resembles the absent, in that he sees neither of them.

To summarize, we see that children do not accept death. When anyone goes away, he is considered as dead. Death is thus a departure. To die also means the same as living on but under changed circumstances. If someone dies no change takes place in him, but rather our lives change since we can no longer see the dead person as he no longer lives with us. This does not mean that children have no disagreeable sentiments concerning death because the most painful thing about death for them is the separation idea itself.

Most children, however, are not satisfied when someone dies that he should merely disappear, but want to know where and how he continues to live. Most of the children connected the facts of absence and funerals. In the cemetery one lives on. Movement is to a certain degree limited by the coffin, but for all that the dead are still capable of growth. They take nourishment, they breathe. They know what is happening on earth. They feel it if someone thinks of them and they even feel sorry for themselves. Thus the dead live in the grave. However, the children realize—with a resulting aversion for death—that this life is limited, not so complete as our life. Some of them consider this diminished life exclusively restricted to sleep.

This general point is similar to one expressed in psychoanalytic thinking where sleep and death are considered as synonymous in the unconscious. In death as in sleep separation stops and unity with the mother, which was complete in the intra-uterine life, is restored. In primitive peoples, too, we find widespread illustrations of the identification of death and sleep. The natives of West Africa, for example, have no special word for sleep. The verb for sleep is written "to be half dead." If the dead live they do this principally in dreams where they can return and visit with the living. The extent to which death is merely a removal is also shown by the fact that in many places food and drink are put beside the deceased, even clothing and arms. Servants and wives are sometimes buried with them, so there should be someone to look after them in the next world. Even within our own culture this outlook finds expression in the language. If someone dies we say he has "passed on." The deceased returns to his dear "mother — earth." We "take our leave" of the dead, wish him "peaceful repose." And if our feelings were consistent about there only being a dead body in the grave, our funeral rites would lose much of their meaning.

b. Death is gradual, temporary. A good proportion of the children aged five and six years no longer deny death but are still unable to accept it as a definitive fact. They acknowledge that death exists but think of it as a gradual or temporary thing.

L. B. (5, 6): "His eyes were closed."

"Why?"

"Because he was dead."

"What difference is there between sleeping and dying?"

"Then they bring the coffin and put him in it. They put the hands like this when a person is dead."

"What happens to him in the coffin?"

"The worms eat him. They bore into the coffin."

"Why does he let them eat him?"

"He can't get up any longer because there is sand on him. He can't get out of the coffin."

"If there were no sand on him could he get out?"

"Certainly, if he wasn't very badly stabbed. He would get his hand out of the sand and dig. That shows that he still wants to live."

In the beginning this child sees death realistically. He does not say, as the previous children, that "he closes his eyes," but that the eyes were closed. He sees only exterior differences between sleep and death. This would be evidence of a denial of death were it not that immediately afterward he speaks of worms. He does not state that the dead cannot move, merely that the sand hinders them from moving. On the other hand, he attributes a desire for life to the dead person—though only when he is not "very badly killed." Thus there are degrees of death.

T. D. (6, 6): "My sister's godfather died and I took hold of his hand. His hand was so cold. It was green and blue. His face was all wrinkled together. He can't move. He can't clench his hands because he is dead. And he can't breathe."

"His face?"

"It has goose flesh because he is cold. He is cold because he is dead and cold everywhere."

"Does he feel the cold or was it just that his skin was like that?"

"If he is dead he feels too. If he is dead he feels a tiny little bit. When he is quite dead he no longer feels anything."

This child's explanation begins realistically. The dead person cannot move or breathe. He explains the cause of the cold childishly. He is cold because it is chilly. He feels the cold, however, only when not entirely dead. This has no relation to the process of the death agony, as he saw his sister's godfather only at the funeral.

That gradualness in death is not merely a matter of insufficiency of expression and is not related to the processes of death can be seen from the case of a ten-year-old, to whom this early childish impression remained as an incoherent element in what otherwise was an entirely realistic conception:

"Until he disappears from the earth he knows everything. Until they have thrown three shovelfuls, three handfuls of earth on him, he knows if they say anything about him."

In the beginning he describes realistically the physical changes which take place in death; then states, that until he is put into the earth the dead person knows everything. Thus the time between dying and being buried is a transitory state between life and death.

G. P. (6, 0): "He stretched out his arms and lay down. You couldn't push down his arms. He can't speak. He can't move. Can't see. Can't open his eyes. He lies for four days."

"Why for four days?"

"Because the angels don't know yet where he is. The angels dig him out, take him with them. They give him wings and fly away."

"What stays in the cemetery?"

"Only the coffin stays down there. Then people go there and dig it up. They take out the coffin for it to be there if somebody dies. If they couldn't make one quickly it would be there. They clean it up, good and bright."

"What happens to him?"

"If it's a woman, she does the cleaning. If it's a man, then he'll be an angel. He brings the Christmas trees. Who doesn't, bakes cakes in the sky, and brings toys. It's bad to go to heaven because you have to fly. It's a good thing to be in heaven. You can't get wet, don't get soaked if it rains. It only rains on the earth."

"Well, what are you going to do if you ever get there?"

"I'm going to bake cakes the whole year. Each angel has got his own stove."

"Won't there be an awful lot of cakes if you bake the whole year round?"

"Lots of houses. Lots of children. If the cakes are done we can play hide-and-seek. Then the children hide in the clouds. You can hide very well up there. One flies up, the other flies down."

This child describes death realistically. The activities of life are missing. He says that one remains only four days in the tomb, then goes to heaven. (This is not belief in a life in the world beyond, but simply living on, because while the former knows about the body's dissolution, the latter fantasy does not.) Thus death lasts four days. He imagines heavenly life in quite a childish way. They play and eat cakes.

The children of this group already accept death to a certain extent. The distinction between life and death is, however, not complete. If they think of death as gradual, life and death are in simultaneous relation; if as temporary, life and death can change places with one another repeatedly. These conceptions are of a higher order than one which entirely denies death. Here, the distinction between the two processes has already begun. Alongside their wishful desires the feeling for reality also plays a role. Thus a compromise solution occurs: while death exists it is not definitive.

Rivers [5] reports a similar outlook in the Solomon Islands. The inhabitants there have a word—*mate*—which they translate as death though it cannot be used as the contrary of *toa*, which is their expression for life. *Mate*-ness is a state which can last for years. It is not the period before death because for them there is no death but a transition between two modes of existence. The person designated as being in a state of *mate* is accorded funeral rites. However, the burial is not the burial of the dead body but a festive transposition from the *toa* state into the *mate* state. It is a great turning point in life, like pubescence, the founding of a family, etc. The distinction between life and death has the same vague quality noticed in the children of this group.

Stage Two: Personification of Death

In the second stage, the child personifies death. This conception, although appearing in all ages of the children studied, seems to be most characteristic between the ages of five and nine. Personification of death takes place in two ways: death is imagined as a separate person, or else death is identified with the dead.

Some illustrative examples follow.

B. M. (6, 7): "Carries off bad children. Catches them and takes them away."

"What is he like?"

"White as snow. Death is white everywhere. It's wicked. It doesn't like children."

"Why?"

"Because it doesn't like to see them."

"What is white about it?"

"The skeleton. The bone-skeleton."

"Is it really that way or do they only say so?"

"It really is. Once I talked about it and at night the real death came. It has a key to everywhere so it can open the doors. It came in, messed about everywhere. It came over to the bed and began to pull away the covers. I covered myself up well. It couldn't take them off. Afterwards it went away."

"You only pretend it was there. It wasn't really there."

"I was ill then. I didn't go to kindergarten. A little girl always came up. I always quarreled with her. One night it came. I always took raisins though it was forbidden."

"Did you tell your mother?"

"I didn't dare to tell my mother because she is afraid of everything."

"And your father?"

"Papa said it was a tale from the benzine tank. I told him it wasn't any fairy-tale."

The child sees death as a kind of skeleton-man who carries people off because he is bad-hearted. Dying is consequently thought of as a bad thing. Talk of death is responsible for its magical advent. Also, death comes when you do "wrong" things.

P. G. (8, 6): "Death comes when somebody dies, and comes with a scythe, cuts him down, and takes him away. When death goes away it leaves footprints behind. When the footprints disappeared it came back and cut down more people. And then they wanted to catch it, and it disappeared."

For this child, death is so much a person that it even leaves footprints. Like a child, it teases people. He wants to exterminate death.

B. T. (9, 11): "Death is a skeleton. It is so strong it can overturn a ship. Death can't be seen. Death is in a hidden place. It hides in an island."

He thinks of death in fairy-tale style. It hides in an island. Its strength is tremendous. Death is invisible. He doesn't say whether it is invisible of itself or whether it is only that people don't see it.

V. P. (9, 11): "Death is very dangerous. You never know what minute he is going to carry you off with him. Death is invisible, something nobody has ever seen in all the world. But at night he comes to everybody and carries them off with him. Death is like a skeleton. All the parts are made of bone. But then when it begins to be light, when it's morning, there's not a trace of him. It's that dangerous, death."

"Why does it go about at night?"

"Because then nobody is up and it can come undisturbed."

"Is it afraid of people?"

"No. It doesn't want people to see it."

"Why?"

"Because they would be frightened of it."

Death is invisible because it goes about at night. Others imagine death as ill-intentioned; this child supposes it to have good intentions. It goes about secretly because it does not want to frighten people.

B. G. (4, 9): "Death does wrong."

"How does it do wrong?"

"Stabs you to death with a knife."

"What is death?"

"A man."

"What sort of a man?"

"Death-man."

"How do you know?"

"I saw him."

"Where?"

"In the grass. I was gathering flowers."

"How did you recognize him?"

"I knew him."

"But how?"

"I was afraid of him."

"What did your mother say?"

"Let us go away from here. Death is here."

This boy imagines death as a man whom he saw when gathering flowers. He could be recognized by his fearfulness. Afterwards he says he would like to know death's address; he would go and shoot him. "Kill the death-man so we will not die" is a frequent comment by children.

K. P. (6, 1): "Puts on a white coat, and a death face."

"Who?"

"Death. Frightens the children."

"Has he frightened you already?"

"I'm not afraid. I know it's just a man who has put on a death face. He was in the circus once."

"Now don't tell me about that man but about real death. What is death, really?"

"Real death? I don't know. It has big eyes and white clothes. It has long legs, long arms."

"But that's not really death. That is an 'uncle' dressed up like death."

"No. I went to church. I saw the real death. He went toward the park."

"But that was a man dressed up like death."

"But death has eyes as big as the squares on this table. Death is also only a man, only it has bigger eyes."

Death is considered the same as an actual, existing person. It is interesting to note the effect of a circus clown on this boy.

S. D. (8, 3): "It's like a man."

"How?"

"Well, when its time comes it dies. Then it comes down from heaven and takes him away."

"Who?"

"Death."

"It's like a man?"

"Sort of like a man. Lives up in heaven."

"Is death good?"

"I think it's bad because it stops people from living."

"How is it like a man?"

"It's like a man in its body. In its way of thinking it's different. People think that death is bad. Then death thinks now it is going to do good if it takes people up to heaven."

"Then does it think too that it is doing good when it takes people to Hell?"

"No. People are afraid of death, but death isn't afraid of itself. It certainly takes them up in some kind of carriage. It surely takes a lot of people at a time. So it couldn't take them otherwise than in a carriage."

Death is a man, living in heaven. In body he resembles mankind, in thought he is different.

H. G. (7, 9): "When someone dies the death angels carry

him away. The death angels are great enemies of people. Death
is the king of the angels. Death commands the angels. The angels
work for death."

Death is the angels' king.

T. S. (7, 6): "What is death? A ghost. You can't see him,
he just comes, like that. Like something that flies in the air."

"What is a ghost?"

"Somebody invisible. An invisible man. In the form of a
ghost. Comes in the air."

Death is an invisible man, a ghost.

H. G. (8, 5): "I don't know if it is alive, if it is a person.
If it is a man it is like the woodcutter. It has a white cloak on, a
scythe in its hand, as one imagines it in a picture. It's not something you can see. I'm not sure if there is really any such thing."

"If there is, where is it?"

"Spirit forms haven't any country."

"Haven't angels either?"

"Yes, but they are good spirits. I only mean the bad ones.
Bad men haven't any home. They come and go, wander about,
loiter around, doing damage."

"Is death a bad spirit?"

"Yes."

"Why?"

"Because somehow it's cold. I imagine it would be terrible if
you saw it. You would kneel down, pray to it, and still death
would make you die. I've often imagined I ran away from death."

"Ran away?"

"In my room, by myself, I imagine it. I don't dare to go out.
I shut the door after myself so he can't catch me. It's as if he were
there. I play like that, often."

"Is it a game?"

"I don't know. I often pretend about him."

"Are you afraid when you are alone?"

"No, I just pretend to myself."

"The whole thing isn't true?"

"No."

"Why are you afraid if it isn't true?"

"Somehow I'm afraid. Death is the most powerful ruler in the world, except the good God. Death is a companion of the devil. Death is like a ghost. If death has servants, then the ghosts are its servants. If death dances, then a lot of ghosts come in white cloaks and dance the ghost dance. It could be so beautiful."

"What would be beautiful about it?"

"I don't know, but there's something so beautiful about it. Death and ghosts go together, like fairies and angels. Spirits and the devil go together with death. But the most terrible of all is death."

"Do you often think of death?"

"I often do. But such things as when I fight with death and hit him on the head, and death doesn't die. Death hasn't got wings."

"Why?"

"I imagine somehow that he hasn't. The angels have, and the fairies in the stories, but death hasn't. But he can fly for all of that. He can fly without wings, too. Death has got some kind of invisible wings. In reality they can't be seen."

In the beginning this child denies that death is a personal reality, but then imagines it in characteristic day-fantasies. He runs away from death, hits it on the head, but it doesn't die.

S. J. (9, 10): This is a boy who accepts death quite realistically. He tells how at home he always plays ghosts with the smaller children. He shakes the bushes and says that death is going about there. When they hear this the small children run away, while he gathers up their toys and the whole playground is his. He stretches cords so the little ones cannot come back. He tells about this incident concerning himself.

"I stayed there, lying on the ground. I fell into the cord myself.

I stayed for a quarter of an hour lying on the ground. Only later I dared to get up. I was afraid that death was really there and perhaps I would die too."

He doesn't believe in the death-man, but starts to be afraid of him during an evening's play. It is noteworthy that 15 per cent of the children studied stated they were accustomed to think about death at evening. They supposed a relationship between death and darkness. The death-man goes about principally at night.

Another form of personifying death is when death is identified with the dead. Here the word for death is used in place of the word for the dead person. This is the more extraordinary because in Hungarian the two words are essentially different (halal—halott) and even in sound could never be confounded as in other languages (der Tot—tot; la mort—mort, death—the dead.)

W. L. (6, 8): "It is a superstition about death because it doesn't go about at night, anywhere. It's in its coffin. Death isn't true. It isn't true that it goes about on earth and cuts people down."

"Then where is it?"

"It's in the coffin, always; death lies in the coffin."

This child doesn't believe in death as a distinct personality. He identifies death and dead people.

A. C. (7, 11): "Death can't speak or move. I was often at the cemetery. It's very sad."

"What is sad?"

"When I see a grave there's death in it. That's sad."

"Is death in the grave, or a dead person?"

"A dead person. . . . I never saw death, only heads and bones."

"What is death?"

"A dead person who hasn't any flesh any more, only bones."

According to her twin brother, "Death is a skeleton."

"Is it real or is it only that one makes an image like that of it?"

"It exists, too. If a person dies, that will be death."

Death as identified with the dead exists for both twins.

B. M. (8, 2): "Death can't talk. Death can't talk because it isn't alive. Death has no mind. Death can't think because there isn't any mind in him. Death can't write because there isn't any soul in him. Death can't read because there is no living soul in him."

"What is the difference between death and the dead?"

No answer.

"What are the dead?"

"The person who dies."

"What is death?"

No reply.

In a childish way this boy describes in detail all the things the dead cannot do. His ideas of life and soul are confused. He cannot express the difference between death and the dead, nor define death.

To summarize: between the ages of five and nine, children generally personify death in some form. Two-thirds of the children studied in this group imagine death as a distinct personality. Either they believe in the reality of the skeleton-man, or individually create their own idea of a death-man. The death-man is invisible for them. This means two things: (a) it is invisible in itself, as it is a being without a body; (b) we do not see him because he goes about in secret, mostly at night. However, they do feel that death can be seen for a brief moment by the person he carries off.

In comparison with the first stage where death is denied, we find in this second stage an increased sense of reality. The child already accepts the existence of death, its definitiveness. On the other hand, he has such an aversion to the thought of death that he casts it away. From a process which takes place in us death grows to a reality outside us. It exists but is remote from us. As it is remote our death is not inevitable. Only those die whom the death-man catches and carries off. Whoever can get away does not die.

One-third of the children in this stage conceive of death as a person and identify it with the dead. These children use the word "death" for "the dead." This conception also evidences a desire to keep death at a distance. Death is still outside us and is also not general.

Although the tendency of the child to personify is a well-known phenomenon of his development, it is surprising how little attention the literature on this subject pays to this with respect to death.

Stage Three: The Cessation of Bodily Activities

It is only starting at the age of nine and thereafter that the child reaches the point of recognizing that death is the cessation of corporeal life. When he understands that death is a process operating within us he realizes its universal nature.

F. E. (10, 0): "It means the passing of the body. Death is a great squaring of accounts in our lives. It is a thing from which our bodies cannot be resurrected. It is like the withering of flowers."

Death is the destruction of the body. It is also a reckoning. This girl utilizes both a natural as well as moral explanation.

C. G. (9, 4): "Death is the termination of life. Death is destiny. We finish our earthly life. Death is the end of life on earth."

This boy expresses its regularity by the word destiny.

F. G. (9, 11): "A skull portrays death. If somebody dies they bury him and he crumbles to dust in the earth. The bones crumble later and so the skeleton remains all together, the way it was. That is why death is portrayed by a skeleton. Death is something that no one can escape. The body dies, the soul lives on."

This boy knows that the portrayal of death is not death itself. Indeed, he also explains why the skeleton becomes the symbol of death. Death is universal.

S. T. (9, 4): "What is death? Well, I think it is a part of a person's life. Like school. Life has many parts. Only one part of it is earthly. As in school, we go on to a different class. To die means to begin a new life. Everyone has to die once, but the soul lives on."

The themes of inevitability and universality predominate here.

GENERAL SUMMARY

There are three major stages of development in children concerning their ideas about the nature of death.

The first stage, which characterizes children between the ages of three and five years, highlights the denial of death as a regular and final process. Death is a departure, a further existence under changed circumstances. Death is also envisioned as being temporary. Indeed, distinction is made of degrees of death. The child knows itself as a living being. In his egocentric way he imagines the outside world after his own fashion; so in the outside world he also imagines everything, lifeless things and dead people alike, as living. Living and lifeless are not yet distinguished. He extends this animism to death, too.

The second stage, which typifies children between the ages of five and nine, indicates that death is personified, considered a person. Death exists but the children still try to keep it distant from themselves. Only those die whom the death-man carries off. Death is an eventuality. Fantasies are also present, though on a less frequent scale, where death and the dead are considered the same. Some of the children consistently employ the word "death" for "the dead." Here death is seen as still outside us and not universal. The egocentric, or anthropocentric, view plays a role not only in the birth of animism, but in the formation of artificialism. Every event and change in the world derives from man. If in general death exists, it is a person, the death-man, who "does" it. We get no answer as to why, if death is bad for people, he does it.

Finally, in the third stage, which becomes prominent in children in their ninth and tenth years, death is recognized as a process which takes place in all of us, the perceptible result of which is the dissolution of bodily life. By then children know that death is inevitable. In this stage not only does the conception of death become more realistic, but the child's general view of the world veers in this direction. Indeed the child's conception of death reflects in a large measure his general picture of the world.

A final thought based on clinical experience is that it is really not possible to conceal death from the child nor should concealment be permitted. Natural behavior in the child's presence can greatly diminish the impact of his acquaintance with death.

REFERENCES

1. Anthony, S.: *The Child's Discovery of Death,* Harcourt, Brace and Company, Inc., New York, 1940.
2. Chadwick, M.: "Die Gott-phantasie bei Kindern," *Imago,* **13:** 383–394, 1927.
3. Chadwick, M.: "Notes upon fear of death," *Intern. J. Psychoanal.,* **10:** 321–334, 1929.
4. Cousinet, R.: "L'idée de la mort chez les enfants," *J. Psychol. Norm. Pathol.,* **36:** 65–76, 1939.
5. Rivers, W. H.: *The History of Melanesian Society,* Cambridge University Press, New York, 1914, vols. I and II.
6. Schilder, P., and D. Wechsler: "The attitudes of children toward death," *J. Genet. Psychol.,* **45:** 406–451, 1934.
7. Stern, W.: "Zur Psychologie der reifenden Jugend," *Z. pädagog. Psychol.,* **28:** 1–10, 1927.
8. Weber, A.: "Concerning children's experience with death," *Monatsschr. Psychiat. Neurol.,* **107:** 3–4, 1943.

7 ROBERT KASTENBAUM

Time and Death in Adolescence*

Certainly there is nothing dark or sickly about the adolescent you observe playing football, repairing his car, and cutting up with friends. Death and dying appear to be a long way from him—it seems rather odd even to bring up the subject. Longevity statistics indicate that he can reasonably expect approximately three more years for each one he has already experienced. Ahead of him lies a long future in which he can apply his energy and fresh mind to the actualization of his life values. Here is youth on the threshold of the adult world: why consider death?

Yet when we add one other common observation some curious possibilities present themselves. It is widely acknowledged that the adolescent lives in a transitional world vacillating between the roles of a dependent child and an independent adult, an in-between state that is marked by changes in virtually every aspect of functioning. He is trying to locate himself with respect to his past and future, to "shape up" emotionally and intellectually, to attain a new footing as an individual and as a member of social units.

Considering jointly these two characteristics of the

* Valuable assistance in processing the data reported herein was provided by F. Harold Giedt, Ph.D., chief of the research psychology service of the Veterans Administration Hospital, Sepulveda, California.

adolescent period can illuminate the significance of death attitudes as one aspect of a person's general psychological functioning, and more besides. Something of rather unsuspected practical importance may be involved.

Approximately two hundred and sixty high school students in a medium-sized Southern California community cooperated in our exploration of adolescent death attitudes and their implications. What we learned from them will be more meaningful if a few of the notions that guided this investigation are now introduced.

Picture a person moving along his "life line" from birth to death. From position to position (from age to age) he changes in appearance and behavior, sometimes moderately, sometimes grossly. A fantastic way in which to account for these changes would be to imagine that each region of time has its own dynamic field that somehow operates upon the individual as he enters its radius. Each field selects certain aspects of the person's behavior for emphasis, others it minimizes. As he progresses along his life line from one "time field" to the next the traveler may impress us as much with his changes as with his consistencies.

This notion is somewhat extravagant because we know that time per se has not the substantial basis for providing a dynamic field. But the imagery is provocative, and the logical defect can be swiftly remedied. Although the objective life line of an individual possesses no such wondrous powers, each person constructs for himself a subjective life line in which his knowledge and ignorance, hopes and fears, thoughts and feelings play a part. He invests each point of his life line—past and future as well as present— with personally meaningful characteristics. Aware of it or not, he owns a psychological model of his own life line, divisible into just those peculiar "time fields" described above. When he moves into each future time field of his own creation his behavior at that point of his life is influenced by the nature of the field he has projected forward—or at least that is our assumption. Direct evidence has yet to be gathered, but the circumstantial case is strong from many sources in psychology.

Before proceeding to the next theoretical notion let us give particular attention to the place of death along an individual's life line of subjective time fields. The further along a person has moved, the less distance remains between his present life-line position and death. As the prospect of death becomes a matter of realistically closer concern the subjective time fields quite possibly could come more and more under the influence of the individual's attitudes toward death. The subjective time field in which the high school student dwells may or may not be determined to an appreciable extent by the manner in which he has come to grips with the prospect of death; but sixty years later this seems likely to be a most potent determinant.

If there were no way of determining the make-up of a person's subjective time field at a given point until that point were reached in actuality, then we would be seriously limited in theoretical and practical efforts. As death looms ever more prominently as a realistic prospect, will a given individual continue to find meaning in life and function productively, or will he become depressed, apathetic, demoralized? We could not know until the time was at hand and the range of possible interventions drastically reduced. But if the way a person comes to terms with death—as reflected in the structure of his subjective time fields—could be gauged "ahead of time," then knowledge and change are genuine possibilities.

"Structuring principle" is another notion we have found useful in exploring the implication of death attitudes. The time fields a person constructs for himself constitute just one special case of a more general tendency to organize. At any cross-sectional slice of life the individual presents not a random collection of events occurring in every which way, but a more or less cohesive functional entity. A scientist with enough knowledge and skill should theoretically be able to study an adolescent and find a common theme, directional force, or structuring principle in terms of which a host of specific behaviors could be understood. Nobody seems to have that much knowledge and skill as yet. Perhaps the closest we ever come to seeing such a structuring principle or principles unearthed is when a particularly gifted clinical psychologist or psychiatrist picks up from a bewildering variety of information the essential shaping-and-driving force in an individual's life. Experimental approaches tend to be clumsier and less vital as they go about the necessary step-by-step work of science.

The experiment reported here began with a tentative putting together of these two notions of subjective time fields and structuring principles. Assuming that a way could be found to study empirically both of these constructs, we asked ourselves three questions: (1) Is the average adolescent's attitude toward death part of the structuring principle dominant at this point of his life, or does it belong to a second, discrete, psychic organization? (2) Does the nature of the subjective time fields constructed for past, present, and future areas of the life line reflect the operation of a single structuring principle or of several? (3) Whether unitary or multishaped, does the structuring of time fields by the adolescent involve his attitudes toward death, or are these seemingly left out of the picture?

Elucidation of these questions and their implications can be accomplished simultaneously with an account of the experimental results obtained.

Inspection of the way these 260 young men and women responded to a technique designed especially for this experiment provides a tentative answer to our first question. (Conclusions regarding problems of such large scope are best regarded as tentative until verified by additional research.) Within the limits of this one investigation a rather clear-cut phenomenon can be observed: the adolescent has one frame of reference in terms of which he regards most things; but death is separated from this dominant view, and structured much differently.

This result was obtained chiefly by asking the experimental subjects to make a set of judgments. A stimulus word was presented to them, and they were given the task of relating this term to a set of fifteen paired-opposite words. For example, the stimulus term might be *good*. Beneath this term would be found the set of paired opposites, one pair being much–little. In deciding whether *good* was more like "much" or more like "little" the subject had his choice of four response categories: extreme or qualified preference for either alternative. No neutral choice was permitted. The same procedure was repeated for five other stimulus words each of which was judged separately in regard to the identical set of paired opposites.

In effect this procedure forces the subject to make use of his present psychological organization in differentiating and grouping a number of significant concepts. He will structure these ideas in one way or another, and the results can be interpreted as one manifestation of his structuring principle or principles. *Death* was one of the six stimulus terms used; the others were *good, real, life, bright,* and *myself*.

The impressive fact emerging from this data is that while all of the other five concepts are structured comfortably within a single framework, death stands off by itself as a second, self-contained organization that differs diametrically from the former in almost every regard. That tendency within adolescents which leads them to cluster all of the concepts except death we can designate S(structuring) P(principle)/dominant. The smaller, isolated pattern of death judgments can be designated SP/death.

We can now return to our curiosity about the type of structuring involved in past, present, and future time fields. Does the individual shape his entire life line on the basis of SP/dominant, or only certain parts? Is SP/death represented everywhere along his life line, in certain areas, or not at all?

Fortunately there are experimental data available here. As part of the same investigation a rather thorough study was made of these adolescents' structuring of their own past, present, and future. A variety of objective techniques were used and will be described elsewhere. The following conclusions appear to be warranted by the data thus obtained:

1. The adolescent lives in an intense present; "now" is so real to him that both past and future seem pallid by comparison. Everything that is important and valuable in life lies either in the immediate life situation or in the rather close future.

2. Extremely little explicit structuring is given to the remote future by most of the adolescents tested. Those attitudes toward the distal region of the subjective life line that do become manifest are of a distinctly negative character. Most of these fifteen-, sixteen-, and seventeen-year-olds regard their remote time fields as risky, unpleasant, and devoid of significant positive values.

3. More explicit structuring is given to the past than to the remote future, suggesting a greater place for the past in conscious awareness. Curiously, however, the past time fields which can be assessed at a surface level of functioning bear a remarkable similarity to the remote-future time fields which do not lend themselves to such direct observation. The past, too, is seen as a risky, unpleasant place. It is also a vague, confusing place where the adolescent is none too sure of his personal identity.

Evidence is clear that the present time field and that of the proximal future are shaped by SP/dominant. If we describe these time fields as having the subjective connotations of fullness, activity, and reality, we have also described the content of SP/dominant. Moreover, the adolescent regards himself as being at an initial point, at a first position in a series, as a beginner in some all-important but dimly conceived progression toward whatever may be valuable in life.

By contrast, the last point, the terminal position in a series, the end of a progression toward whatever may be valued in life are components of SP/death. The distal—and relatively unstructured—regions of the subjective life line thus appear to be prevailingly under the domination of SP/death. Death is empty, not active—the end. Correspondingly, the remote time fields are weakly structured, at least by conscious efforts, and are considered to be devoid of values. We shall examine the past time fields a little later.

We have seen that the time fields which the adolescent has cared to structure on a conscious, straightforward basis are shaped by that tendency which groups together all concepts but death. We have also seen that the distal future which is weakly structured on a conscious basis is shaped by that tendency which sets death aside as a separate conceptual unit. One possible objection to any conclusion that might be reached from this state of affairs should be considered before proceeding further. The discerning reader might comment that death would perhaps not be such a singular concept if a different set of stimulus terms had been sampled. Despair and oblivion, for example, might well be companions under the same conceptual roof. This consideration is worth mentioning as a corrective to an impression that might otherwise erroneously emerge from the present data, namely that death necessarily has meanings completely unique unto itself. But the possibility that different experimental operations might yield different results is no special cause for concern. The important point is that death, as a representative of one particular class of emotionally loaded ideas, does stand diametrically opposed to another class of emotionally loaded ideas which we know to include the adolescent's identity (*myself*), sense of urgency and significance (*real*), and positive value (*good*), etc.

Examination of the way the adolescent has constructed his present time field and of that dominant structuring principle which includes his attitudes toward himself, reality, goodness, etc., reveals no incongruity, no problem. But now let us project into the future and imagine this same adolescent in his sixth or seventh decade. The peaceful harmony that once existed between SP/dominant and the current subjective time field no longer exists. From our knowledge of the individual's time-structuring and death attitudes at adolescence we would predict a definite disruption at this later point. Here, that which is real, good, bright, throbbing with life, and consistent with self-identity lacks a counterpart in the existing subjective time field. The life line at this position has for years and years been regarded by the individual as a region completely antithetical to the experiences he has known and the values he has cherished.

Conflict rages and the manner of solution has profound implications not for one nook of behavior or cranny of feeling, but for the entire personality of our now aged time-traveler—and for the society in which he lives. Logically there are four alternative outcomes: (1) the death-determined subjective time field prevails; (2) the previous SP/dominant prevails; (3) both prevail on a temporary, pendulum-swing basis; or (4) some sort of compromise is effected.

The four corresponding alternatives, writ large, *might* seem to be (1) a society whose senior generation is dispirited, unproductive, and a grim, forbidding model for its younger contemporaries; (2) a vital, productive, older group that contributes to its society and encourages the younger generation; (3) an unstable, shaky, senior generation that shows flashes of life alternating with a confused and confusing withdrawal; or (4) a toned down, unobtrusive group of aged citizens.

However, the relationships could conceivably be more subtle. If we take into consideration not only the subjective time field the individual has constructed for his advanced years but also the objective changes in his life situation that are likely to occur (diminished physical strength, for example), then we might wonder if unaltered structuring of life according to the principle dominant since adolescence is necessarily the most realistic and productive alternative, or compromise necessarily a mediocre outcome.

It might be that failure to modify one's *Weltanschauung* as the normal changes with age occur and the prospect of death assumes greater imminence will lead to an admirably determined but anachronistic and inappropriate pattern of behavior that has not adapted itself to the unique existential situation of human life at dusk. Similarly, compromise might involve for some individuals a totally new organization of personality in which interplay of the values dominant throughout life and the present, death-shaped time field produces a wise and valuable synthesis that could be achieved at no other time.

The best way to determine how well these outcomes can be differentially predicted from adolescence would be to follow in actuality a person upon whom adolescent data is available all the way along his life's journey. There is no insurmountable obstacle to carrying out such an investigation; but for the moment we must use less direct means.

Compromise between SP/dominant and SP/death when the latter is strongly influencing the time field would seem to depend upon the magnitude of the force by which the individual has characteristically separated these two realms. It might be that the typical adolescent structures death and related meanings differently than he does the dominant meanings in his life, yet not have any investment in actively keeping these two frameworks apart. Were this the case, then compromise and synthesis when the SP/dominant intersects with the SP/death time field would be a highly plausible outcome. But if for some reason he is exerting intrapsychic pressure to keep SP/death away from SP/dominant, then we might expect a more intense conflict with less possibility for compromise solution.

One way to test these alternatives would be to give the adolescent an opportunity to show us the extent of his concern with putting death out of his mind and out of his life. We gave the young people in our sample just such an opportunity by means of another technique developed especially for this study. The three specific items of our interest were embedded in a longer twenty-item test concerned with judgments of time units. The students were asked to regard the width of the test page, from margin to margin, as representing all the time that was available to them. To answer each item they were to draw a line beginning from the extreme left margin of the page to indicate how much of the total (spatialized) time they cared to use for their answer. The lines could be very brief, or could extend clear across the page, although the instructions emphasized that the entire width should be used only in those cases in which they were quite sure they wanted to indicate by their answer all the time possibly available. The thoroughly objective scoring of this test consisted of measuring the lines drawn with rulers graduated in millimeters.

The results? Two of the items had been selected with the emotional meaning of death in mind. What is a long time to be alone? What is a long time to be in a dark room? These two experiences appeared to be as close as most of us have come in our daily lives to living through certain major facets of implicit death expectations. Exploratory study indicated that being alone and being in a dark room were frequently associated with the individual's idea of what death must be like.

The third item asked, "How long is it from youth to old age?" Here was the adolescent's opportunity to indicate how much distance he would be comfortable in having between his present self and the subjective time field over which death casts its shadow.

Both of the death-experience items received almost identical treatment from the experimental subjects: the lines they drew were of virtually equal length. This marked similarity of responses further indicates that both items were tapping the same reservoir of feeling and ideation. It is of course the direction of the results that commands our interest: exceedingly short lines were drawn for the death-experience items, and the longest lines possible were drawn for the death-distance question (despite the instruction to use such extreme responses sparingly).

These results imply on the one hand a very low tolerance for acceptance of death-connoting experiences and, on the other hand, an extreme, active rejection of the SP/death–shaped time field. Being alone or in a dark room is something the adolescent can tolerate for a very brief time only; while he wants to put all the time that he can lay his hands on between himself and his remote-future time field. Thus, compromise in later life between these two structuring principles for the average adolescent (insofar as our sample is representative) seems less likely than domination of one by the other. Inner turmoil followed by radical—rather than gradual—shifts in behavior might therefore mark the entrance of today's adolescent into his remote-future time field.

But there are some adolescents who do not fit this picture, adolescents who are consciously concerned with both death and their remote future. This minority, amounting to about 15 per cent of the total sample, seems to be doing quite a different thing psychologically than their peers who share the consensual view. Instead of keeping the thought of death separate from their present functioning, they attempt to structure their life in terms of goals and experiences far removed in time. The prospect of death is very much alive for them; it enters actively into the decisions they are making while still in the transitional world of adolescence.

When such a person ages it is highly doubtful that he will face death in the manner of his peer who has characteristically refrained from including in his dominant life view the fact of his mortality. Having for years perceived himself within a long-range perspective that emphasizes the place of death in human values, he need not be disorganized by the realization that he has relatively little time remaining between himself and personal death. The actual differences (in the manner of relating to death when the prospect becomes strong) between two adolescents whose outlooks are those described above cannot be determined without further research. We can, however, add two further bits of information: (1) The death-oriented students tend to be more outspokenly religious, church activities being important in their lives. (2) There are no differences in general intellectual ability, suggesting that the way young people integrate the meaning of death into their lives involves something other than IQ alone.

We have not ventured to say at what specific chronological age the individual considers himself to be in this region of the life line where change is to be expected. Common observation informs us that some of the people we know begin thinking and behaving like old-timers when they are as young as forty or fifty, while others apparently regard old age as something that happens to somebody else far into their seventies and eighties. Research specific to this point is needed.

But on the basis of the available data another speculation can be ventured, one that takes us on a backward journey through time in addition to the future projection we have already attempted. Earlier we learned that the adolescent structures his past in a rather curious way, compared with his structuring of the remote future. He has the same sort of negative feelings toward the past as he does toward the distant future—but these feelings about the past seem to be more vivid, more consciously accessible to him. It is as though he were grappling actively with the image of his personal past, not pleased with what it means to him yet unable to put it entirely out of mind.

The qualitative impression this experimenter received in working with the subjects further supported the notion that the past was something they were trying hard to forget, but with only partial success thus far. More resistance and feeling in general was engendered by requests to consider aspects of their past than in any other area of the investigation.

A sense of inner relationship between the ways the past and remote future are handled by the adolescent comes to us when we consider a pair of well-known principles of contemporary psychology:

1. The more ambiguous and unstructured the situation, the

more the individual will impose upon it a personal structure compounded of his own needs and expectations.

2. Emotionally powerful concerns do not evaporate when the individual chooses to bar them from consciousness. Rather they continue to operate unconsciously and influence behavior in divers ways often unknown to the individual himself.

Relating these ideas to our findings suggests the following formulation: The adolescent in his transitional, search-for-identity state, is uncomfortable with his memories of a past in which he lived a role that he is now trying to transcend. He remembers himself as confused, inept, undifferentiated, bound to the wishes of others. As he attempts to repress these unacceptable aspects of his past, the feelings do not disappear but are available for displacement elsewhere, for other areas of expression. It would be difficult to imagine a more likely place for these feelings of cloudy dread and inadequacy to gather than in the subjective time field of the remote future. With all the realistic uncertainty surrounding it, the remote future stands as an unstructured "temporal ink blot" as it were, ready to receive those feelings the adolescent is trying to dislodge from consciousness.

It is as though the adolescent were seeking to throw away his past, but that this unwelcome subjective entity acts as a boomerang which meets him in his conception of the remote future. This "boomerang effect" leads him to attribute in his later years and to the encroachment of death all the dysphoric and terrifying feelings that have made his notion of the past unacceptable to him.

Elsewhere in this volume it has been pointed out that our society tends to discourage straightforward appreciation of the fact of death. This attitude no doubt creates a climate which fosters the "boomerang effect," frightening people away from the sort of honest, conscious contemplation of death that would serve to reduce its ambiguity and terrors. A further contributing factor on a culture-wide level might well be the clustering of values at an early point of the life line. Many have commented on the skimpy, unrewarding role that is offered by and large to our senior citizens. The adolescent who develops in this cultural atmosphere is likely to pattern his own subjective life line along the same model, so that his later years contain little to which he can look forward. Because the future is realistically ambiguous, it can to a large measure be shaped by the wishes and fears the individual projects forward; the expectation selects and prepares future experiences. The wheel comes full circle as the behavior of the once-adolescent, now-aging individual influences the next generation in the development of its attitudes toward later life and death.

The adolescent thus occupies a pivotal position. His maturing outlooks on life and death are strongly influenced by the existing cultural matrix, and the resultant configuration of personal beliefs will strongly influence his future experiences. But it would be a mistake to suppose that the individual is passively shaped by the external forces which operate upon him. We take here the view that on every level of functioning—from the biochemical to the psychological—organisms tend to achieve a synthesis of outer and inner forces.

Yet among humans there are striking differences in the extent to which the individual imposes his own structuring upon external circumstances or engages instead in environmental following. Such differences have been demonstrated with regard to the electrical activity of the brain, visuomotor orientation to the environment, and conscious reaction to emotional stimulation. Possibly, differences at these levels can be related to differences in the structuring of ideas and feelings concerning death. Adolescents who fearfully evade and encapsulate the subject of death seem in effect to have organized their mental lives along the lines of dominant cultural attitudes. Further study of the ways in which they differ from those who have developed more idiosyncratic beliefs would be worth pursuing. This approach could be used to explore the interplay between individual and society which appears to have resulted in a dysphoric outlook toward later life and death.

Examination of this cultural design for a fearful, unproductive, valueless senior generation could be an immensely useful enterprise; within the limitations of the scant data reported here we can already read signs of profound disturbances as the reality of death increases through the years for the young men and women who are even now just stepping over the threshold of adult life.

8 HERMAN FEIFEL

Attitudes toward Death in Some Normal and Mentally Ill Populations

A discerning passage from the Talmud states that "for all creatures, death has been prepared from the beginning." To be alive is to face the possibility of death, of nonbeing. As far as we can determine, man is the only animal who knows consciously that he has to die. Death is something which we all must, sooner or later, come to grips with. Life insurance, Memorial Day, the belief in immortality—all attest to our interest and concern. Historical and ethnological information [6] reveals that reflection concerning death extends back to the earliest known civilizations and exists among practically all peoples. Some investigators [7, 26] hold that fear of death is a universal reaction and that no one is free from it. Freud [12], for instance, postulates the presence of an unconscious death wish in people which he connects with certain tendencies to self-destruction. We have only to think of sports like bobsledding and bullfighting, the behavior of the confirmed alcoholic or addict, the tubercular patient leaving the hospital against medical advice, etc. Melanie Klein [17] believes fear of death to be at the root of all persecutory ideas and so indirectly of all anxiety. Paul Tillich, the theologian, whose influence has made itself felt in American psychiatry, bases his theory of anxiety on the ontological statement that man is finite, or subject to non-being [24]. Others [15] feel that time has meaning for us only because we realize we have to die. Stekel [21] went so far as to express the hypothesis that every fear we have is ultimately a fear of death.

Death themes and fantasies are prominent in psychopathology. Ideas of death are recurrent in some neurotic patients [5, 23] and in the hallucinations of many psychotic patients [3]. There are the stupor of the catatonic patient, sometimes likened to a death state and the delusions of immortality in certain schizophrenics. It may well be that the schizophrenic denial of reality functions, in some way, as a magical holding back, if not undoing, of the possibility of death. If living leads inevitably to death, then death can be fended off by not living. Also, a number of psychoanalysts [11, 19, 20] are of the opinion that one of the main reasons that shock measures produce positive effects in many patients is that these treatments provide them with a kind of death-and-rebirth fantasy experience.

In broader perspective—the meaning of death is no side issue but the central theme at the core not only of the Babylonian epic of Gilgamesh but of some of our most important present philosophicoreligious systems, e.g., existentialism and its striking preoccupation with dread and death; Christianity, where the meaning of life is brought to full expression in its termination. This orientation has enormous practical consequences in all spheres of life, economic and political, as well as moral and religious.

Death is one of the essential realities of life. Despite this, camouflage and unhealthy avoidance of its inexorableness permeate a good deal of our thinking and action in Western culture. Even the words for death and dying are bypassed in much of everyday language by means of euphemisms. It is not the disquieting, "I die," but rather the anonymous, "one passes on," "one ends his days." The *Christian Science Monitor,* one of our outstanding newspapers, did not permit the word to be mentioned in its pages until recently. American movies, for the most part, shy away from tragedy and death and give us "happy endings." Forest Lawn, a cemetery in Los Angeles, proudly claims to minister "not to the dead, but to the living." And one of our industries has as its major interest the creation of greater "lifelike" qualities in the dead. Geoffrey Gorer, the English anthropologist, has commented [13] that death has become, in a certain sense, as unmentionable to us as sex was to the Victorians. He points out that in the nineteenth century most Protestant countries would seem to have subscribed to Pauline beliefs concerning the sinfulness of the body and the certainty of an afterlife. With the weakening of these concepts in the twentieth century, there appears to be a concomitant decrease in the ability of people to contemplate or discuss natural death and physical decomposition.

The underemphasis on the place of the future in psychological thinking is surprising because, in many moments, man responds much more to what is coming than to what has been. Indeed, what a person seeks to become may, at times, well decide what he attends to in his past. The past is an image that changes with our image of ourselves. It has been said that we may *learn* looking backward—we *live* looking forward. A person's thinking and behavior may be influenced more than we recognize by his views, hopes, and fears concerning the nature and meaning of death.

Both theology and philosophy have grappled with the problem of death and its meaning. A review of the psychiatric and psychological literature, however, highlights the lack of any systematic endeavors to bring this area into the domain of controlled investigation. I want to indicate some general findings on attitudes toward death resulting from a continuing series of research investigations [9, 10] which I am now carrying on. They will have to be considered in the nature of an interim report, tentative and subject to change. It should also be kept in mind that they pertain more to conscious and public attitudes than to the "deeper layers" of the personality. The results are based on three major groups: (1)

85 mentally ill patients—mean age, 36 years; (2) 40 older people —mean age, 67 years; and (3) 85 "normals" consisting of 50 young people—mean age, 26 years; and 35 professional people— mean age, 40 years.

In response to the question, "What does death mean to you?" two outlooks dominate. One views death in a philosophic vein as the natural end process of life. The other is of a religious nature, perceiving death as the dissolution of bodily life and, in reality, the beginning of a new life. This finding, in a sense, broadly mirrors the interpretation of death in the history of Western thought. From these two opposite poles, Marcuse (Chapter 5) has suggested, two contrasting ethics may be derived. "On the one hand the attitude toward death is the stoic or skeptic acceptance of the inevitable, or even the repression of the thought of death by life; on the other, the idealistic glorification of death is that which gives 'meaning' to life, or is the precondition for the 'true' life of man."

The philosophic outlook is primary in all groups except the group of normal young people. It is noteworthy that in all the groups, particularly that of mentally ill patients, some find thinking about death so anxiety provoking as to deny having any ideas at all about it. One aspect of the patients' concept of death is also worthy of comment: this is their frequent depiction of death as occurring by violent means. The conjecture is that a violent conception of death mirrors self-held feelings of aggressiveness toward others as well as toward oneself.

When faced with hypothetical situations suggesting the imminence of death, e.g., "If you could do only one more thing before dying, what would you choose to do?", the characteristic choices of the mentally ill patients tend to give priority to activities of a social and religious type, e.g., "give my belongings to charity," "stop war if possible," "know more of God," etc. This is in contrast to the responses from the normal groups which emphasize personal pleasures and gratifications, e.g., "travel all over the world," "live in a new home," etc.

The groups were asked at what age periods they thought people most fear and least fear death. (A study I recently completed shows that there is little difference between subjectively held attitudes in this regard and those generally attributed to others.) The patients and older people select the age period of the seventies and beyond as the time when people most fear death because "you are close to it then"; "you're at the end of your rope." The age periods of the forties and fifties, however, are the ones chosen by the normal group because "death is now a definite possibility and you cannot brush it away," "you want to enjoy your accomplishments," and "your achievement and reproductive life is ending." Interestingly, the patients rank childhood second to the seventies in this respect. Their frequent choice of childhood as a time when people most fear death is somewhat surprising. We have indications that attitudes toward death are strongly influenced by experiences of early life. We also know that children's connotations of death revolve around the idea of deprivation. Since evidence from several directions suggests that, more than the average, mentally disturbed patients come from homes where they experience early deprivation and rejection, it is conceivable that in many such persons, the impact of the fear of death may come to the fore earlier than in most people. Another possible contributing factor is suggested in the psychoanalytic thinking that anxiety concerning death is, in essence, a repetition of previous childhood castration fears. With regard to when people least fear death, all the normal groups choose childhood because "you don't know what it is" and "life seems all ahead of you." The frequent singling out, in this connection, of old age, the period of the seventies and beyond, by the older people is somewhat less expected. The main reasons are "you accept and are resigned to it," "you've lived your life," and "you've least to live for." The inference from the responses of some of the older persons is that certain people fear idleness and uselessness in old age more than they do death.

The *degree* of mental disturbance per se in the patients, apparently, has little effect on their over-all attitudes toward death. Neither neurosis nor psychosis produces attitudes toward death which cannot also be found in normal subjects. The emotional disturbance seemingly serves to bring *specific* attitudes more clearly to the foreground. These results reinforce the findings of Bromberg and Schilder [5].

Examination of the data along lines of sex suggests that women tend to think more *frequently* about death than do men. Exactly what this means needs further study. We should not forget that there is no necessary relationship between thinking about death and fear of death.

In response to the query, "What specific disease do you most often think of in connection with your own death?" a majority in all groups answer "none"—except for the physicians and psychologists among the professional people. Both of these select "heart disease"; the physicians because "it's an occupational hazard" and "I'm suffering from it now"; the psychologists because "it's prevalent in the family" and "I've got trouble with it now." The second most frequently mentioned disease is "cancer" because "my parents died from it," "it's frequent," and "it sneaks up on you." Incidentally, few normal people visualize themselves as dying by means of an accident. This is in contrast to the findings for mentally ill patients, a good proportion of whom see themselves as dying by "crashing in a plane," "being run over by a tractor," "getting shot," etc.

When asked to express their preference as to the "manner, place, and time" of death, an overwhelming majority in all the groups want to die quickly with little suffering—"peacefully in your sleep" as most put it or "having a coronary." The remainder want to have plenty of time in order to make farewells to family and friends. "At home" and "bed" are specifically mentioned by the majority as the preferred place of death. There are, naturally, personal idiosyncracies—"in a garden," "overlooking the ocean," "in a hammock on a spring day." About 15 to 20 per cent in each group say it really doesn't make much difference to them where they die. One wonders whether these responses do not reflect, on some level, a reaction to our modern way of dying. No longer do most of us receive death in the privacy of our homes with the family about and attending us and with a minimum of medicine to prolong life. We die in the "big" hospital with its superior facilities for providing care and alleviating pain, but also with its impersonal intravenous tubes and oxygen tents. It is as if death's reality were being obscured by making it a public event, something which befalls everyone yet no one in particular.

With reference to the time of death—most people say they want to die at night because "it would mean less trouble for everyone concerned"—"little fuss." This concern about "fuss" is also conspicuous in the attitudes of seriously ill patients. Our cultural pattern seemingly fosters a sense of guilt in most of us when we are placed in the dependent role. This is further extended in the dying patient because of his feeling that he will be hated for forcing the living about him to face the necessity and finality of death. The choice of night, outside of the contemplated peaceful end of life it connotes, has many engrossing symbolic overtones. Homer in the Iliad alludes to sleep (Hypnos) and death (Thanatos) as twin brothers—and many of our religious prayers entwine the ideas of sleep and death. Orthodox Jews, for example, on arising from sleep in the morning thank God for having restored them to life again.

While the data were being collected and evaluated, the implication suggested itself that certain persons who fear death strongly may resort to a religious outlook in order to cope with their fears concerning death. I thought it would be fruitful to get comparative data on religious and nonreligious persons, particularly taking into account the "judgment" aspect after death as a possible important variable. The mean age of the religious group (N = 40) was 31.5 years; that of the nonreligious one (N = 42) was 34 years. The main beliefs which characterized the religious group, as distinguished from the nonreligious one, were credence in a divine purpose in the operations of the universe, in a "life after death," and acceptance of the Bible as revealing God's truths. One should be cautious in considering the religious person as invariant; the same holds true for the nonreligious person. Individuals may derive values (sociability, emotional support, sense of belonging, etc.) and need-satisfactions from religious membership and participation that are not necessarily related to religious belief and commitment. Also, individuals may frequently express a religious identification (tradition) without formal membership or commitment. And often, there may be a difference between the value commitments of the individual and those required by the "official" theological structure of his particular faith [14]. In other words, some people may profess religious tenets but not practice them. Others may adopt religion as a kind of defense against "the slings and arrows of outrageous fortune." Then, there are those who incorporate their religious beliefs into the activities of everyday living. Sharper and more definitive categorization is needed in this field. For example, attitudes toward death may well vary among differing denominational groups. Our purpose, however, at this stage, was to get some general measure of fundamentalist or nonfundamentalist outlook.

The religious person, when compared to the nonreligious individual, is personally more afraid of death. The nonreligious individual fears death because "my family may not be provided for," "I want to accomplish certain things yet," "I enjoy life and want to continue on." The emphasis is on fear of discontinuance of life on earth—what's being left behind—rather than on what will happen after death. The stress for the religious person is twofold: concern with afterlife matters "I may go to hell," "I have sins to expiate yet"—as well as with cessation of present earthly experiences. To check whether religious persons, perhaps, were being more honest in admitting to personal fear of death, I thought it would be enlightening to determine the relationship between the individual's fear of death and his belief as to whether he personally was going to heaven or hell. The data indicate that even the belief that one is going to heaven is not sufficient to do away with the personal fear of death in some religious persons. This finding, together with the strong fear of death expressed in the later years by a substantial number of religiously inclined individuals, may well reflect a defensive use, so to speak, of religion by some of our subjects. In a corresponding vein, the religious person in our studies holds a significantly more negative orientation toward the later years of life than does his nonreligious peer.

Along this line, I believe that the frenetic accent on, and continual search for, the "fountain of youth" in many segments of our society reflects, to a certain degree, anxieties concerning death. One of the reasons why we tend to reject the aged is because they remind us of death. Professional people, particularly physicians, who come in contact with chronically and terminally ill patients have noted parallel avoidance tendencies in themselves. Counter-phobic attitudes toward death, for example, may be observed frequently among medical interns. Now this reaction on the part of the physician is understandable—the need to withdraw libido investment, the reality that others may benefit more from his time, etc. But I would submit that some physicians often reject the dying patient because he reactivates or arouses their own fears about dying—that, in some, guilt feelings tied up with death wishes toward one's own parents may play a role, not to speak of the wounded narcissism of the physician, whose function it is to save life, when he is faced with a dying patient who represents a denial of his essential skills. I think it would prove interesting to pursue the relationship aspect of choice of occupation here—where the "saving of life" is paramount, with the personal attitudes concerning death in physicians. In truth, most healthy people feel anxious and guilty at seeing someone else die. Being faced directly with the existential fact of death seems to cast a blight on ego functioning.

It is also relevant to observe that when anxiety about death is noted in the psychiatric literature it is often interpreted essentially as a derivative and secondary phenomenon. Freud derived his fear of death from castration anxiety and from fear of losing the love-object, i.e., anxiety about separation from the mother. There is good clinical evidence that this type of displacement does occur. But, as Wahl (Chapter 2) points out, one wonders whether this formulation also serves in part a defensive need on the part of psychiatrists themselves.

Be that as it may, I think one of the serious mistakes we commit in treating terminally ill patients is the erection of a psychological barrier between the living and dying. Some think and say that it is cruel and traumatic to talk to dying patients about death. Actually, my findings indicate that patients want very much to talk about their feelings and thoughts about death but feel that we, the living, close off the avenues for their accomplishing this.

The democracy of death encompasses us all. Even before its actual arrival, it is an absent presence. To deny or ignore it distorts life's pattern. Some will say "Don't waste time thinking about death—live well the time you have, forget that it ends. To remember that there is an end does something, in spite of good intentions, to cut the nerve of present effort." But what kind of adaptation is it not to consider the end of individual consciousness, which is pertinent to every undertaking of the individual? [16]. Our concern with death is not the sign of a cult of indifference to life or a denial of it. Rather, in gaining an awareness of death, we sharpen and intensify our awareness of life. Augustine in his *Confessions* [1] implies that it is only in the facing of death that man's self is born. Man can completely understand himself only by integrating the death concept into his life. In the first century, Seneca, the Roman philosopher, put it this way: "No man enjoys the true taste of life but he who is willing and ready to quit it." In 1956, the American poet Jesse Stuart [22], recovering from an almost fatal coronary attack, phrased it: "No man really begins to live until he has come close to dying." One of Lael Wertenbaker's perceptions in her book *Death of a Man* [25], a moving account of how her husband faced his impending death, is also relevant here. She writes:

. . . I am reminded of one of those high moments in the New York theatre. In S. N. Behrman's adaptation of Giraudoux's *Amphitryon 38*, Jupiter, the immortal god, takes on the disguise of Amphitryon's mortal flesh in order to make love to Amphitryon's mortal and faithful wife. "And then suddenly," Jupiter says afterward to his fellow god, Mercury, "she will use little expressions—and that widens the abyss between us—" "What expressions?" asks Mercury. Alfred Lunt, acting Jupiter, read the lines so tenderly that they still echo in my memory: "She will say—'When I was a child'—or 'When I'm old'—or 'Never in all my life'—This stabs me, Mercury." Then Jupiter says of the gods: "But we miss something, Mercury—the poignance of the transient— the intimation of mortality—that sweet sadness of grasping at something you cannot hold. . . ." I realize now that mortals miss it, too, when they do not seriously think about death. [27, pages 56 and 57]

Attempts to expel death or not to take death into account are a deception committed by man on himself. No matter how hard man tries to shelve and hush up knowledge of the inevitable end of his earthly life, he never quite succeeds. Knowledge of finiteness may make time the fatal enemy of lasting gratification and introduce a repressive element into all libidinal relations [18]. At the same time, however, it can serve man positively as a galvanizing force—an Aristotelian *vis a tergo* if you will—pushing him forward toward creativity and accomplishment. For human maturity brings along with it a recognition of limit, which is a notable advance in self-knowledge. In a certain sense, the willingness to die appears as a necessary condition of life. (We are not altogether free in any deed as long as we are commanded by an inescapable will to live. In this context, the everyday risks of living, e.g., driving downtown, taking an airplane trip, losing one's guard in sleep, become almost forms of extravagant folly. Life is not genuinely our own until we can renounce it [16]. Montaigne has penetratingly remarked that "only the man who no longer fears death has ceased to be a slave.") This condition has, in large measure, been responsible for many of the advances of our science, medicine, and technology. Not until man overcame the fear of death could he permit himself to be bitten voluntarily by a mosquito infested with yellow fever germs, sail the seven seas, master the art of flying. And tomorrow, this condition will bring into our ken knowledge of vast new worlds of space.

In line with some of the above material, some preliminary thoughts and hypotheses issuing from the initial stages of a research program dealing with attitudes toward death in terminally ill patients, in which I am presently engaged along with a few psychiatric colleagues, may be of interest. A goodly number of terminally ill patients prefer honest and plain talk about the seriousness of their illness from their physicians. They evince a sense of being understood and helped, rather than becoming frightened or panicking, when they can talk about their feelings concerning death. There is truth in the idea that the unknown can be feared more than the most dreaded reality. When the study was initially broached, questions were raised as to the possible negative effect and "stress" aspects of the interviews and testing procedure on the patients. In resulting fact, the vast majority of them showed no untoward reactions. Some of them actually thanked the project personnel for affording them the opportunity to discuss their feelings concerning death. There is almost nothing as crushing to a dying patient as to feel that he has been abandoned or rejected. This realization not only removes support and prevents the patient's getting relief from the guilt feelings of various kinds which he has, but does not even permit him to make use of the denial mechanisms which he may have been able to use until then. It seems that in many circumstances it is not *what* the patient is told, but rather *how* it is done that counts. Patients can accept and integrate information that they are to die in the near future but want a gradual leading-up to this rather than a "cold-shower" technique as one patient put it.

In certain people, fear of the dying process, because of its associations with extreme dependency, the sense of shame, and experiencing of pain, may be more frightening than the idea of death itself. In addition, clinical observation prompts the reflection that, for many individuals, perception of death from a temporal distance and when it is personally near may be two quite different matters. Also, knowledge of the "external" degree of threat alone seems to be an insufficient basis on which to predict with any certainty how a person will react to it. The person's character structure—the type of· person he is—may sometimes be more important than the death-threat stimulus itself in determining reactions. Information that you are to die in the near future does not necessarily constitute an *extreme* stress situation for *specific* individuals. In our ongoing work, we hope to scrutinize closely the existing relationships here, i.e., relating attitudes toward death to the *kind* of person who has them. It is apparent that such a study can serve as a valuable source for enriching and deepening our grasp of adaptive and maladaptive reactions to other types of stress and disaster situations.

My own tentative thesis is that types of reaction to impending death are a function of interweaving factors. Some of the more significant ones appear to be (I strongly support the outlook of Jerome Beigler [2] here) (1) the psychologic maturity of the individual, (2) the kind of coping techniques available to him, (3) variables of religious orientation, age, socioeconomic status, etc., (4) severity of the organic process, and (5) the attitudes of the physician and other significant persons in the patient's world.

The research in progress reinforces the thinking that death can mean different things to different people. Death is a multifaceted symbol the specific import of which depends on the nature and fortunes of the individual's development and his cultural context. To many, death represents a teacher of transcendental truths incomprehensible during life. For others, death is a friend who brings an end to pain through peaceful sleep. Shakespeare expresses it in Macbeth's comment about the murdered King Duncan—"After life's fitful fever, he sleeps well"; Heine in the thought, "Death, it is the cool night." Still others, like the late Lord Balfour, visualize it as an adventure—a great, new oncoming experience. Then there are those who see it as the great destroyer who is to be fought to the bitter end. This is beautifully described by Dylan Thomas, the Welsh poet, "Do not go gentle into that good night . . . rage, rage against the dying of the light"; and expressed in more earthy manner by a dying American general of Revolutionary War fame, Ethan Allen, who, when told by his parson, "General Allen, the angels are waiting for you," replied, "Waiting are they? Waiting are they? Well, God damn 'em, let 'em wait!"

As Bromberg and Schilder [4] have indicated, death may be seen as a means of vengeance to force others to give more affection to us than they are otherwise willing to give us in life; escape from an unbearable situation to a new life without any of the difficulties of our present life; a final narcissistic perfection granting lasting and unchallenged importance to the individual; a means of punishment and atonement—a gratification of masochistic tendencies in the idea of a perpetual self-punishment, etc. One leitmotiv that is continually coming to the fore in work in this area is that the crisis is often not the fact of oncoming death per se, of man's unsurmountable finiteness, but rather the waste of limited years, the unassayed tasks, the locked opportunities, the talents withering in disuse, the avoidable evils which have been done. The tragedy which is underlined is that man dies prematurely and without dignity, that death has not become really "his own."

Systematic research efforts concerning attitudes toward death are definitely in order along the paths of observational survey, depth clinical interview, and experimental and laboratory studies, among others, to illumine effects of the prospect of imminent and not-so-imminent death upon the human individual. Certain aspects (to be studied) come immediately to mind: (1) longitudinal and depth investigation of early and later life attitudes toward death with focus on their origin and development (The adaptation of the older person to dying and death, for example, may well be a crucial aspect of the aging process.); (2) the temporal factor— role of nearness and distance of personal death; (3) the impact of sudden knowledge and the cumulative effect when told that personal death is probable in the near future; (4) the influence of varying frames of reference, such as religious orientation, sex, age, intelligence, socioeconomic status, etc.; (5) relation of death anxiety to self-concept and ego mechanisms; (6) place of attitudes toward death in the psychogenesis of mental illness; (7) role of "public" and "private" ways of dying; (8) the effect of the reactions of a family to dying and the death of one of its members; changes in family structure and attitudes toward death as byproducts of death of a member; (9) cross-cultural differences; (10) relations between attitudes toward death and choice of occupational roles as physician, mortician, executioner, etc.

Fortunately, it will be possible to relate the findings to already existing theory in the fields of learning, perception, stress, reference groups, and social organization—as well as to the powerful theoretical line of psychoanalytic thinking and propositions of behavior theory.

In conclusion, a man's birth is an uncontrolled event in his life, but the manner of his departure from life bears a definite relation to his philosophy of life and death. We are mistaken to consider death as a purely biologic event. The attitudes concerning it, and its meaning for the individual, can serve as an important organizing principle in determining how he conducts himself in life [8]. I think that it is a much-needed step forward in recognizing that the concept of death represents a psychological and social fact of substantial importance—that attitudes toward death can provide us with additional clues in understanding the behavior of the individual—and that the dying words attributed to Goethe, "More light," are particularly appropriate to the field under discussion.

REFERENCES

1. Augustine, Saint: *The Confessions of Saint Augustine,* Sheed & Ward, Inc., New York, 1943.
2. Beigler, J.: "Anxiety as an aid in the prognostication of impending death," *A.M.A. Arch. Neurol. Psychiat.,* **77:** 171–177, 1957.
3. Boisen, A., R. L. Jenkins, and M. Lorr: "Schizophrenic ideation as a striving toward the solution of conflict," *J. Clin. Psychol.,* **10:** 389–391, 1954.
4. Bromberg, W., and P. Schilder: "Death and dying: a comparative study of the attitudes and mental reactions toward death and dying," *Psychoanal. Rev.,* **20:** 133–185, 1933.
5. Bromberg, W., and P. Schilder: "The attitudes of psychoneurotics toward death," *Psychoanal. Rev.,* **23:** 1–28, 1936.
6. Caprio, F. S.: "Ethnological attitudes toward death: a psychoanalytic evaluation," *J. Criminal Psychopathol.,* **7:** 737–752, 1946.
7. Caprio, F. S.: "A study of some psychological reactions during prepubescence to the idea of death," *Psychiat. Quart.,* **24:** 495–505, 1950.
8. Eissler, K. R.: *The Psychiatrist and the Dying Patient,* International Universities Press, Inc., New York, 1955.
9. Feifel, H.: "Attitudes of mentally ill patients toward death," *J. Nervous Mental Disease,* **122:** 375–380, 1955.
10. Feifel, H.: "Older persons look at death," *Geriatrics,* **11:** 127–130, 1956.
11. Fenichel, O.: *The Psychoanalytic Theory of Neuroses,* W. W. Norton & Company, Inc., New York, 1945.
12. Freud, S.: *Beyond the Pleasure Principle,* International Psycho-Analytic Press, London, 1922.
13. Gorer, G.: "The pornography of death," *Encounter,* **5:** 49–52, 1955.
14. Hager, D. J.: "Religious conflict," *J. Social Issues,* **12:** 3–11, 1956.
15. Heidegger, M.: *Sein und Zeit,* Max Niemeyer Verlag, Halle, 1927.
16. Hocking, W. E.: *The Meaning of Immortality in Human Experience,* Harper & Brothers, New York, 1957.
17. Klein, M.: "A contribution to the theory of anxiety and guilt," *Intern. J. Psychoanal.,* **29:** 114–123, 1948.
18. Marcuse, H.: *Eros and Civilization,* The Beacon Press, Boston, 1955.

19. Schilder, P.: "Notes on the psychology of metrazol treatment of schizophrenia," *J. Nervous Mental Disease*, **89:** 133–144, 1939.
20. Silberman, I.: "The psychical experiences during the shocks in shock therapy," *Intern. J. Psychoanal.,* **21:** 179–200, 1940.
21. Stekel, W.: *Conditions of Nervous Anxiety and Their Treatment,* Liveright Publishing Corporation, New York, 1949.
22. Stuart, J.: *The Year of My Rebirth,* McGraw-Hill Book Company, Inc., New York, 1956.
23. Teicher, J. D.: "Combat fatigue or death anxiety neurosis," *J. Nervous Mental Disease,* **117,** 234–243, 1953.
24. Tillich, P.: *The Courage To Be,* Yale University Press, New Haven, Conn., 1952.
25. Wertenbaker, L. T.: *Death of a Man,* Random House, Inc., New York, 1957.
26. Zilboorg, G.: "Fear of death," *Psychoanal. Quart.,* **12:** 465–475, 1943.

PART 3

Death Concept in Cultural and Religious Fields

9 FREDERICK J. HOFFMAN

Mortality and Modern Literature*

A subject of this kind requires both a series of suggestive terms and, to begin with, a few assertions concerning its status as a valid and useful source of insights into literature.† I believe that much may be seen and said of modern literature in terms of the variations upon the figure of death observed in it.[1] But the range of suggestion is vast and one runs the risk of saying either too much or too little about it if he does not see his way clear to certain elementary notions of order.

1

The first of our necessary assertions is that the disposition toward death in twentieth-century literature is different from that in any other. This is true not only because of the phenomenon of total war, with its calculus of impersonal killing,[2] but also because the balance of expectation in the human physical and spiritual organization has been considerably changed. Generally speaking, the integration of death with the tolerance of present time and the expectation of future (that is, postmortem) time has been upset. This is because we have either lost the focus of

---

 * Reprinted (with elaboration by the author) with permission from the *Virginia Quarterly Review*. "Grace, Violence, and Self," **34:** 439–454, 1958.

 † All footnotes are at the end of this chapter.

belief or dispersed our talent for belief over too wide an area of possible objects. The idea of "mystery" has been considerably changed in its nature. In a sense, we are now more than ever dominated by the mysteries of our nature because we know so much; it is possible for us "scientifically" to trace our origins, birth, growth, decline, death, and dissolution to a nicety of explanation. But this development has revealed a serious need that the mystery of both origin and destination had formerly satisfied, the need of an illusion that conceals, postpones, or absorbs knowledge of vital or fatal matters. Death was explained in one or another kind of *myth* or "story," in which superior natures accounted for the moral deficiencies of inferior ones, sacrificed themselves so that the moral economy might be better balanced, or superintended areas of punishment, purgation, or reward. In these circumstances, controlled by whatever systematic theology, death (however disagreeable as a physical experience it might be) was considered a point in time on the way to eternity, or the conclusion of time and the beginning of eternity. The thought of death was also less unpleasant because of the strong conviction of an actual continuance of physical being into eternity.

While these promises and sanctions are not entirely removed from our moral landscape, they are less and less believable. For one thing, since they are not provable, they must either be discredited altogether as "superstitions" or tolerated amiably as allowable indiscretions. One of the major aims of science was to work toward the final elimination of death as a necessary human experience. It is true that no scientists claimed either the ability to remove death or the hope that it might be alogether eliminated. The more realistic ambitions of science were to eliminate disease, to facilitate movement, and to increase comfort. The first of these was a move toward the postponement of death; the second was supposed to reduce the incidence of human misunderstanding; the third was a step on the way to creating a surrogate heaven on earth. This very real and laudable (though certainly shortsighted) ambition tended to distort the human physical and moral economy by eliminating or ignoring certain basic elements of the traditional religious view. The myth of Satan is one of the most powerful in Christian history. The struggle between Satan and God, with its complex allocations of guilt, evil, defection, and contrivance in the human drama, is an indispensable part of the texture of life. To equate evil with disease, discomfort, or "remediable circumstance" is to remove from human psychology the sanction of man's complicity in the development of a moral sense.[3]

Because human passion was not considered an unpredictable, irremediable cause of evil, and because Satan had lost his status as a mythical figure, reflecting and dramatizing the moral imbalance of man, the most blatantly optimistic visions of what science might do by way of postponing death, encouraging benign human intercourse, and establishing a heavenly city on earth were responsible for grievous disillusionments in the twentieth century. The pattern was somewhat as follows: generalities concerning progress, the rational society, and so forth became "battle cries" of the destructive drive; the energies of science, which were supposed to bring about the great society, were turned toward the perfecting not of man but of weapons to destroy men (emancipators became, almost unwittingly, destroyers); most disastrous of all, the *occasion* of death lost the mitigation of the important relationship between man as victim and death as assailant. One could no longer "prepare for" death. Survival became a matter of chance, of "luck." There was little or no possibility either of calculating the moral, physical, and spiritual responsibilities for the event or of adjusting oneself to the range of "illusion" clustered about the hope of immortality.

Since no one has experienced death and survived to describe the experience, the actual nature of death (aside from physical and perhaps psychiatric notations of the degeneration of tissues, etc.) must always depend upon imaginative speculation. Much energy has been expanded upon the metaphors of death as event and death as beginning. Many of the images attaching to death have long been stratified and catalogued, but the need for fresh metaphor remains. There are two principal ranges of image: one is thoroughly realistic, the other as thoroughly "idealistic." In the one case we have the *memento mori,* the conqueror worm, and other paraphernalia of maggotry.[4] In the other case, the imagination strives to eliminate as much as possible the evidences of physical dissolution by substituting for them suggestions of spiritual beginnings. In other words, we have in this second view the idea of death as *transcendence.* All transcendental illusions have at their source the desire to deny the corporeal nature of man, even though sometimes physical and natural details are coyly cherished.[5]

Of course, this is not all that needs to be said about the literary perspective upon mortality. The *choice* of image and metaphor depends upon current milieu sanctions and determinants; upon the relative ease or difficulty of belief; upon the nature of man's realization of his condition at any stage of his progress toward death; and upon the forcefulness of systems of eschatology. One of the most important of all elements in the literature of mortality is the time-space relationship that for any given sensibility governs a specific human nature. This relationship is indispensably associated with eternity and its effect upon the measurement or the sensing of time. One may say that if eternity is definitely credited, the sense of time will be more easily generalized. That is, a man expecting and believing in eternity will be less concerned with his temporal experiences, will see them less in depth than in linear progression toward the beginning of eternity. As the belief in immortality (which is eternity individualized) becomes less and less certain, more attention is paid to time, and time achieves a spatial quality. The passing of time becomes a spatial object or a succession of objects; it is their spatial quality that attracts and not their sequential nature. An age whose people are little convinced of immortality or little comforted by the hope of it is likely to produce a literature that emphasizes the spatial qualities of life. This literature is also concerned with the density of objects, with their texture, with the specific values residing in experiences. If death is a wall and not a doorway, the pace of experience diminishes, the attention to time is translated into an absorption in space, and every detail of change is noted and treasured. Instead of a metaphysic dependent upon an infinite extension of the given, we get an ontology of objects and experiences. Death turns us toward life and forces us to admire or cherish it (even though we despair of it as well), to begrudge the passing of time (which is signified by changes occurring in objects), and eventually to despair of conclusions.

This alteration of perspective is perhaps most easily seen in such a poem as Stevens' *Sunday Morning*. The burden of the poem is its emphasis upon death as a state in time that has to be recognized, is inevitable, and cannot be mitigated by visions of a postmortem paradise. Death becomes "the mother of beauty" in this case, and it is a beauty of objects or of experiences with objects. Similarly, Stevens says in another poem (*Peter Quince at the Clavier*) [6] that

> Beauty is momentary in the mind—
> The fitful tracing of a portal;
> But in the flesh it is immortal.

And the poem describes the kind of spatial immortality that we also see in the last stanza of *Sunday Morning*. Unfortunately, this essay is not the place for more than an abbreviated comment upon Stevens' treatment of this absorbing theme. I believe it to be one of the dominating themes of modern literature. It is, for example, in part responsible for such curious perspectives upon time as we get in Gertrude Stein's *The Making of Americans*. Indeed, Miss Stein's objectives seem, first, to be a kind of spatialization of history (that is, if you can identify parallels in historical events you can all but do away with time and enjoy immortality in a persistent present), and then, to develop a method and style designed as nearly as possible to perpetuate immediacy.

2

I wish to present the major sections of my study according to these three major terms: *Grace, Violence,* and *Self.* I list them in a rough chronological sequence; one may say that the violent destruction of the possibilities of grace has forced upon the self the responsibility of adjustment to death. At any rate, there is some justice in assuming that the terms represent three essential phases of our thanatology.

Grace is a condition of allowance. The human energy can depend upon it. It is a form of assurance of immortality, with various restrictions and rules. Grace requires an imaginative effort; we must believe in "miracles as things." Its effect is to aid us in distributing our native energies; they need not be expended entirely upon current demands, but can be allocated and "deposited," arranged and postponed. In the expectation or hope of grace, we do evil on an installment basis; we are always aware of the necessary compensatory forms of remorse and penance. If we believe in grace, we also believe in immortality; in short, we *believe.* Such a circumstance has a remarkable influence upon our power of metaphor. We expend as much of it upon our vision of the postmortem world as upon the description of the world as a way to death. This does not mean that the world is slighted; on the contrary, the assurance of immortality often makes sin more vividly possible; we sin not from despair but in the expectation of a saving grace. It also affects the quality of sin, and in any event makes both the commission of it and the atonement for it more specifically, concretely, and vividly active in the range of self-judgment and self-criticism.

It is possible to think of blasphemy as an expression of the need of grace. This idea is of course most cogently suggested in T. S. Eliot's essay on Baudelaire (1930), in which he describes "genuine blasphemy" as "a way of affirming belief." One way of reading Baudelaire is to suggest that the predominance of death, darkness, and sordidness in the poems is a way of crying out against the loss of grace in modern life. It is of course very wrong to assume that belief in grace conveniently settles all fears; no literature is a more eloquent testimony of the opposite reading of the role of grace in human life than that of modern Spain. While, on the one hand (in Unamuno's fiction), we have a desperate drive toward sustaining the illusion of immortality (in one of his stories he suggests that to deny a persistent skepticism may be a way of sustaining the illusion), we also have (in Lorca's plays) the imagery of death both announcing the agony of mortality and reminding those who sense it of the elementary compensations of grace. This makes for a very complex portrait of a culture, which can only be suggested here; it has at least been touched upon by almost every commentator upon modern Spain.

I do not suppose that there was ever a time in twentieth-century life when expectations of an eternal life, with proper and discernible sanctions of conduct, were universally or even widely held. It is a matter of *degrees* of credibility, forms of imaginative effect, phases of partial or almost total suspension of such assurances. Most writers who have concerned themselves with the presence of grace have done so in metaphoric terms. Some have put the *time* of grace in the past, have borrowed the most vividly effective metaphors of grace from history and tradition. Others have conceived of grace as an almost purely personal issue: the search for a *means* of defining the reality of man's life demands a scope of metaphor that exists not as the sign of belief but as the area of imaginative speculation concerning mortality.

The secularization of man's self-judgment has had an important effect upon his view of grace. Grace is sometimes seen as health, physical or social. That is, it is what we deserve if we are "scientifically" or "verifiably" good. In this sense, personal immortality is dissolved into a social immortality. A state is progressively strengthened; evil is gradually purified out of it; and I as citizen, in working toward that future condition of bliss (not for myself but for my children's children), share posthumously in it. This concept of grace depends upon an almost absolute faith in futures. Only future time is important in this case; the past is valuable only in showing what we ought to avoid in the present to make the future pure. An exact and exacting discipline of *known* procedures and sound hypotheses is here mixed with an almost blind faith in the linear progress toward a condition infinitely better than exists in the present. Disillusionment comes hard in a matter such as this and is likely to lead to a change from secular to religious values out of desperation.

It is possible of course to see immortality as a purely secular abstraction. The most materialistic of social systems often has the most purely dedicated martyrs. This kind of immortality, expected not on the other side but on this side of death, is a common enough phenomenon in a time when "the other side" is hard to realize, to imagine, or to *see*. It involves the most rigidly doctrinaire and rational discipline as well as the most thoroughly sentimental, even irrational, trust in futures. All of life is in this case governed by a secular monasticism. Death is a proper conclusion, not a beginning at all. It is a sacrifice paid to the future. All men are Christs, suffering so that an idea of what society should be will be actualized.

There are several superficial similarities between secular grace and spiritual grace: the ways in which each acts to provide sanctions and directions for behavior on this earth; the idea (rather hesitantly entertained, it is true) of a postmortem state of blessedness (for secular grace, it is "postmortem" in the sense of existing in a future beyond the deaths of those who are working for it); and the sense of dedication, commitment, surrender of self. The basic *difference* lies in the extraordinary value put upon history in secular grace, the absence of that value in spiritual grace. Eliot can dramatize the situation of Thomas à Becket (in *Murder in the Cathedral*) almost as though neither he nor the situation had ever existed in history. Indeed, any historically grounded temptation offered Thomas is scornfully turned aside; only spiritual temptations affect him. In the best of modern literature devoted to problems of secular grace the reverse is true. Rubashov's major concern (in Koestler's *Darkness at Noon*) is with history; all of his acts, selfish or self-sacrificial, are referred to history, and the question that haunts him to his death is that of the two forms of historical relevance: the humanitarian concern over persons living in the present (that is, *are* people living now a *part* of history or do they merely antedate it?) as against the impersonal view of history that puts ends entirely in the future and thus abstracts them. Thus the definitions of secular grace are constantly being modified in particulars but strengthened and hardened in generalities. It is all but impossible for a literature treating of secular grace to be grounded upon a form of discourse similar to the theological grounding of religious literature. Yet one ought to note, at least for future consideration at this point, that conflicts not altogether dissimilar from those suffered by Rubashov have appeared in the literature of spiritual grace. The temporal and spiritual powers have not always been so neatly differentiated as they are in Eliot's play.

Grace may also be seen as the essence of a *culture*. This is another form of abstraction. At one extreme it is a kind of exalted *tourisme*. Americans are especially vulnerable; sensing that there is something "spiritual" lacking in skyscrapers, they search for it in cathedrals. The literature of the First World War (or part of it) had many examples of this kind of grace. Here it was the architecture, the gardens, the visible forms of a cultural state that inspired. Young men from Nebraska died for "good taste" in France. It is not so easy to speculate upon the terms of immortality in these cases, but I believe that grace does successfully influence the relationship of life-death-immortality here as well. The cathedral and the abbey are symbols of tradition, forms of immortality;

when they are destroyed man is reduced to despair. The culture is linked to goodness, to virtue, to a spiritual world that was otherwise not clearly seen. The young men who died so that culture might survive did not expect an eternity of abbeys and string quartets. Their expectations were otherwise grounded, but they *were* vaguely associated with the classics, and with France. God was dimly seen as a man of taste; it was only proper that men should fight to preserve his best expressions of it.

I should say that one of the best ways of *seeing* grace as culture is to explore the meaning of architectural symbols in literature. This is suggestive of a complex of examples that is beyond the scope of this essay, but I can mention a few possibilities. Cathedrals for Henry James, for example, have several roles: touristic interest in them is lampooned on occasion (as in the case of Christopher Newman's companion on his tour of monuments, in *The American*); Isabel Archer's journey through the streets of Rome (*The Portrait of a Lady*), after her shocking realization of what her husband really is, makes her see buildings for the first time as objects symbolizing experience rather than as mere cultural signs. (She sees the buildings as she sees herself for the first time, the seeing and the moral awareness uniting.) Many minor pieces in modern literature have scoffed satirically at *tourisme* (none more effectively than Eliot's poem, *Lune de Miel*); but there is enough evidence, particularly in the war literature of World War I, to suggest that architecture symbolized a culture, that cultural grace was a real and powerful source of values, and that destruction of abbeys and cathedrals led to despair similar to that suffered by sinners untimely caught by devils. John Dos Passos' Martin Howe (*One Man's Initiation*), seeing a German shell destroy an abbey, is plunged into despair; his John Andrews (*Three Soldiers*) is hospitalized in a "kind of Renaissance hall," and the appropriate ironies are lavishly supplied; but perhaps the most urgent sense of architectural verities is seen in Edith Wharton's several books which touch upon this subject (her novel, *A Son at the Front,* and her essay, *French Ways and their Meaning,* are the most noteworthy) and in Willa Cather's contrasting sense of Nebraska and France. Miss Cather's illusion of cultural grace was extraordinarily strong; Claude Wheeler of *One of Ours* testifies to it abundantly, but one notes again and again, in the posthumous *Willa Cather in Europe,* her own strength and obstinacy in living the illusion, carrying it back with her intact from the first actual experience of Europe. Except for Irwin Shaw (*The Young Lions*) and John Hersey (*A Bell for Adano*) this rather naïve balance of culture and immortality is not entertained in the literature of World War II.

Let me try to suggest some of the meanings of grace in modern literature. It is first of all influential even in extremely naturalistic cases as a spiritual residue. Even blasphemy and profanity testify to its persistence. Some of the most extreme forms of what appear to be "non-Christian" literature give evidence of its endurance. They are Black Masses[7] which follow the form of the ritual for apparently perverse aims. Secondly, the presence of grace testifies to a continuity of tradition. Grace is usually held, in modern literature, to be a condition of the past. We are reminded of the past when we think of immortality. Several ambiguities appear, and they may well provide one of the clues to the meaning of modern literature. Secular conversions often have many of the characteristics of religious conversions. The case of Joaquín on El Sordo's hill is pertinent (Hemingway's *For Whom the Bell Tolls*): his conversion to the Communist ideal had been so thoroughly along Christian lines that in the end it changed over into a Christian faith. So that often modern literature follows the forms of conventional illusions of immortality while at the same time it appears to be renouncing them. The *true* occasions of grace in modern literature, however, are linked to the image of a past that is as much unlike the present as possible.

More specifically, immortality has a profound effect upon the description of death scenes, of dying. Consider, in any number of cases, the scene and what it involves. While death is linked to life as its cause (since living is a succession of devices for bringing life to a close), it is also linked to a postmorten future. The dying man is at the edge of learning the secret of that future.[8] His body, corrupt, is to be given up, his soul to be transported into space, which at the beginning is limited but ends by being infinite. Most important, death is a means of purification. No immortality has been conceived which perpetuates the impurities of the body. There are stages along the way, which may be compared with the religious experience of a devout worshiper. The most vivid of these experiences is the expansion of space—*pure* space, uninhabited, undefiled. The soul "enters into" space, no matter how constricted the actual scene of the dying may be.[9] This is the most significant of the qualities of the death scene. It is what gives much discussion of "the spirit" a sense of spaciousness. The mystic talks not only of the loss of material consciousness, but also of the great expension of space, of air, of light. Immortality begins, then, by gaining space and light at the expense of life. There is also the anthropomorphic sense of the absorption of an inferior by a superior being. Death is thought of as a rebirth into another life, quite unlike this life but with certain metaphoric associations with it. It also is considered a "wedding" of the spirit with God. These metaphors are essentially nonspiritual in their origin, linked to the anthropomorphic aspects of belief.

To these conjectures concerning death much of the literary view of mortality is indebted. The basic ambiguity of the death scene lies in the struggle to the end with the devil; for death is not only a way to eternity, it is also an entrance to the place of judgment. The devil is associated throughout with the senses, with the pleasures and dissipations of the body. The dying man must therefore be purified; hence the predominating representations of whiteness, of spaciousness, of purity, of emptiness. This is a state devoutly to be desired, but it is also one much feared; and it casts a pall upon those who must calculate all offenses in terms of relative and absolute purification. Basically, modern literature, in treating of the phenomena of death, contrasts the images of space and congestion (uncongested space is pure, crowded space is foul). Slum death occurs with every reminder of the constrictions of the grave. The grave is a crowded place, and uncomfortable, as are a jail cell, a flophouse room, a hospital ward, a trench, a city street. None of these places is a proper one for communing with God. Many of the modern images which specify the loss of belief in immortality emphasize this kind of space-congestion: furnished rooms, gutters, passageways, subways, etc. They are forms of hell on earth, a terrestrial hell.[10] Conversely, immortality (which must save persons from these congested areas) is thought of in terms of the most expansive spatial senses: ocean, sky, church (where the spatial sense moves upward, unifying ritual object with infinity), desert spaces, "wide open spaces," or "God's country." [11]

The significance of grace depends upon the predictability of the relationship between the dying man and his expectation of immortality. He must know in advance that he will die, that death while inevitable is also an event for which he has the privilege of preparing. If he dies suddenly, the nature of the assailant as well as his complicity in the pattern of events leading to his death must be comprehensible. The ambiguities of dying should be reduced to personal complexities; he must understand them well enough to accept them. In short, he must be in command of both the space and the time in which his life reaches its conclusion.

3

Violent death does not in itself need to involve the destruction of a belief in immortality. It is not really so much a question of violence as it is one of the passion of committing it. If the violence of one's death (either as actor or as victim) bears a discernible relationship to passion—that is, if the circumstance of death is

consistent with the energy of one's earning it—then the balance of
life, death, and immortality may still be maintained. Most concrete
visions of hell have some fairly intelligible design of punishment
according to the quality and intensity of the deaths that have preceded it. One entertains a metaphor of punishment or purgation
consistent with the nature of sin.

There are two kinds of violence, however, in which this balance is not achieved: violence in excess of expectation ("sentimental violence") [12] and impersonal violence. One may say that any
violence is comprehensible if it is inflicted upon another by personal means within view of the victim, or at least within the range
of the victim's expectation. Any violence which goes beyond these
limits is not comprehensible, and it upsets the calculus of understanding in the matter of dying. One must know from what and
from whom one is dying, or he will not be able to cast up his
accounts. The obvious next step leads us to a consideration of the
"mechanics" of death. The history of death moves from the circumstances of calculated risk or predictable consequence to the condition of the impersonal, unreasonable, unreal, and unseen assailant.
All moral and religious systems depend upon at least a core of
reality and prediction in these matters. One must at least imaginatively, if he cannot literally, accept the circumstances of his death.
Kafka's earnest heroes suffer from a failure of imagination, or at
least they are designed to warn us of the dangers of a too literal
expectation from reality.

The history of our culture is quite adequately clear in these
matters. Once physical law has described the limits of our world,
our literature begins to work within these limits, to borrow the
broad, vague metaphors of fate and destiny, to invoke images of
vast natural forces which overwhelm man. Naturalism so directs
man away from the moral, confessional, and willed levels of his
life that events must take place in a world and in a way that cannot be understood. As a result, naturalist literature fumbles over
the question of motivation, because motivation is no longer clear

if "forces" dictate beyond the power of man to accept and adjust. One of the simplest examples is that of Clyde Griffiths in Dreiser's novel, *An American Tragedy*; his failure to make a decision, while Dreiser tortures his text in an effort to explain it, is a form of motiveless violence; he *allows* a crime to happen (as distinguished from Raskolnikov of Dostoyevsky's *Crime and Punishment*, who *forces* it to happen), and the crime is therefore a consequence of criminal indecision. Naturalist violence of this kind is very close to being impersonal, and one may draw an interesting parallel with other forms of impersonal violence in our literature.

Impersonal violence upsets all of the equilibriums noticeable otherwise in the relationship of life, death, and immortality. There is neither a cause nor a corpse. And since in the overwhelming majority of cases both are necessary to sustain a belief in immortality, most of the sanctions which support a faith in something beyond the self are entirely lacking. Our literature therefore treats of violence in terms of the psychological equivalents of the distance between assailant and victim. There is a direct relevance in the matter of passion expended, both to deal blows and to suffer them. Intellect cannot be substituted for passion. In fact, most of the ambiguities associated with death in modern literature arise because intellect *has* replaced passion as an agent of death. Since the intellect is accessible to almost infinite expansion, the ratio between cause and corpse becomes more and more disproportionate. The credibility and acceptability of death are both dependent upon one's knowing, suspecting, sensing, or imagining the cause. If death comes as a "surprise," it may still be understood as a consequence of one or another kind of inadequacy of body, mind, or spirit. Violent death, however, destroys all expectations, reasonable or imaginable. The history of violence in the twentieth century (and in its literature) follows somewhat along these lines, in terms of the character of the assailant: the assailant as human being, as instrument, as machine, as landscape. In this last case, the assailant is neither human nor mechanical but the entire en-

vironment, the land itself, or the world or the solar system: whatever extent of space the instrument of the assailant has put at his
disposal. Many of the literary expressions of this circumstance have
been given in terms of vast landscapes of desert, or icebound
images of terror, or mountain perspectives.[13] These have the
double function of separating man from time and eliminating most
associations with ordinary reality. The strategy of adjustment to
this kind of violence usually takes the form of making the generalizations defending it as vast, unreal, and unavailable to rational
explanation as the circumstance itself. The natural reaction to
them is to trust nothing that is vague, abstract, and not associated
with immediate experience. Most of the poetry written about the
Second World War considers the landscape of violence that is
the metaphor of that war as a space suspended between the past
the soldier has left and the future to which he hopes to return. The
past and future are identical and together they are antithetically
opposed to the present. A soldier is given a number; he is asked
to be anonymous—that is, he is asked to *give* his passion to the
army so that it may be regulated to the strategies of its military
needs. Having lost or temporarily suspended his identity, he exists
in a state of unreality, of anonymity, which constitutes the circumstance of his death, should he meet it there. This means that
he must risk the chance of death without identity.[14] He is an "unknown soldier" in a vividly statistical sense. The shock of dis-
location is much more vivid in the literature of the First World
War than it is in that of the second. This is because the violence
had little or no precedent and it was therefore not expected. Both
the occasion and the shock of it were a violent separation from the
reality to which the soldier was accustomed. Further, the occasion
of violence on a vast scale had the double result of destroying
precedent and setting up circumstances of violent tension. Much
of our literature is a literature of tension caused either by unexpected violence or by the expectation of violence that does not
occur.

4

We are left with self. The basic mode of adjustment to the phenomena of modern dying is that of self. The self, considered as identifiable entity (it has a name, a sex, a set of qualities identifying it) had once existed in "partnership" either with God or with a philosophy that denied or accommodated Him. It is this association that Unamuno, for example, insists upon, against all dissuasions of reason and logic (*The Tragic Sense of Life*). The history of Kierkegaardian existentialism and of the literature which recalls it is abundantly supplied with issues involving the self and God, belief and acceptance in the face of overwhelmingly discouraging evidence. The shock of violence unaccounted for, unseen, unreal, and unreasonable, meant that the self was separated from most doctrines of sufficient reason; it had to make its "separate peace." Since the self cannot be sustained without some viable code or some illusion, there were many contrived readjustments. The history of religious and emotional "fads" in the years between the wars is well known. The search for a sustaining illusion also led into the byways of mythopoeic research and availed itself of archetypal resources. The modern self tries also to reread the past in terms of its present situation. This is unusual only in the intensity with which it is done. Revivals in literature conspicuously emphasize the heroic struggle with evil, or seize upon dramatizations of force in the near or remote past, or try to reaffirm old religious orthodoxies by combining them with resources in mysticism.[15] In addition, the devotion to technique is a sign of the failure of substance; the mind wishes to live in texture because of its terror of structure. That is, it values objects for their own sakes.[16]

It is not so much that the self needs a God, but that it cannot (or does not wish to) stand alone. It is a comfort to know that patterns of behavior, actual or imagined, are repetitious, shared archetypically with the entire history of the race, are actually a part of a "collective unconscious," to which each self may attend if the need occurs. This is not to defeat death but to gain a kind of immortality in the sharing of undying patterns.

The role of the self in modern literature has undergone one of the most thorough histories an age might contrive. It begins with the "pure, practical" consciousness of William James, developed in a time when self-awareness was something little more than a pleasant game. It begins also in Bergson's *élan vital,* available as it was to only the most exquisite of metaphysical scruples. The pre-eminence of self, or of sensitive self-awareness, could not long endure without its own scorching ironies. Shortly after the beginning of the twentieth century the ironic modes of Laforgue, Corbière, and, occasionally, of Rimbaud became popular and seemed necessary. Some such form of ironic contemplation is evident in at least one phase of the work of most of the modern "giants": Eliot, Pound, Joyce, Gide, even the very early Faulkner. In any case, the self is separated from the "herd," the "mass," the "mostarian" by some contrivance or other, or by virtue of a powerful *non serviam* gesture, or a "separate peace," which requires redefinition of the terms of an enduring armistice. In the 1930s, when the self was not absorbed by the state, it became an isolated intelligence looking on hopelessly upon the wasteland as ever did Eliot's Tiresias, though here with even less prospect of salvation because it was associated with no system whatsoever of therapeutic values.[17] Religious exertions on behalf of the self are conspicuous in this and the following decade. Eliot's is perhaps most notable, but one must also note the Christian fable of William Faulkner, which makes the torturous path described for his early heroes seem like a secularized Ash Wednesday. The Catholic assertion in modern literature, independently avowed in the psychological circumstance of conversion, is also of great importance. This is like a reexamination of the Catholic orthodoxy done over entirely from the perspective of an ego formed from quite different sources. In Robert Lowell, for example, the Calvinist condemns, the Catholic saves; both are indispensable, the Catholic only more so. Many of the Catholic views of the self, while they stay within the knowledge of the Catholic judgment of evil, make dramatic substance of the very real conflict between doctrine and human fallibility. Graham Greene again and again takes his characters on the most complex and tortured of journeys to an end which can be called neither salvation nor damnation but appears to be an intolerable mixture of both.

The most important, and in many ways the most· "realistic" adjustment of the self in recent years is that of the existentialist. It is more persuasive because it does not require an appeal to religious forms to explain the self and because it begins with the naked fact of an isolated self. In these terms, the problem of the "absurd," which is after all what the violence of our century has given us, can be and must be considered. It is related to the defeat of rationalist expectations, begins with the acceptance of such a defeat. In these circumstances, the entire growth of the sensibility is seen with death as a terminus. At least for the purpose of present realization, there is nothing beyond death. It is important that there be nothing, because self-awareness ought not to be mitigated by promises or soothing prior knowledges. The terror of immediate self-realization is an experience of death-in-life which, at least in some of its manifestations, is consonant with the century's violent history. In terms of it, Sartre, at least, has developed a cosmogony, an eschatology, an earth, and a hell—solely along lines of the immediate issues of existence in space and endurance in time that emerge from the abandonment of immortality. One endures, not because man is good and "will prevail," but because he exists, because he will die sometime but meanwhile must live.

One needs to point out that Sartre does not stress the "death-as-terminus" theme with nearly the strength of Heidegger. Nevertheless, the role of death and its effect on the range and limits of human expectations are sufficiently important to occupy a rather high place in Sartre's thinking. While the major Sartrean terror is nothingness (void, emptiness, despair over the chance of achieving continuity), death is one of the most important figures in which this nothingness is imaginatively realized. Both the story *The Wall* and the play *The Victors* testify to the overwhelming effect upon man caused by the certainty of death. And the final decision of the hero of the play *Dirty Hands* is motivated by his wish to control the image of death as it applies to a man he has killed.

What I have given here is only a small portion of the speculation necessary in any exact and thorough study of death and modern literature. My principal objective has been to show that each of the three major terms—grace, violence, and self—has a determining influence upon the ways in which death as event is invested with image and metaphor, and that the pattern of life-death-immortality is distinct in each case. We have in the first of these cases a clearly seen development of the human consciousness; the images of death are borrowed from those of life, and there is a close relationship between primary and secondary qualities (between abstractions and sensuous detail). In the second case, the ordinary expectation of immortality is violated, and the balance of assailant and victim, of cause and corpse, is upset. As a result, death ranges from statistical loss to complete annihilation, but in any event the calculus of proper and responsible judgment of death as a predictable result of understandable causes no longer obtains. Finally, the various mutations of the self in the twentieth century lead us perhaps to the present and to the pin point of existence as the irreducible starting point. This is a reconstructive beginning, perhaps; it is prefigured in a number of ways in twentieth-century literature. In any case, self, defined by existence as prior law, is a pervasive and often an obsessive notion underlying much modern literature.

NOTES

1. I wish to express my gratitude to my students in English 548 at the University of Washington, during the summer term of 1957, with whom I discussed many of the ideas analyzed in this paper. They are not responsible for any mistakes I may have made.

2. A number of minor literary ironies have played upon this fact: see especially Randall Jarrell's poem *Losses* and the last sentence of Chap. 1 of Hemingway's *A Farewell to Arms*.

3. One of the most affecting explorations of this condition is to be found in the work of Wallace Stevens, conspicuously in the long poem, *Esthétique du Mal*, and in the essay, *The Noble Rider and the Sound of Words*. But the need for a figure like Satan, who embodies much or all of the evil as well as dramatizes some of the uncertainties of our natures, is revealed in a number of other "modern" texts. Perhaps the most provocative of these is the alter-ego devil of Ivan Karamazov, who bears a much more traditional relationship to theological disputes of Dostoyevsky's time and ours than does the Faustian creation of Adrian Leverkühn in Mann's *Doctor Faustus*. It is interesting to note that Sartre's devil of *No Exit* is reduced to the status of a valet in hell, and hell is itself an interior landscape of the mind and self; this is consistent, of course, with Sartre's theory of the self and his avoidance of theological supports for the imagination.

4. Perhaps one need not point up the fascination with corpses in modern literature; this is in part a product of naturalist influence (there is in this respect a discernible line leading from Stephen Crane to Norman Mailer), but it is also and more importantly a result of experience, particularly the experience of World War I. The most immediately interesting of the "studies" of corpses seen in attitudes of sudden and surprising death is Hemingway's *A Natural History of the Dead*.

5. Both of these approaches to death are brilliantly represented in Mann's novel, *Buddenbrooks*. Indeed, death as transcendence gives way to death as dissolution as the distinction of the Buddenbrook family declines and collapses. Thomas Buddenbrook's toothache is a signal of the disaster (a collapse of decorum more than of the spirit) that occurs almost immediately after his strenuous bout

with his dentist. The toothache as a metaphysical sign of the body eroding the spirit is also a rather elaborate motif in Arthur Koestler's novel, *Darkness at Noon.*

6. W. Stevens, "Peter Quince at the Clavier," *The Collected Poems of Wallace Stevens,* Alfred A. Knopf, Inc., New York, 1954.

7. A conspicuous example is Joe Christmas' appearance in a Negro church (William Faulkner's *Light in August*); his behavior there culminates a complex irony directed against the perversion of religious values. In contrast, the Negro Easter service in Part IV of *The Sound and the Fury* is endowed with qualities of grace and simplicity; but the scene is itself described as two-dimensional, as though the final dimension were to be postponed to the "other world," which is brilliantly and emphatically promised by the Reverend Shegog, imported from Saint Louis to assure Dilsey and her friends of the "ricklickshun en de Lamb."

8. One thinks of the deathbed scene of Father Lucero (Willa Cather, *Death Comes for the Archbishop,* Alfred A. Knopf, Inc., New York, 1950.): "Among the watchers there was always hope that the dying man might reveal something of what he alone could see; that his countenance, if not his lips, would speak, and on his features would fall some light or shadow from beyond."

9. Perhaps it is not too extravagant to suggest at this point the interesting spatial figurations in E. M. Forster's novel, *Howards End.* Howards End itself, presided over by Ruth Wilcox and after her death by the Schlegel sisters, is spatially related to immortality and its requisite acknowledgment of death in the human economy. As a country house not too far separated from the rapidly growing city, it is constantly threatened by roads, motors, and industrial developments; dust, smog, and smoke similarly threaten the horizon. But it is there, where one has a *feeling* of space, that the soul is nourished and prepared for its entrance into death. The recognition of death will save man, as against his horrifyingly naïve and urgent effort to deny it. The novel brilliantly illustrates many of the ideas I discuss in this essay.

10. Examples are numerous and their meanings complex: Eliot's *Preludes, Rhapsody on a Windy Night,* the London tube of the *Quartets;* Allen Tate's *Subway;* Hart Crane's *The Tunnel,* next to last poem of *The Bridge* (though Part II of his *For the Marriage of Faustus and Helen* suggests the jazz rhythms of a secular

heaven); the scene of E. E. Cummings' *The Enormous Room,*
"unmistakably ecclesiastical in feeling" but now reduced in space
and abominably crowded.

11. These images are much more conventional than those which describe the hell of disbelief. There is a strong line from Whitman
through modern poetry describing both death and immortality in
terms of the sea (for example, Hart Crane's *Voyages,* Marianne
Moore's *A Grave,* Eliot's *Dry Salvages*). As for desert spaces, one
need only observe the very effective imagery of retreat into death
and immortality in Willa Cather's *The Professor's House,* or contrast many of the love scenes of D. H. Lawrence's *The Rainbow*
and *Women in Love* with his portrayal of the soul's *mise en scène*
in *St. Mawr.* Perhaps the most elaborate use of the sea symbol is
found in Mann's *Death in Venice.* Premonitions of death begin
with the cemetery as setting; Venice and the sea are at the beginning of Aschenbach's decline (before he knows of it), framed
neatly, though even then there are omens of disaster; as he falls
in love with Tadzio, the sea acts as background of the "perfect
form" of his beloved; eventually we see the terrifying conflict between Aschenbach's notion of "perfect form," which in itself is
empty, and the chaos described both in the sea and in the plague-
infested streets of Venice.

12. A remarkably successful example of "sentimental violence" is
found in the figure of Robert Cohn, in Hemingway's novel *The
Sun Also Rises;* here Cohn's skill as a boxer propels him into
violence against his friends for "romantic" purposes. His romanticism (a naïve failure to read human situations correctly, a literal
earnestness concerning literary clichés) is powered by his skill,
which had originally been acquired for unrealistic purposes. These
subtleties are entirely missing in the recent film version of the
novel.

13. One thinks especially of W. H. Auden's early poems (*Poems, 1930*)
and of such plays as *The Ascent of F-6;* the terror of impersonality
in situations demanding consideration of death is implicit in images either of vast desert or high mountain peaks. In another context, the characters of Paul Bowles' novel, *The Sheltering Sky,*
experience the desolation of impersonality in terms of vast ex-
panses of desert scene. Eliot's *The Waste Land* borrows this impression from ancient symbolic use of it, but something of the
same terror is felt, especially in the opening lines of Part V.

14. One thinks of certain poems of Randall Jarrell, Karl Shapiro, Hubert Creekmore, Charles Butler, and Harry Brown; and, by contrast, some poems of Richard Eberhart, which attempt to "understand" death and almost succeed in doing so. One gets the same haunting sensation of war as an anonymous interim between two existences in much of World War II fiction: in Mailer's *The Naked and the Dead,* Brown's *A Walk in the Sun,* John Holmes Burns' *The Gallery,* for example.

15. Perhaps this phenomenon will prove to be the most rewarding of all to examine. It is not so much the fact of these revivals as the peculiarly personal nature of them that is so striking. Just a glance at Eliot's and Pound's reviews of Dante and of their reasons for admiring him might prove extremely profitable. The point that need be made here is that the reasons for taste are personal and are closely linked to reactions of the self to violence. Other examples are Sartre's play, *The Flies,* Simone Weil's little pamphlet on *The Iliad;* and, in the light of recent stresses upon religious examination, the increase of studies of Dante's *Purgatorio,* as compared with the dominating popularity of *Inferno* two or three decades ago.

16. This is a matter of tremendous importance. It is linked with my discussion of death and space. While formalist criticism can scarcely be explained historically in so simple a way as this, it is undeniably true that concentration upon form (together with the "imagist" development in poetry) does stem from a distrust of generalizations that are identified with a simple religious confidence.

17. Perhaps the most conspicuous example is the "Camera Eye" technique of Dos Passos' trilogy, *U.S.A.* It is actually an expression of despair over every "communal gesture" toward progress. In a sense, the self discussed in Sartre's persuasive essay on *U.S.A.,* "The Camera Eye," and the sensitive reader of the trilogy are one and the same person.

10 CARLA GOTTLIEB

Modern Art and Death*

Art generally seeks its inspiration from the important in human life. Along with birth and marriage, death marks a definite peak in an individual's existence. Small wonder, then, that the theme of death is a common subject in art, found in all styles and dating back to the creations of the cave man.

Our present age has witnessed mass murder and mass death overriding the disasters wrought by the plagues at the end of the Middle Ages, a period exceptionally rich in the creation of death images. Yet, surprisingly, the representation of death is underplayed in much of modern art, except for certain artists active at the end of the nineteenth century. Entire groups of artists have avoided it, such as the Impressionists, Matisse and the Fauves, Bonnard, and Vuillard, etc. An important section of modern art has tended to spotlight the incidental and the marginal. Take, for example, the painter Degas: he shows us the laundress not laundering but yawning or tipping the bottle; and the woman at her toilet no longer an object of beauty for the admiration of the connoisseur—but scratching her back.

Modern art, with its rejection of the death image as important, may indicate a need to counteract the spirit of dejection caused by the dreadful events witnessed during

---

* All footnotes are at the end of this chapter.

the last hundred years. Matisse stated that he would like his art to function as a mental soother for the human race.[1] If the above hypothesis be true, then it appears that our age fights oppressive thoughts by burying them while the fourteenth and fifteenth centuries sought release by materializing their horrors. The one period of intense interest in death during the last hundred years, viz., the last decades of the nineteenth century, seems related to the apocalyptic feeling that something was about to end and to be buried. Literature is full of references to the *fin du siècle*. Not only the nineteenth century, but a way of life was coming to an end. The bourgeois-*rentier* of the industrial age was giving way to the adventurer-explorer of the space age. This poses the question as to whether the coincidence between the preoccupation with death and the end of an era is accidental. It is not possible to give a definite answer. But it is suggestive that the fifteenth century was likewise a turning point in the history of mankind: it marked the end of the Middle Ages and ushered in the modern age. Perhaps the use of the theme of death was caused not merely by the hecatomb of dead, as is commonly believed, but by some special power of the artist to sense a coming change.

All visual themes, whatever their nature, can be developed in several ways: they can be exalted, satirized, or registered impartially. Additionally, the individual theme poses specific problems for the artist. In the case of death, the artist can deal either with the abstract idea of death or with a specific event of some person or persons meeting death. As an abstract idea, Death can be personified or referred to by symbols. The specific event permits variations in the choice of time, place, and circumstances. As his pregnant moment, the artist may select the before (the dying) or the after (the dead). As circumstance, he may depict the lonely and voluntary death of a suicide or the communal and ordered death of the soldier; the normal death of an old man, the untimely death of a child, or murder. Death may arrive for us as a deliverer or as ravisher; it may be courted or feared. Each artist in making his choice thereby reveals his attitudes toward life and death and hence permits certain insights into his character. The personal reasons for favoring the theme of death are likewise manifold, such as an inclination toward violence as well as an abhorrence of violence; a feeling of impending doom; preoccupation with the fundamentals of life as well as a love for the macabre, fantastic, and burlesque. My goal will be to uncover iconographic motifs within the period 1850 to 1950 and, in contrasting them with those used by earlier ages, sum up their meaning.

PERSONIFICATIONS OF DEATH

The Old Testament speaks of death as an angel sent by God (II Kings, 19: 35–37), the New Testament as a rider on a pale horse (Revelations, 6: 8), and the Iliad as the brother of sleep carrying away the body of the deceased Sarpedon (XVI, 668 ff., etc.). These descriptions have their parallel in the visual arts. Many graves are adorned with the angel of death, and a goodly number of ancient vases are decorated with the image from Homer. Dürer's two prints, *The Four Horsemen* and *Knight, Death, and Devil,* exemplify the rider on a pale horse. To these representations, the late Gothic period added a new and most compelling portrait of death: the corpse. First, a mummified, shrunken body was shown, but within fifty years this had evolved into a skeleton from which the flesh had rotted away. There is an interesting contrast here. The images of the Old and New Testaments depict death as an angel or rider—with poetical license in visionary form;[2] those of the Iliad and the 1400s represent death as the twin brother of sleep or as a skeleton—as the living person ordinarily sees his own kin when dead.

Modern art has made no contribution to the portrayal of death personified. Modern painters and sculptors both shy away from allegory as literal and rely rather upon symbols. It is in this latter domain that we find their imagination at work.

TRADITIONAL SYMBOLS FOR DEATH

Some of the traditional symbols for death are the scythe and hourglass borrowed from the god Chronos (Time), the bow and arrow borrowed from the god Eros (Love), the inverted torch, and the sword. Skulls and bones are other obvious references to death. Such *mementi mori*—to give them their official title—have been employed widely by artists. Yet the purpose for which they were shown has varied with the age concerned. Silver skeletons or simulated corpses in coffins were passed around at Egyptian and Roman feasts (Herodotus, II, 78; Petronius, *Satyricon,* 34). By reminding the guests of what lay in store for them, they served as an incentive to enjoy life while it was possible. These *mementi-mori* were based upon "Enjoy the day," the motto immortalized by Horace's ode.

Medieval Christian art had quite a different aim when it showed skulls and bones. It wanted to remind us of the transitoriness and unimportance of earthly life. As expressed in a famous Latin antiphon by Notker Balbulus of St. Gall (A.D. 830–912): "In the middle of life we are in death." Christian *mementi mori* preach the *Vanity* theme. The 1400s added a particularly grisly motif to the repertoire of Vanities: the deceased shown on his funeral monument as a mummy, a decaying corpse, or a skeleton. This image was supposed to be interpreted as a likeness of the dead since it substituted for the portraits used on tombstones up to this time. The best-known example of this kind is the tomb of Cardinal Lagrange (d. 1402), now in the Musée Calvet, Avignon. The inscription expostulates as follows: "Wretch what reason hast thou to be proud? Ashes thou art, and soon thou wilt be like me, a fetid corpse, feeding ground for worms." [3] In some cases two effigies were carved, one showing the deceased as he looked when still alive, the other representing him as a mummy, corpse, or skeleton. This variant has a further meaning in addition to that of vanity: it opposed life to death. Such an idea was also expressed by paintings which showed a child facing a skull or similar motifs.

A good many modern artists have used the established symbols of skull, scythe, or inverted torch—even Cézanne whose subject matter is quite traditional when compared to his strikingly new form. Twice in his life Cézanne was interested in the *Vanity* piece composed of skull, candle, and closed book: as a young man in his middle twenties (1865–1867) and in old age during his last decade of life (1894–1905). One of his paintings, executed about 1894–1896 (Barnes Foundation, Merion, Pennsylvania), shows a youth opposed to a skull, thus revealing a philosophical preoccupation with the meaning of human existence. This is one of the rare instances when Cézanne meets on common ground with his great contemporary antipode, van Gogh. In September, 1889, van Gogh painted a cornfield with a big sun and a reaper with scythe (Kröller-Müller Museum) on which he commented as follows: ". . . a vague figure fighting like a devil in the midst of the heat to get to the end of his task—I see in him the image of death, in the sense that humanity might be the wheat he is reaping. So it is—if you like—the opposite to that sower I tried to do before. But there's nothing sad in this death, it goes its way in broad daylight with a sun flooding everything with a light of pure gold . . ." (letter no. 604).[4] Van Gogh permeated traditional subject matter with personal interpretations; this was characteristic of the man.

Another artist haunted by the problem of life and death was Gauguin. However, he rejected the use of instituted symbols, finding it franker to state his meaning through the titles of his paintings, e.g., *Where do we come from? What are we? Where are we going?* which was completed in 1897 (Museum of Fine

Arts, Boston). Picasso too was not immune to metaphysical anguish. But in this giant it is possible to trace several approaches conjointly. Starting out with the use of a symbolic title in the manner of Gauguin (*Life,* 1903, Cleveland Museum of Art), he followed up in the vein of Cézanne with the use of traditional symbols (juxtaposition of a youth and a skull in the first sketch for the *Demoiselles d'Avignon,* 1906; Vanities with skulls, 1939, 1942, 1945, 1951). After the Second World War he equated Life and Death with *War and Peace,* 1952 (Vallauris). War and death had become synonymous for many artists.

In addition to the symbols borrowed from personifications of death, there had always existed—and still exist—other symbols derived from different pertinent domains. They may be listed in four groups:

1. Motifs drawn from death in other realms than the human, such as leafless trees, trees struck by lightning, ruins, or wintry scenes. Modern paintings of this kind are Cézanne's *Quarries,* which belong to his old age, and Erich Heckel's *Spring in Flanders,* done in 1916.

2. Motifs based upon the cemetery and its inventory of coffins, sepulchral urns, and vultures. Here belong van Gogh's cypress trees and his crows, motifs which appear in his art after his first attack of madness; Picasso's *Woman Kissing a Crow,* 1904 (Toledo Museum of Art); and Klee's *Purple Asters,* completed in 1919.

3. Motifs referring to slaughter, such as the amputated limbs in Goya, Géricault—and continued in modern art by Hyman Bloom, Picasso, etc. While the preceding sets of symbols do not contain any indication of violence, since death, ruin, and decay come about in course of time, the last-named shows death despoiling the human being of his dignity. In that resides its gruesomeness.

4. Instruments which can cause death: weapons, knives, etc. These are conspicuous in Max Beckmann's paintings.

All these motifs will become symbols of death only within a conducive context; otherwise the spectator reads them on their first level of meaning. This is true even of dismembered joints which—as ham in Pieter Claesz. or Gauguin—are seen simply as pieces of meat. In Picasso's *Still Life with Blood Sausage* (Figure 1), the hidden meaning has become obvious only because the artist confided to the dealer Janis that the knives and forks which spill over the table's drawer are for him ". . . like souls out of Purgatory."[5] Thus this innocuous still life acquires an ominous significance. Two equally distasteful interpretations present themselves: man is an instrument of death, and objects are our equals and will encounter bliss or damnation at the end of time.

THE CLOCK AS A MODERN SYMBOL FOR DEATH

The modern equivalent for the hourglass is the clock or watch, and this motif recurs in modern art in widely disparate circles. I shall discuss its meaning for Cézanne, Klee, Dali, and Chagall.

About 1870, shortly after his early *Skulls,* Cézanne painted a still life, *The Black Clock* (Niarchos collection). In it are displayed a collection of bric-a-brac, prominent among them an ormolu clock that lacks hands. Cézanne has time stand still as in eternity. This motif was never repeated by the artist.

Klee's life philosophy is shaded slightly differently, stressing afterlife rather than eternity. He used timepieces in several paintings, even juxtaposing in the same work clock and hourglass, old and new motif. However, Klee's clocks usually have hands which are set in several instances at the hour of ghosts, twelve to one o'clock. In his water color *Heavenly and Earthly Time* (Figure 2), the church is inscribed ¾ 1 while the clock itself is blank. Hourglass shapes are strewed around generously. Through his title Klee stated explicitly that for him "Heavenly Time" exists.

Dali has chosen the watch instead of the clock. With him the motif is incidental as it is with Cézanne,[6] but his *The Persistence of Memory* (Figure 3) is so well known that this is often over-looked. In this painting the watches are broken in one way or another and thus arrested. One watch, suspended from a barren tree which grows out of a barren table, is bent in two. Folded over the edge of the table lies another bent watch. Next to it is a watch that crawls with insects. Yet another limp watch is wrapped as a blanket over the back of a form that resembles not only a sea lion but also a hand and lies on an absolutely barren ground with stones as pillows. The background to this scene is formed by an empty sky and an empty mountain range. In the title of the painting, Dali alludes to those who live with memories instead of in the present. His image illustrates the danger of such an attitude. The dead past contaminates the present, twisting it into a likeness of death. By means of the lifeless watches, Dali is not referring to eternity or afterlife but to deadness. He sees death as waste—ruin and barrenness and instead of worrying about meta-physical questions, he is pointing a moral.

On the other hand the timeless clock, though referring to eternity, may not refer to death. Chagall's *Time is a River without Banks* (Figure 4) uses this motif. On a broad river floats a tiny boat, apparently a symbol of human life carried on the back of the stream of time. Two lovers lie on the river's border. They are outside of time's stream, oblivious of the passing hours. "To the fortunate time stands still . . ." says Schiller in *Wallenstein*. This is symbolized by the large pendulum clock without hands which floats in the center of the painting. Above it flies a winged fish which plays the violin. He, like the lovers, has escaped from the confining stream of time—his music endowing him with wings: the artist lives forever through his art.

NONOBJECTIVE WAYS TO EXPRESS DEATH

A great many modern works of art are abstract and nonobjec-tive. This poses the question: can death be expressed by form alone? I believe that color, line, and shape—isolated or in conjunction—can convey the idea of death as well as any realistic image. The most obvious examples that come to mind are the color black, lacerating crisscross lines, and jagged, sharp shapes. Care should be taken, however, not to generalize that any of the above are per se a reference to death. The context in which they appear is all-important for understanding their message. Sometimes the artist clarifies his intention by titling his work or by making a statement.

Many modern artists have worked with black and its derivatives. Louise Nevelson has built constructions from painted black wood. She has called one *Sky Cathedral,* 1958 (Museum of Modern Art, New York), another, *Moon Dial.* These titles reveal that she has chosen black for denoting the ignorance of what man faces after death. Picasso's *Still Life with Blood Sausage* (Figure 1) is a grisaille. The artist wished to convey "an atmosphere like Philip II, dark and dismal." [5] Hence gray signified to Picasso obscurantism and the oppression which is the death of the mind. Painted during the German occupation in 1941, the meaning of the reference is self-evident. Since death may be equated with nothingness as well as with life in a better world, chromatic colors are not the only ones to express it. Ethel Schwabacher's *Dead Leaves,* 1956 (Parsons Gallery), are painted in jubilant, joyful reds. As she did not title her painting *"Autumn" Leaves* or *"Fallen" Leaves* but *"Dead" Leaves* we conclude that death for her is glorification, intensification of earthly life. Moreover, a chromatic color may even stand for a "black" mood. During the years 1949 to 1955, Kline had painted black hieroglyphs. His recent works are done in yellow. Far from meaning sunshine as many people thought, they are a way of communicating his depression.[7]

Crisscross lines convey two ideas: deliberate hurting and imprisonment. Jean Bazaine, Mark Tobey, Willem de Kooning, Carzou (Figure 5), Jimmy Ernst, and many other artists have utilized these. The figure is left impotent in the grip of powerful, external, incalculable forces. Bazaine speaks of ". . . the anguish of a man turned in on himself, dispossessed of a world he no longer recognizes." [8] Black symbolizes the stillness after man has died. The lacerating line symbolizes the fight between a hostile world and man driven into a corner; it is the moment before death when there is no hope left for escape. Crisscross lines may be employed in representational and nonrepresentational images. Let us examine their expressive value in the art of the representational French painter Carzou within the context of his subject matter. Carzou's themes deal with two opposite things: dead glories and present-day achievements. He depicts churchyards of ships, dead places like Venice and Versailles, outmoded tools such as ploughs. But he also portrays instruments which scarify man and nature such as cannons and oil wells. Built after the likeness of the cathedral spire, the latter are the unnatural emblems of faith of the modern world. In Carzou's *The Forest,* 1957 (Artist's collection), enormously tall, thin trees surround and overshadow a group of workmen. Even nature has turned against man.

The sensation of wounding is also induced by shapes in the form of thorns, barbed wire, or shears. These appear in the art of Chadwick, Lipton, Graham Sutherland, Herbert Ferber, and Georgia O'Keeffe. An even stronger odor of death is felt in shapes reminiscent of bones and skeletons as used by Hare, Noguchi, Lassaw, Amino, and the Surrealist artists. The evocation is particularly forceful if an upright human figure underlies the image shown. In some cases the reference to death is not provoked purposely by the artist, but comes out of his unconscious so that he may even be unaware of what his image actually conveys.

The foregoing is a short survey of formal means utilized to express death. Certainly many more examples could be found. It is sufficient, however, to indicate that nonobjective art can approach the portrayal of death from many different angles and associate it with liberation from earthly toil (Schwabacher), the gloom of Hades' world of shadows (Kline), mystery (Nevelson), the vanity of earthly life (Noguchi, Amino), torture (Carzou), and peace (Nevelson).

THE ARTISTIC TEMPERAMENT REFLECTED IN THE PORTRAYAL OF DEATH

Death is the great mystery and excels in controversial associations, several of which have already been encountered. The artist will meet it according to his natural disposition, be it that of philosopher, moralist, dreamer, humorist, or terrorist. Three reasons may impel him to turn to the theme of death: a personal experience, an historical event, or a state of mind. Even where the death image appears sporadically, it may still be founded upon a state of mind. And even when it refers to a specific historical event, the latter may be only a pretext for veiling the real reason for its use. Picasso's *Guernica* was completed within six weeks after the bombing of the Basque city by German planes in 1937. Yet, as Brendel has shown,[9] only the mother and child are new symbols in Picasso's art. The constellation of bull and horse and the loose arm of the soldier had appeared in his works before the annihilation of the civilian population of Guernica. Out of old material, drawn from disparate sources, Picasso has made a pertinent, coherent, deeply moving statement.

Philosophy is considered the queen of disciplines. In studying the variety of artistic temperaments as revealed in the representation of death we shall therefore begin with the philosopher. The nineteen-year-old Chagall composed in 1908 his *Death* or *Candles on a Dark Street* (Artist's collection). In 1909 he painted the *Wedding* (Paris, private collection), another *Wedding* in 1910 (owned by the artist), also *The Birth* (owned by the artist), and in 1913 the *Pregnant Woman* (Municipal Museum, Amsterdam). Within this sequence Chagall's *Death* is revealed as part of the cycle of life. Chagall is old-fashioned in that he likes to depict special events in our existence—birthdays, honeymoons—searching out the exalted moments of human life, not the everyday events. This is true of his art even today.

More moralistic artists utilize death to point up our social and political evils. Their subjects are the untimely death of the unwed mother, famished orphan, and soldier. To enforce their meaning, they frequently produce in series, stating the same truth again and again. They dwell on repulsive details, hoping to strengthen their case through shock. Dix's *Dying Soldier* (Figure 6) may serve to illustrate this approach. It epitomizes cruelty and the wanton waste of something precious. The moralist attitude is particularly strong among German and Mexican twentieth-century artists. While the Germans center on the human being in its extremity (Kollwitz, Grosz, Dix), the Mexicans focus on the next movement in temporal succession, on bones and the debris of what once had been a human being (Siqueiros, Orozco).[10]

The depiction of death may also be a means to give vent to fantasies which in turn can be either macabre or burlesque. Arising at the turn of the century, a whole group of artists saw death in these terms (Ensor, Willette, and Rops in Western Europe; Posada in Mexico). To a great extent these artists rely upon the incongruous effect produced by skeletons which mix with and behave like living beings. It is not always easy to differentiate between grotesque and gory in a work of art, or in the body of works of an artist, since the demarcation line is thin and depends upon the temperament of the spectator. The purpose for which the work was done counts for much. Hence Willette's menu card for the banquet of the *"Old Montmartre"* society, held on June 18, 1898, strikes me as funny. It shows a dead nude with lyre, surrounded by ravens against a background of the famous Montmartre windmill, and a cross under which lie skull and bones. Posada's Calaveras (skeletons), directed against the social and political abuses in Mexico, impresses me as macabre. Much of this grim and farcical production was in prints rather than in the major

1. PABLO PICASSO: *Still Life with Blood Sausage,* 1941. (From H. and S. Janis, *Picasso. The Recent Years,* Doubleday & Company, ·Inc., New York, 1946.)

2. PAUL KLEE: *Heavenly and Earthly Time*, 1927. Philadelphia Museum of Art—Louise and Walter Arensberg Collection.

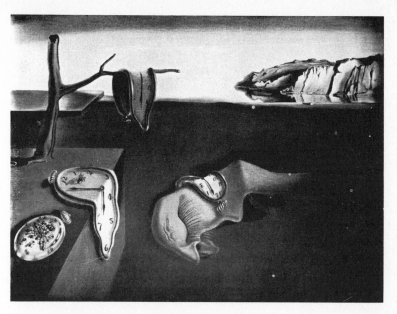

3. SALVADOR DALI: *The Persistence of Memory,* 1931. Museum of Modern Art, New York.

4. MARC CHAGALL: *Time is a River without Banks*, 1930–1939. Museum of Modern Art, New York.

5. JEAN MARIE CARZOU: *The End of the Day*, water color,
1957. (*Reproduced courtesy of the artist.*)

6. OTTO DIX: *Dying Soldier* (No. 26 from the series *Der Krieg*), lithograph, 1924. New York Public Library, Prints Division.

SQUELETTE.

7. JAMES ENSOR: *My Portrait in 1960*, etching, 1888. Reproduced from B. Rousseau et al., *James Ensor*, Librairie de la Société anonyme, "La Plume," Paris, 1899, p. 18.

8. MAX BECKMANN: *Departure*, triptych, 1932–1935. Museum of Modern Art, New York.

9. GUSTAVE COURBET: *Historical Painting of a Burial at Ornans*, 1849–1850. The Louvre, Paris. Photographed by J. E. Bulloz.

10. Detail from Dipylon Vase. Athens National Museum, No. 990. (*Courtesy Deutsches Archäologisches Institut, Athens.*)

11. CASPAR DAVID FRIEDRICH: *Cemetery of a Monastery in the Snow*, 1819. National-Galerie, Berlin.

12. EDOUARD MANÉT: *The Funeral*, c. 1870. (*Courtesy The Metropolitan Museum of Art, New York, Wolfe Fund*, 1909.)

13. EDOUARD MANET: *The Shooting of the Emperor Maximilian*, 1867. Städtische Kunsthalle, Mannheim.

14. GEORGE GROSZ: *Dedication to Oskar Panizza*, c. 1917–1918.
Staatsgalerie, Stuttgart.

15. MARC CHAGALL: *The Gate to the Cemetery*, 1917. Collection Mme. Meyer-Chagall, Bern. (*Reproduced courtesy of the artist.*)

16. ABRAHAM RATTNER: *The Valley of Dry Bones,* triptych, 1953–1956. The Downtown Gallery, New York. (*Reproduced courtesy of the owners.*)

17. ALBERT PINKHAM RYDER: *Dead Bird,* c. 1890–1900. Phillips Collection, Washington, D. C.

18. EDVARD MUNCH: *Death in the Sick Chamber*, 1892. National Gallery, Oslo.

19. IVAN LE LORRAINE ALBRIGHT: *Woman*,
1928. Museum of Modern Art, New York.

art of painting. There was one exception: the Belgian Ensor. It is with him that this trend can be studied best.

Ensor belonged to the humorist section of fantasts. If you have not yet met him, be introduced now to the king of masks and skeletons. He selected the skeleton and the mask because of their terrifying aspect, a trait common to both. While the classicist externalizes the beautiful soul by showing it in a perfect body— a concept in conformity with the Old Testament credo in which we are warned of those marked by the hand of God—Ensor, a perverted classicist, externalizes man's moral ugliness by means of fearsome visions: masks, skeletons, and frightening monsters. Ultimately his art also has a moral content, like that of Dix, but the fantast-humorist attitude should be distinguished sharply from the moralist one. Ensor does not show, but insinuates; he does not preach, but amuses. In 1888 he made an etching which he entitled *My Portrait in 1960* (Figure 7). Ancestor to this image is the funerary monument of the Lagrange type, but Ensor transformed it from the medieval *Vanity* theme to the ancient *Carpe diem*. He repeated the motif of the self as skeleton in another etching in 1889, and the German artist Alfred Kubin picked it up in a drawing (August 13, 1908, letter to Hans von Müller), while the Norwegian Munch composed a variant in a lithograph *Self Portrait,* 1895, showing his face combined with a bone instead of an arm.

It has been asserted that every classicist is a repressed romantic. If contrary emotions fight within man's breast, an artist who paints disasters may be moved by either attraction or repugnance —or by both. I shall make no attempt to differentiate between these subtle nuances, but will classify all artists who selected the theme of death for its ingredients of violence and catastrophe as terrorists.

A terrorist may arrive at his vision through the apocalyptic feeling of coming disaster. This seems to be the case with the

German poet and painter Meidner whose *Burning City,* 1913
(May Collection, St. Louis), foreshadowed the afflictions of World
War I. A terrorist may arrive at his vision through a wish to
record historical events. This seems to be the case with Meidner's
compatriot and contemporary Max Beckmann who painted the
Sinking of the Titanic, 1912 (May Collection, St. Louis), and
the Nazi tortures in his nightmarish *Departure* (Figure 8). Although Beckmann, like Dix, chronicles contemporary events, his
presentation is not realistic as is the latter's but couched in fantasies. However, his invented tortures, which take place in crowded
space under blaring noise, seem more fearsome to watch than
the most shocking agonies in Dix and Grosz. The torturer's presence
makes a voluntary act out of the horror which in Grosz and Dix
is caused by accident. Hidden depths of ignominy are plumbed
so that the frightened beholder tries to turn ostrich and hide his
face in the sand.

Goya and Picasso are also attracted to violent death. But
what is important to them is death's brutal, unrivaled strength,
not the registration of events. Both painters have glorified the
bull, another symbol of fierce power. But the two Spaniards are
better psychologists than Beckmann. They knew where to draw
the line in showing horrors, excluding from their pictures the
perpetrator of the violent acts. The human mind seems able to
tolerate butchered limbs, even to witness the butchering, as long
as the butcher himself is an abstract quantity. I believe the same
distinction obtains between dropping a bomb and stabbing with
a bayonet.

Philosophers, moralists, humorists, and terrorists have always
existed. Their divergent tempers have colored the representations
of death through the centuries. We have already discussed the
philosophical and moral *Vanities,* the macabre funerary monument, and presently shall introduce the terrorist *Triumph of
Death.* There is then nothing new in the themes described above
from this point of view. Modernity can be found not in the reason

why they have been chosen but rather in their presented form. Ensor's (and his followers') motif of the *Self Portrait as Skeleton* differs from the funerary monuments from which it derives in that it deals with the self. Chagall, Beckmann, and Dali differ from earlier artists in that they release private fantasies. The self and the private fantasy are recurrent subjects in twentieth-century art. It may be surmised that there also exists a modern attitude toward life reflected in the choice of theme. This is our next field of discussion.

OLD THEMES ON DEATH

Sometimes one artist discovers a theme which his contemporaries bypass. In other cases, however, he strikes a chord to which his contemporaries respond joyfully as though released from a burden. The new theme is taken up and reproduced in many versions. For the historian of art the birth of a theme is always a fascinating object of study. Why did this specific theme come into existence at this particular time, in that special place; what is the reason for its vogue or neglect—these are questions which occupy his mind. Before turning to an investigation of modern themes on death, it might be helpful to survey briefly the period 1300 to 1500. The outline of its iconography will serve as a backdrop against which to see our own.

Besides the Vanities discussed previously, the fourteenth and fifteenth centuries have bequeathed to us four other important themes which deal with death.[11] Three developed in the North, the last in Italy. They are *the Encounter of the three Living with the three Dead, the Dance of Death, the Art of Dying,* and *the Triumph of Death.* In its most common form, *the Encounter of the three Living and the three Dead* deals with three knights out hunting who come across three corpses in their coffins. This theme is merely another admonitory *Vanity* motif. A further variant depicted a young and beautiful girl who looks into a mirror to discover a skull as reflection. *The Dance of Death* carries beyond the idea of *Vanity* another connotation, viz., the equality of man in the face of death: pope and usurer, old man and child, monks and lovers—none are spared. Writers on the subject usually refer to the equality in social status of those claimed by death. But the social status is maintained in the sequence of the dance, reaffirmed by remarks of the victims, and implicitly admitted in the abusive addresses by Death. It is rather the equalization of good and evil, the lack of distinction between those who had lived a good and those who had lived an evil life, which is expressed. That the conduct of the individual in his earthly life has no influence upon his fate is a disturbing and dangerous thought. The examples of Christ, the martyrs, and Job do little to assuage the damage it causes to our morale. Doubts about the existence of God are created; these in turn lead to fear of the beyond. That fear of death ran high is proved by another, coeval, theme—the *Ars Moriendi*. This consisted of a series of deathbed scenes in which the moribund is beset by all sorts of monsters who try to bar his access to the kingdom of the blessed by tempting him to sin. Fortunately, their bad intentions can be defeated with the help of God and His deputies. For us, these monsters externalize the dangers of the unknown which worry man.[12] As regards the Italian *Triumph of Death,* it shows death no longer as a delegate of God but as His substitute. Revolt at the injustice of fate, dread of the unknown, the abdication of God in favor of Death—these are the moving ideas of the fourteenth- and fifteenth-century themes.

The *Ars Moriendi* and *the Encounter of the three Living and the three Dead* have vanished from the artistic repertoire. But the *Dance of Death* and the *Triumph of Death* still remain, though in modified forms. The plague is no longer a threat, so war (Rethel, Kollwitz) or chance (Kubin, Kollwitz, Klinger) provide the reasons for a *Dance of Death.* War (Rousseau, Barlach), and a nameless cause (Solana, Ensor) also dictate the persistence of the *Triumph of Death* in our time. To these inherited themes dealing with death modern art has added six of its own: the *Burial,* the *Funeral,* the *Cemetery,* the *Death of a Bird,* the *Death Chamber,* and the *Decay of a living Being.*

NEW THEMES ON DEATH

The burial as a subject in art is found in the chapter on the *Mass for the Dead* in illuminated manuscripts of the fifteenth century. At that time, 1424, the churchyard of the Innocents in Paris had been recently decorated with a *Dance of Death,* causing a good deal of comment. This motif can often be identified in the illuminations. Hence it was the holy place rather than the burial scene which dictated the choice.[13] Another instance of the interment in art is El Greco's *Burial of Count Orgaz* (Toledo). Iconographically, this painting is an adaptation of an *Entombment* which in turn modifies Raphael's *Entombment,* the latter being based upon the ancient *Death and Sleep carrying away the deceased Sarpedon.* In 1849 to 1850, Courbet presented the world with his *Historical Painting of a Burial at Ornans* (Figure 9). It acted like a thunderbolt out of a blue sky. Courbet referred to his work as the "Burial of Romanticism." Actually, the painting's repercussions were more far-reaching. It would be more appropriate to speak of the "Burial of Premodern Art." While El Greco's *Burial* had dealt with the end of a hero, Courbet showed the end of his own grandfather—a commoner who had died a timely death of old age, unimportant from the viewpoint of history. Yet the artist called it an "historical painting" and used for his painting canvas of the size reserved for great events. Moreover, the burial was depicted in epic grandeur with full attendance by all the villagers in rows of stately mourners dressed in historical costumes. By form and presentation Courbet raised the event to heroic stature, making the death of his grandparent the equal of the death of Christ or a king. Thus he applied to art the idea of equality taken from the French Revolution, abolishing the existing

hierarchies in subject matter which until his time had placed
religious and historical painting at the top of the list, still-life
and genre at the other end.[14]

While Courbet's painting is in one respect a cornerstone of
modern art and thought, it belongs at the same time to the ideology
of the past because the artist had to choose a climactic moment in
dramatic presentation in order to obtain heroic stature for genre.
Whatever the presentation be, however, its climactic nature made
the *Burial* theme incompatible with the trend which modern art
was to take, and it was soon replaced by a related theme, the
Funeral. Contrasted with deathbed and interment, the funeral procession is an unimportant and transitory state in man's encounter
with death. It was thus exactly suited to the taste of nineteenth-
century art.

The *Funeral Cortege* had been a fashionable motif in the
history of art once before (Figure 10). It is a frequent adornment
on the Dipylon funerary vases of the Greek Geometric age; later
Greek funerary art preferred the funeral banquet. On the Dipylon
vases the deployment of the obsequies has a dramatic and emotional character. Despite its abstract stylized form, the figure on
the bier can be identified with a specific person, the defunct whose
tomb the vase adorned. His funeral procession is like a triumphal
march and the tearing of hair by the mourners a suitable accom-
paniment to it. A second version of the funeral theme is found
in Poussin's *Funeral of Phocion* (Louvre). In it the Dipylon
rhetorics are replaced by a lyrical quality that is attained through
the grandeur of the setting in which the procession moves. But
here also a specific hero is laid to rest. A third version on our
theme was given by the German painter Friedrich (1774–1840).
His *Cemetery of a Monastery in the Snow* (Berlin, National-
Galerie) no longer shows the funeral of a specific hero but that of a
type of human being which he considered to be heroic. For him this
is the person withdrawn from worldly affairs. The mourners with
the coffin move slowly in a wintry scene toward a ruined Gothic

church. The grandiosity of this setting rivals that of Poussin's painting. Itself a double allusion to death as ruin and death as winter, it gives the unknown monk something of the standing of the unknown soldier (Figure 11). Like Courbet, Friedrich belongs partly to the past and partly to the future. They commemorated a hero (premodern approach) but it is their personal one (modern).

The modern *Funeral* takes a different form from all those discussed above. It is presented as a minor event, lost in the landscape. It is anonymous—cause of decease, name, and nature of defunct are unknown. This permits us to remain impassive in contact with death without appearing callous. Manet's *Funeral* (Figure 12) is a beautiful illustration of what the theme meant to the nineteenth century. The procession is merely a spectacle, like a race, like the World's Fair, like a concert or a cabaret— yet another glimpse caught of man's world on a rainy day. The dark clouds and grayness carry a stronger sense of wistfulness than the passing procession. Death is voided of emotion and drama, completely depersonalized, so that it can be watched with detachment. It should be noted here that Manet deheroized even the heroic death. *The Shooting of the Emperor Maximilian* in Mexico (Figure 13) is watched by the spectators upon the wall impassively, like a brawl between street urchins. The import of the event is quite lost, even upon the soldiers; one of them is attending calmly to his rifle. In contrast to Courbet who had raised the lower classes of subject matter to the importance of the higher, Manet —reversing the process—reduced the higher to the level of the lower.

When death had been divorced from associations of apotheosis as well as grief or alarm, the jester could take over. We met him in Ensor's *My Portrait in 1960;* the funerals of the Spanish painter Vayreda (1843–1894) and the Swiss Vallotton (1865–1925) belong to the same class. Vayreda's *The Funeral Cortège* (private collection, Barcelona) transports us into the realm of the child mourner; children carry the corpse of their dog in solemn procession to its grave. Vallotton harps on man's pettiness of mind which even death cannot cure. His print *The Awkward Step* depicts a group of people who try to carry a casket down a stairway which is too narrow for adequate manipulation of their burden. What may happen if they stumble scares them to such an extent that their minds have no room for any other thought—not even that death in itself is a much more serious calamity than the one which might befall them.[15] The end of the century seems to have been the era of jolly jokers. After exalting death, then treating it as just one event among others, the artist ridiculed it.

By the advent of the twentieth century, the *Funeral* had been absorbed into art and henceforward stood for the traditional. Its use then denotes a rather retrogressive attitude on the part of the artist. For example, it is found in Rouault, who valued it for its religious overtones. It is also utilized by Grosz whom we met with as a moralist in the company of Dix (cf. Figure 6). To Grosz it presented the advantage that a moral lesson can be taught better with known symbols than with novel ones. In his *Dedication to Oskar Panizza* (Figure 14) (Staatsgalerie, Stuttgart), the rites are again linked with a specific person who is a type and a hero of thought rather than action, reminding us of Friedrich, not Manet. For Grosz the hero is the artist. His funeral cortege is modeled upon the *Triumph of Death* but added to this old motif is a sharply discordant background of caroling people. The moral lesson to be drawn is obvious. Valuable people, like the poet Panizza, lose their lives. Another section of society enjoys itself at their expense, thriving parasitically upon the flow of blood which colors the whole scene in red. Death seems to have made with them an infamous pact to let them live if only they supply Him with sufficient butcher material. In our time Death can be vanquished as in Petrarca's, but not by Fame. Death is circumvented by money and moral depravity.

The theme of the *Cemetery* is related to those of the *Burial* and *Funeral*: all three have selected the "after" as their pregnant moment. The *Cemetery* is nearer to the *Funeral* than to the *Burial* because it does not center on a climax; but neither does it depict a passing state. It has something permanent, eternal, lasting. The deceased is anonymous and one of a crowd indicating that death is the fate of all men. The *Cemetery* theme was discovered in the twentieth century, not in the nineteenth.

Cemeteries occur in art prior to the twentieth century but are usually shown as objects of curiosity or beauty, e.g., Jacob van Ruisdael's *Portuguese Jewish Cemetery at Oudekirk* (Detroit). As such they excite aesthetic emotions or thirst for knowledge. Friedrich's *Cemetery* belongs in this category. Poussin's *Et in Arcadia Ego* (Louvre) must also be considered as a forerunner. He shows a group of shepherds standing around a tombstone and reading the inscription. Here, even in Arcadian realms, the al-mightiness of death is celebrated. But, contrary to the concepts of Goya and Picasso, death is a peaceful event. Poussin saw it with the eyes of Leonardo da Vinci: "As a well-spent day brings happy sleep, so life well used brings happy death." (*Notebooks,* Tr. 28a.)

But the new twentieth-century *Cemetery* is a churchyard with-out documentary value or aspirations toward beauty.[16] Chagall's *Gate to the Cemetery* (Figure 15) is a case in point. Its importance resides in the religious and philosophical meaning of a com-munity of graves. This painting, and another version, *The Cemetery* (owned by the artist), were completed in war-torn Russia at the time of the revolution in 1917. Chagall had also suffered personal losses then. Russia had gone unequipped into the First World War with disastrous results and a Russian artist had thus as much—if not more—reason than a German one to decry the ignominy and absurdity of war. Yet Chagall's burial places do not have moral or social overtones. The one illustrated in Figure 15 shows a large portal in the foreground and next to it a strong and healthy green tree. Through the gate and a break in the fence a group of graves appear small and far away. On the gate is inscribed the famous

passage from Ezekiel 37: 12–14, referring to the resurrection:
". . . Behold, I will open your graves, O my people, and cause
you to come up out of your graves, and bring you into the land
of Israel . . . and ye shall live." [17] For Chagall (as for Milton and
the medieval Christian), death is the gate through which man
enters into true life. It is interesting to compare Chagall's iconography with that of the sculptor Bartholomé as used for the *Monument aux Morts* (Père Lachaise cemetery, Paris), which was un-
veiled in 1899. Bartholomé's relief also shows a gate. Through
it disappear the souls of the dead while outside of it a group of
people display their emotions. Some exhibit fear, others longing,
and still others mourn for those passed away. Bartholomé's work
depicts man's reactions in the face of death. Chagall's painting has
none of these premodern histrionics. It is the modern equivalent
of *Christ in Glory* or the *Virgin Enthroned*. It embodies a great
peacefulness in the sense of wishlessness. Death is for Chagall
neither ecstasy nor mourning, but continuation of life under more
just conditions and his *Gate to the Cemetery* is a token of this.[18]
The cruel waste of human lives in war or the pogrom is also
brought home with sharpness and clarity by the army of graves in
Chagall's other *Cemetery*. But even here, in contrast to the German
works and their pessimistic mood, the emotion of horror is over-
laid with a belief in an otherworldly reward for those who have
behaved justly. The same belief in the greatness of afterlife as
against the smallness and unimportance of life on this earth
speaks to us from Chagall's *Mirror* of 1916 (Russian State Collection). It shows his first wife Bella, who has fallen asleep in a
chair, seated at the side of a table upon which her head reposes.
Behind the table, facing us, is a mirror. Bella is a tiny figure, but
in the background of the mirror is seen in enormous size the
reflection of a lamp, symbol of the eternal light.

Chagall's approach to life is not twentieth-century though his
theme is new. This becomes obvious if his *Gate to the Cemetery*
is compared with Rattner's triptych *The Valley of Dry Bones*

(Figure 16), inspired by the same passage in Ezekiel. Not being poetically inclined like Chagall, Rattner rendered the prophet's words literally by depicting a heap of skeletons on the ground and the shapes of the resurrected in the air. The white angelic forms in the upper portion are, however, not comforting; they look too vaporous to reassure our shaken faith. Moreover, the presentation of bones and the formal angularities convey an anguish absent in Chagall. Next to the self and private fantasies, metaphysical anguish is a third recurrent theme in twentieth-century art.

Another modern way to treat death is to shift it from the human world to the world of birds. Dead birds had been depicted in art previously but in a different context. They appeared in still lifes and thus were a part of the world of man for whom they served as food. One is not even aware of the fact that they are dead, killed by man for his use. The modern *dead bird* has only a superficial resemblance to this still-life motif. In Ryder's *Dead Bird* (Figure 17), perhaps the first instance of this new theme, the bird is made an individual and its death an event that assumes the proportions of a human death.[19]

Animals who act like human beings have been popular at least since Aesop's time. But in Aesop, *le Roman du Renard,* La Fontaine, etc., the substitution is made so that the author can say overtly what—if the image of man were utilized—would have to be stated less directly. Thus the device served moral ends. This is not true of Ryder's *Dead Bird* and similar bird images in modern art. When the modern artist replaces the human being with an animal, as for instance Henri Rousseau does in his *Jesters,* c. 1906 (Philadelphia Museum of Art), where monkeys act out the beloved modern role of clown, he does so without aiming to drive home a moral lesson.

But why choose from among all animals a bird for the representation of death? I believe it is because "deadness" can be easily shown in a bird. If a nonviolent death has to be depicted, man's attitude in it is similar to the one he takes in sleep, viz., a relaxed, supine position; hence death and sleep cannot be easily distinguished from one another. The same is true of quadrupeds. Not so the bird. It sleeps standing on one leg, with head placed under its wing. A dead bird, on the other hand, stretches out its legs and lies on its back. Hence sleep and death cannot be confused if the bird is the subject. It so happens that a dead bird is also a more poignant image than a dead quadruped. A quadruped on the ground can be experienced as having come to rest in its natural setting. The bird's realm is in the air. Earthbound it is a lost soul in a foreign land. This is why Ryder's *Dead Bird* looks infinitely sad. It conveys a mood of resignation because the end is the same for those who crawled on the ground (vulgar crowd) and for those who soared up into the air (artist).

Ryder has apparently left only one image of a dead bird but in Graves's work, which falls into the twentieth century, it is used repeatedly. Graves (born 1910) seems to consider death an affliction. His dead birds appear next to stricken birds, e.g., the *Blind Bird, the Moon Mad Bird*. Yet these afflictions are treated as a distinction which sets it aside from the ordinary bourgeois bird. We are reminded that blindness and madness go together with the gift of prophecy. Thus the limitation becomes a positive value and death loses its tragic content. It is merely a mystery. Reflected against Graves's image, Ryder's pathos appears antiquated, i.e., premodern.

We come now to two themes which have not found an echo in other artists' work so far. They belong to the twentieth century. One of these two is the deathbed scene. When picked up by modern art, the *Deathbed* was an old, established, and widespread theme; in this respect, too, it differs from the other subjects surveyed which had appeared more sporadically. The *Deathbed* occurred often in medieval art in connection with the *Dormition of the Virgin* and the *Death of Lazarus and of the Miser,* but its apogee was reached in the *Ars Moriendi.* Poussin also takes it up—in a variant upon Petrarca's Renaissance spirit. In his *Testa-*

ment of Eudamidas (private collection, Copenhagen) the dying
man commends wife and daughter to his friends, all assembled
around his couch; thus death is defeated by friendship, Eudamidas
surviving in his friends—as Meyer Schapiro has pointed out in
lectures at the New School. Classicists and Romantics both treated
the *Deathbed* theme. The classic artist liked to dwell on the death
of heroes, e.g., David painted Marat in his bathtub assassinated
by Charlotte Corday and *Socrates Drinking the Hemlock.* The
Romantics, on the other hand, transformed the death of the defeated into a triumph, e.g. Delacroix's *Death of Sardanapalus,*
where the Assyrian king after having lost his kingdom selects his
own way to exit in an orgy of destruction, and his *Massacre at
Chios* where the physically beaten Greeks become the moral victors
of their Turk conquerors. The Classicist likes the straightforward
and obvious, the Romantic the twisted and devious.

When the inherited deathbed scene is treated by the twentieth-
century Norwegian artist Munch, he centers on the everyday death
of a common person who has passed away. This is in harmony
with the values of nineteenth-century modern art. What is new,
and shocking, and twentieth-century in his painting, *Death in the
Sick Chamber* (Figure 18),[20] is the fact that the interest focuses
on the living instead of the dead. The expressions and stances of
the surviving family members are powerful and expressive; and
the bed and deceased are shifted into the background. The second
shocking fact about Munch's interpretation of death is that the
faces are contorted, not in mourning for a beloved lost member,
but in fear of the unknown which has just swallowed the deceased,
fear for themselves who are eventually to meet the same fate. In
this agony, each person is alone; each survivor turns away not
only from the dead but also from the other participants in the
scene. Faced with death, the family bonds fall apart, revealing
their superficial character. Thus Munch experienced death as dissolving the family ties; while Courbet had seen it as a means to
unite not only the family but the whole community.[21] Other paint-

ings by Munch (*Puberty, Jealousy, In Hell, Unwelcome Guests*) inform us that fear of death is for the artist merely one aspect of the fear of things unknown and things without rational explanation.

The nineteenth century had aimed at pleasure; the twentieth century aims at shock. We are shocked by the mutilated bodies in war scenes and by the behavior of the family members in Munch. But in reacting toward these images, compassion mingles with horror. If the decay of the living flesh is shown, one feels only revulsion without any allaying sentiment. The decay of the living is the subject matter of Ivan Le Lorraine Albright (Figure 19). This is the second twentieth-century theme that deals with death. As ancestors for it one may quote three instances: the Gothic decomposition of the corpse, the *Anatomies,* and the rococo love for ruins. But compared with the twentieth-century image, the older themes pale. The ruin of a building can be enjoyed as picturesque. We can even view with detachment the apparent ruin of the paint surface in Bacon's works where the distorted images suggest that the paints have run. Not so with the ruin of the living flesh. This hits too near to the core of human existence. Raw flesh in the cadaver of an *Anatomy* may be viewed with detachment, though some squeamish beholders may object to the subject as unsavory. But a skinned-looking living being scares us. Stronger and more clearly defined sentiments are provoked by the image that shows putrefaction of the corpse. This will appear gory to all and sundry. But to show decay of the living human being is something different again. This is not gory but revolting. We react to the first by shying away from it but the second rouses us to fight back. The black-and-white reproduction of Figure 19 does not do justice to the effect of Albright's painting, since color helps in a subtle way to create it. The painting is held in an over-all dark-gray tonality with purplish accents upon face and hands, and a whitish shade for the neck. Details are overemphasized by means of sharp lights. As a result the detail becomes too vivid, yielding the impression of aliveness. The gray broadtail collar and cuffs and the lace decompose into many small details which look like crawling vermin. The purple-red face and hands appear to be stricken with a terrible disease; and the whitish-green neck foreshadows the corpse.

We saw the nineteenth century withdraw from emotions and pose for one transitory moment on the crest of a wave of pure spectatorship with Manet's *Funeral*. This approach was rejected by the twentieth century which is not attracted toward the visible but toward externalization of the invisible. It records its dreams and fantasies (Redon, Ensor, Surrealists), its extravisual perceptions (Klee, the Fauves, German Expressionists), its emotions of anguish (Munch, Ensor, German Expressionists), and of revolt (Picasso, Surrealists, Futurists). The twentieth century thus reintroduces the emotions of premodern art which had been banished during the second half of the nineteenth century. But these modern emotions have no rational basis like their predecessors; they are connected neither to a drama nor to a hero. Rather, they are joys without causes (Fauvist painting) and fears without causes (Munch).

While it is quite easy to define the philosophical attitude of the modern nineteenth century as detachment, as a statement of facts observed, I hesitate to commit myself on that of the twentieth century because I am myself part of it as yet. If I judge correctly, it is the will to shock us out of the scientific impartiality advocated by the nineteenth century and into fight. Picasso is considered the symbol of our century by admirers and detractors alike—obviously because we all identify with his attitude. Schapiro has epitomized his style as the will to transform.[22] This will to transform is, I believe, not merely unrest—inclination to search for ever-new solutions since, to paraphrase Picasso, it is distasteful to copy oneself (though quite permissible to draw upon other works).[23] It is rather based on a profound awareness that active participation in life is necessary to avoid slipping backward in civilization. "My whole life as an artist has been nothing more than a continuous struggle against reaction and the death of art." [24] This truth had been found by bitter experience after the artist had tried to withdraw into an ivory tower and as a result had foregone his duty toward humanity. In another statement Picasso has summed up what nineteenth-century art stands for as compared with that of the twentieth century. "No, painting is not interior decoration. It is an instrument of war for attack and defense against the enemy." [25]

The attitudes of Manet and Picasso are so startlingly opposed that it may be hard to notice their common denominator of "modernity." It appears to be the following. The importance attached to death by mankind resides in three things: its personal relationship to ourselves, i.e., to the individual and human being, its finality, and its mystery. If any of these three things is eliminated, the importance of death is weakened. This, I believe, is done by modern art in each of the six themes discussed. The *Burial* shows survival in the community and the *Cemetery* speaks of the resurrection—both denying finality to death. The *Funeral* removes death from the individual and the *Dead Bird* displaces it from the human realm to nature as a whole—thus loosening the immediacy of the threat for us. Decay of the living being questions the mystery of death by transposing the living being into the state reserved for death. Munch's fears are not particularized as to death—that means denying it uniqueness. Even the paintings of war scenes do not really harp so much on death as on the perversion of the human mind. I have postulated that modern art keeps away from the portrayal of death. Even where it does show death, modern art minimizes it. And why should it not do this? It is life that is important not death.

Conclusion

The two most important aspects of every work of art are its presentation and its message. Let us now sum up the findings on the theme of death in modern art with regard to iconography and meaning.

The iconography of death can select between the following alternatives: (1) moment chosen—moribund or deceased is shown; (2) victim chosen—Hero or Everyman is shown. Modern art favored the deceased and Everyman because these images are tensionless compared with their opposites. Centering on the themes of the *Burial, Funeral, Cemetery,* and *Dead Bird,* it made death anonymous. Rejection of plots and dramatic situations is a characteristic of modern man. If modern art has recourse to the image of the moribund or the Hero, then the artist belongs to the category of social reformers. Teaching and preaching are easiest understood if established values and familiar terms are used for illustration.

Modern artists do not represent Death by personifications because the spirit of allegory is alien to them. Death with a capital "D" is depicted by symbols. One of these is the clock, a mechanical device substituting for the traditional hourglass. A more revealing modern symbol for Death is the living being in a state of putrefaction like so much refuse out of a garbage can. This "living death" image plays upon the value of shock and upon the surrealistic quality of what is portrayed. A quest for disharmony, tension, the shocking, and a power for imaginative creations are other traits of the modern mind.

As regards the philosophical significance of death, it may mean beatitude as well as nothingness; it may attract or repulse. The believer will be interested in it as the ultimate goal of human life and celebrate it in his work. The unbeliever will be interested in it because, for him, it is part of the inexplicable mystery of creation. He will dissect it to stay his fears which are not allayed by faith in the existence of a divine power. These contrary attitudes coexist in modern art, in representational as well as nonrepresentational works.

A work of art is conditioned by both the personality of the artist and the environment in which he lives. Generalizations are apt to overshoot the mark, yet they are useful. Bearing in mind this weakness of the generalization, it may be postulated that the iconography of death reveals the character of our century, while the philosophical significance embodied by the artist in his representation of death reveals his individual personality.

NOTES

1. "Notes d'un peintre," *La grande Revue,* December 25, 1908. English translation in A. Barr, *Matisse. His Art and His Public,* Museum of Modern Art, New York, 1951, p. 122.

2. The vase paintings usually personify Sleep and Death as winged figures but this is not contained in Homer's reference.

3. Quoted from E. Mâle, *Religious Art from the Twelfth to the Eighteenth Century,* Noonday Press, Inc., New York, 1958, p. 141. In Roman art, skeletons and mummies appear from time to time in the context of tombs. According to L. Guerry (*Le thème du Triomphe de la Mort dans la Peinture Italienne,* Gustave-Paul Maisonneuve, Paris, 1950, pp. 31–32), they represent *lemures*— errant souls which cannot find repose.

4. V. van Gogh, *The Complete Letters of Vincent van Gogh,* New York Graphic Society, Greenwich, Conn., 1958, vol. 3.

5. H. Janis and S. Janis, *Picasso. The Recent Years: 1939–1946,* Doubleday & Company, Inc.; New York, 1946, commentary to plate 60.

6. Dali took the motif up again in 1952–1954 with his *Disintegration of the Persistence of Memory* (Limp Watches), Morse Collection.

7. As the artist confided to Sidney Janis, to whom I owe this information.

8. Statement of the artist published in A. C. Ritchie, *The New Decade,* Museum of Modern Art, New York, 1955, p. 15.

9. O. Brendel in a lecture to my class at the New School, spring 1958. His findings will be published in the *Proc. Am. Council Learned Soc.*

10. The Mexican, Rivera, should also be included here. His pregnant moment, however, is that of the German artists, not that of his compatriots.

11. This period has been dealt with extensively. For information and bibliography see L. Réau, *Iconographie de l'Art Chrétien, II. Nouveau Testament,* Presses Universitaires de France, Paris, 1957, pp. 637–662.

12. Another theme which dealt with the agony of death in that time was the first scene from the *Four Last Things.* However, few instances of this are known.

13. This churchyard and its importance for fifteenth-century Paris is described in J. Huizinga, *The Waning of the Middle Ages,* Doubleday and Company, Inc., Anchor Books, New York, 1954, p. 149.

14. M. Schapiro, "Courbet and popular imagery: An essay on realism and naivete," *J. Warburg Inst.,* **4:** 164–191, 1940–1941.

15. Another painting which, in accordance with its title, should be classified in this group is that of the Spanish artist Viladrich (1887–?), *My Funeral Procession* (Hispanic Society, New York). In presentation it is enigmatic.

16. Of course, some conservatively minded artist may still paint in the old manner. For example, the German Fuhr, *Mountain Cemetery,* 1928 (Städtische Kunsthalle, Mannheim).

17. The passage was identified and translated for me by Dr. Hans Jonas and Mrs. Miriam Alexander.

18. I cannot go into the problem of the *Cemetery* in literature but shall confine myself to a quote from Boris Pasternak, *Dr. Zhivago,* Pantheon Books, Inc., New York, 1958, p. 493: "Perhaps the mysteries of evolution and the riddles of life that so puzzle us are contained in the green of the earth, among the trees and the flowers of graveyards." The life story of Pasternak's hero starts with a cemetery—which is, to say the least, strange.

19. Ryder's preoccupation with the problem of death appears also in his *Racetrack* or *Death on a Pale Horse* (Cleveland Museum of Art) and *Death Rides the Wind* (private collection, New York).

20. Munch has also left a lithograph of this subject (1896) and painted a second version, *By the Death Bed,* 1895 (Oslo, National Gallery). Some Dipylon vases also portray the mourning of the survivors instead of the funeral procession.

21. M. Schapiro, "Courbet and popular imagery: an essay on realism and naïvete," *J. Warburg Inst.,* **4:** 190, 1940–1941.

22. Class lectures at Columbia University.

23. Statement of 1935, reprinted in W. Boeck and J. Sabartés, *Picasso,* Harry N. Abrams, Inc., New York, 1957, p. 505.
24. Statement of 1937, in W. Boeck and J. Sabartés, *Picasso,* Harry N. Abrams, Inc., New York, 1957, p. 232.
25. Statement of 1945, in W. Boeck and J. Sabartés, *Picasso,* Harry N. Abrams, Inc., New York, 1957, p. 505.

DAVID G. MANDELBAUM

Social Uses of Funeral Rites

Rites performed for the dead generally have important effects for the living. A funeral ceremony is personal in its focus and is societal in its consequences. The people of every society have a pattern for dealing with the death of their fellows. No matter how unprepared an individual may be for the fact of a particular death, the group must always have some plan of action in the event of death.

Certain things must be done after a death, whether it occurs in a very simple or in a highly complex society. The corpse must be disposed of; those who are bereaved —who are personally shocked and socially disoriented— must be helped to reorient themselves; the whole group must have a known way of readjustment after the loss of one of its members. These things "must" be done in the sense that they *are* done. When people find that they have no set pattern for dealing with death—as may occur in newly coalesced groups—or when they discover that the former pattern is no longer a feasible one, they tend quickly to establish some clear plan for coping with the occasion of death.

These common purposes of funeral rites are accomplished in a great variety of ways among the different cultures of the world. Death ceremonies often entail central motifs of a culture; their performance usually helps to bolster the solidarity of the social group. I shall describe one

189

funeral ceremony, that of the Kota of South India, in some detail, as an example of rites with complex content and multiple functions. Funeral rites include both the ritual performed immediately after the death of a person and also those rites of mourning and commemoration which, in many societies, are performed weeks or months after the death. In the Kota cases, our interest is mainly in the second funeral, the commemorative ceremony staged once a year in a village for all those who have died in the preceding year.

We shall more briefly examine death rites of other cultures in order to illustrate some general concepts concerning funeral practices. From two American Indian societies come examples showing the possible range in emphasis of death ceremonies. In the one, the Cocopa, the mourning ceremony is the great event of tribal life and one in which tribal wealth—a very meager wealth and therefore all the more precious—is extravagantly expended. In the other society, that of the Hopi, a funeral ceremony is played down and hurried over. From the Hebridean island of Barra, we have an example of funeral rites conducted according to the ritual of the Roman Catholic Church, but performed with significant local characteristics as well.

How funeral rites may reflect psychological ambivalence is indicated in the example of the Apache death observances. An analysis of a particular funeral in a town in Java shows that, under certain circumstances, the performance of a funeral ceremony may rouse social conflict. Discussion of these examples can serve as an introduction to the study of funeral ceremonies, one of the universals of human social experience.

1

The Kotas are a people who live in seven small villages which are interspersed among the villages of their neighbors on a high plateau, the Nilgiri Hills, in South India. The height and inaccessibility of the plateau formerly isolated the tribal peoples who lived on it from the main currents of Indian civilization.

That isolation was first broken during the middle of the nineteenth century, and since then many other peoples, English and Indian, have come to enjoy the cool heights or to work there. As a result of these contacts, the cultures of the indigenous Nilgiri folk have been changed. In many ways, the Kotas are now much like typical villagers of low caste in the surrounding plains, but their funeral rites—though altered in recent generations—still follow much of the ancient form.

The Kotas observe two funeral ceremonies: the first, called the "Green Funeral," takes place shortly after a death and it is then that the body is cremated; the second, called the "Dry Funeral," is held once a year (or once in two years) for all the deaths that have occurred since the last Dry Funeral was celebrated [12]. The terms are an analogy to a cut plant. At the first funeral the loss is green and fresh in the mind; at the second it is dried out, sere.

At the first funeral, a bit of skull bone is taken from the ashes of the pyre and reverently cached away until the second funeral. The Dry Funeral extends over eleven days and comes to a climax when each relic from the year's deaths is carried off to the cremation ground and, after complex ritual acts, the relics are recremated. The first funeral is attended by the close relatives and friends of the deceased. The second funeral is a grand occasion, attended by people from all the Kota villages and by non-Kotas as well.

Why is there a second funeral—why does not the first suffice? The Kotas give two reasons: one religious, the other social.

The religious reason is that the spirit of the dead person does not finally depart for the "Motherland," the Kota afterworld, until the second funeral has been completed. Only then is the spirit purified enough to reach God. The social reason is that the dead man continues to have certain attributes of social personality until his second funeral. Most importantly, a widow is still her late husband's wife up to the conclusion of the Dry Funeral. If she becomes pregnant after his physical death but before his second funeral, the child is his, shares in his name, clan, and property. In this society, biological paternity is considerably less important than sociological paternity. Hence the faithful widow of a man who has died without a son will conscientiously try to become pregnant before the end of his Dry Funeral. The dead man's right to a child of her womb ceases only after her first menstrual period following the second funeral.

In a way, the Kotas endow society rather than nature with the last word on whether a man has really died. The process, to be sure, begins with his physical demise, but it is not until people perform a Dry Funeral for him that his spirit departs from earth and his social status is finally deleted.

The emphasis of the funeral ritual is much more on speeding the departure of the spirit from this world than it is on the "Motherland" beyond. Kotas are not much interested in the other world and have only sketchy ideas about it. They are quite precise about the purification which the spirit and the surviving kin must undergo in order that the spirit may depart for good.

Among the Kotas, as among many of the peoples of India, contact with death is considered to be deeply polluting. A polluted person is debarred from normal social relations until he has been purified by proper and protracted ritual. The spirit of the dead person, too, is polluted in leaving the body, and the dual funeral rites purify the spirit so that it may take up proper relations in the afterworld.

Between the time of the body's last breath and the climactic end of the Dry Funeral, the lingering spirit is dangerous to men, especially to the deceased's closest kin. The climax comes when a pot is smashed, at the proper ritual juncture, in the cremation ground beyond the village. At that signal all who have attended the ceremony—that is to say, most of the villagers and many visitors—run back to the village without looking behind them. The living go one way, the dead another. The rite is always successful, the dead never return to plague the living as occurs in some societies. This says much about Kota self-confidence and cultural assurance.

The Dry Funeral extends over eleven days and involves villagers and visitors in a series of ceremonial roles which they play out in a fixed sequence, like the acts of a play. And any great ceremony is indeed like a dramatic performance. It has well-defined roles and acts because it must be performed over and again, in similar ways, by different players.

There are two broad categories of roles: those of the kinsmen of the dead person and those of his fellows in the community. His kin are the bereaved who are being purified and restored to society; his kith—fellow villagers and other Kotas—help restore the bereaved and help speed the spirit on its way.

On the first morning of the Dry Funeral, a band of musicians gathers and plays a lament. With the opening notes of the funeral tune, it becomes clearly apparent, even to a stranger, which villagers have lost a relative during the past year. Bereaved women stop in their tracks. A rush of sorrow suffuses them; they sit down where they are, cover their heads with their shoulder cloths, and wail and sob through much of that day and the next. Men of a bereaved household have much to do in preparation for the ceremony and do not drop everything to mourn aloud as do the bereaved women. But even they stop from time to time to weep.

Most grief-stricken of all are the widows and widowers. They must observe the most stringent mourning taboos and undergo the most extensive purificatory ritual. Much of the ritual of the funerals revolves about them. The siblings and children of a dead person have important, but less extensive, roles to play in the ceremony. Interestingly, the parents of a dead person have no formal part in the funeral. They may be personally as grief-stricken as bereaved parents can be in any society, but the cultural plan of the ritual does not make special provision for them. They may not even go through the formal gestures and symbols of mourning.

Leading roles in the category of participants who are not bereaved kinsmen are taken by priests. They lead in the ritual, except for certain especially sensitive acts such as setting flame to the funeral pyre. Then a specially chosen boy leads. A boy must lead because he is pure; his youth has preserved him from those defiling experiences which tarnish any man, even a priest. Other ceremonial roles are taken, respectively, by secular officers, fellow villagers, visiting Kota villagers, and by neighboring people who are not Kotas.

The ceremony falls into four main acts: First there is a week during which the year's dead are memorialized one by one. During that week strict mourning taboos are observed by bereaved kinsmen; other villagers dance every night, partly as a distraction for the mourners, partly to show both the viability and the concern of society.

The next act takes place on the day of the second cremation. A procession winds out of the village; in it are men carrying funeral goods to be placed on the pyre. The bit of skull bone is taken out and carried to the cremation ground. There the bone, the goods, and the personal ornaments of the widow or widower are placed on the pyre and it is set alight. The bereaved and some of the participants spend the night at the cremation ground.

The third phase of the ceremony begins when the morning star is seen by those who have spent the night at the funeral place. The mood changes abruptly. There is dancing and feasting; widows and widowers perform rituals in several stages which bring them progressively closer to normal social life. At nightfall the pot is smashed, all run back to the place of life, the village. That night the widows and widowers have sexual relations, preferably with a sibling of the dead spouse, thus symbolizing yet another step back to normal relations.

Finally there are two days of singing and dancing. The village houses are ritually purified. Then the visitors leave and villagers take up the ordinary round of life again.

By these roles and these prescriptions for action, Kota culture provides a way of answering the question which Kota society and every society must answer—what to do about death? The body is properly removed. The bereaved are successfully brought through their shock and sorrow back to normal status and relations. The villagers duly commemorate the death and turn back to everyday pursuits with a sense of having done the right and proper things about the social loss.

These are the manifest purposes accomplished by the ceremony, the purposes which villagers recognize and can explain. But the Dry Funeral celebration has other functions as well which are not so apparent to the participants, which are more implicit than explicit.

One such function is the reaffirmation of the social order. The role taken by each participant has to do with one or another of the groupings which make up Kota and Nilgiri society. These groupings range from the family, through the kinship circle, to the village, the Kota people, the Nilgiri peoples. There are economic and social obligations entailed in each of the groupings. These reciprocal obligations are remembered, reenacted, and thus reinforced in the course of the ceremony.

The cohesion of the family is then clearly demonstrated. All in a bereaved household work hard to provide the necessary goods for the pyre and food for the feast. All in the deceased's family stay together in the house during the first week of the Dry Funeral, dressed in old and tattered clothes, hair unkempt, voices low, sadness heavy over all the household.

Kin relationship beyond the family is also reaffirmed during the ceremony. Relatives come to console the bereaved family and contribute to the funeral expenses. Every Kota who considers himself related to the dead person makes a point of attending the Dry

Funeral and bowing to the relic of the deceased before it is re-cremated.

Other social groupings are represented in the ceremony: clan membership is acknowledged and confirmed; village affiliation—both of the dead and of the living—is shown. At certain points, a representative from each of the Kota villages plays a formal part in the ritual, thus reminding the assembly of the unity of all Kotas. There is also a place in the ceremony for associates of the bereaved families who are not Kotas; representatives of the neighboring peoples attend and, in their proper way, participate. A Kota is thus reminded, in the context of the funeral ceremony, of the parts and personnel of his social order. He can see, demonstrated in action, how its various parts serve him and must be served by him.

Participation in the ceremony has yet another effect on the participants. It gives them a renewed sense of belonging to a social whole, to the entire community of Kotas. The villagers and visitors go in procession, led by music, to clear the cremation ground, build the pyre, prepare the feast, and do other work in preparation for the ceremony. These group activities and the dancing which follows not only bring general enjoyment but enhance feelings of social unison.

There is no inclination to enlarge the intensity or scope of the mourners' grief. The bereaved are given a formal opportunity for complete self-immersion in grief, but there is also an effort to curtail their sorrow, to distract them by pleasing figures of the dance. Funeral dancing is not approved in scriptural Hinduism, and as the Kotas have become more influenced by the practices of high-caste Hindu villagers, they have become more uncertain about the propriety of dancing at a funeral.

The ceremony is being changed in this and in other directions, but it is still an occasion when many Kotas work together and together accomplish a religiously proper and personally enjoyable goal, the successful staging of the ceremony. This joint accomplishment bolsters Kota cohesion and sometimes helps smooth over factional rifts.

A third social consequence of enacting the ceremony is that the order of precedence within Kota society is formally repeated and in that manner officially reinforced. Just as a participant gets from the ceremony a sense of the social whole and of the various groupings within the whole, so does he also derive a sense of the proper order in social life. For example, there is a strict order of precedence in the funeral procession, at the feast, and in all phases of the rite. Briefly put, the order is this: all men come before all women; officials and elders before all other men; officials before elders; religious officials before secular officials. Within any category, seniors in age come before their juniors.

This same order of rank applies in all life situations, as in the serving of an ordinary meal. But at great occasions like the second funeral, the whole assembly of Kotas formally, publicly, and impressively rehearses the proper precedence among the constituent parts of society.

Another social consequence which flows from performing the Dry Funeral is the completion of the proper order of a person's career. Every social transition is marked by some appropriate ritual. Hence the final step should also be celebrated appropriately by a person's kin and fellows. "A proper progress through life means a funeral." This comment by Raymond Firth on the people of the Polynesian island of Tikopia applies to the Kotas as well. "The death of every person must be followed by a reaffirmation of the social character of human existence" [5, page 64].

The Dry Funeral performance also has personal, psychological meanings for individual men and women. A Kota woman whose husband has died, reacts in ways which are the common, human manifestations of grief. She appears shocked and disoriented by her loss; she can think of nothing but her grief, she is bewildered, she withdraws. Her keening is culturally stereotyped, and much of her specific behavior as a mourning widow is prescribed by the cultural requirements for the role of new widow but in seeing her, we understand that there is also personal sorrow and genuine disorientation in her behavior.

For this widow, as well as for other bereaved persons, the performance of the Dry Funeral effectively assuages grief and provides personal reorientation. After the first outburst of grieving at the Green Funeral, there is a period of months of relative quietude. The second funeral provides an occasion for summoning up a person's latent grief, for expressing it, and then for terminating it. In the eleven days of the ceremony there is ample opportunity for venting one's sorrow. Perhaps for that reason the grief is more easily and finally dispersed after the rite. The several phases of the ceremony bring the bereaved back to normal status in gradual and socially approved stages [cf. 5, page 63].

As in any major ceremony, incidental consequences ensue. Young men find occasion then to look over girls from various villages. A mature man who has prospered may take the occasion to demonstrate his achievements by providing lavish funeral goods, perhaps for a distant relative. One man, whose main personal victories came from his wide knowledge of ritual, found special satisfaction in playing a director's role in guiding the complex rites of the Dry Funeral. Such personal purposes, no less than the larger societal needs, are served by the celebration of the Dry Funeral.

2

Comparable purposes, both personal and social, are accomplished by the performance of death ceremonies in other societies. But there are great variations in the manner of bringing about such integrative results. As we examine the range of variation we find that among some peoples, funeral ceremonies are great public events; in other societies they are conducted swiftly, quietly, almost furtively. The whole of a social order may be represented at the funeral, or only a small section of it.

Two American Indian tribes of the Southwest, the Cocopa and the Hopi, respectively exemplify extremes of emphasis and of deemphasis, in the observance of funeral rites. Among the Cocopa, death ceremonies are the major events of tribal life; among the Hopi, they are brief and hurried affairs.

The Cocopa, who lived mainly along what is now the Arizona-Sonora border, practiced some agriculture, but depended largely on hunting and gathering. Theirs was a relatively simple culture; they possessed few goods, they conducted few ceremonies [9]. The whole tribe, in the late nineteenth century, consisted of some twelve hundred people, scattered in small settlements. People from several settlements might come together for a harvest fiesta, but many more would gather for the occasion of a mourning ceremony. The death ceremonies were the principal religious and social events of the tribe.

Soon after a death, the mourning members of the family became transported into an ecstasy of violent grief behavior. They cried, wailed, and screamed from the time of the death, without much interruption, for twenty-four hours or more until the body was cremated. The cremation ritual was directed mainly at inducing the spirit of the dead person to go on to the afterworld. To help persuade the spirit to depart, clothes, food, and equipment were destroyed so that the spirit could have these things in the hereafter.

Some time after the cremation, and with purposes analogous to those of the Kota second funeral, a Cocopa family would give a mourning ceremony to commemorate its dead. Then a large part of the tribe would gather, there would be speeches and lamentations for the dead. At all other times, the names of the dead could not be mentioned; at this mourning ceremony dead relatives were recalled publicly, summoned to mingle with the assembled tribesmen, and impersonated by men and women dressed in ceremonial costumes to resemble specific deceased persons. Presents were given to visitors, and valuable goods, including a ceremonial house and the ceremonial costumes, were burned for the benefit of the spirits. Kelly gives his impression that ". . . this action symbolized a desire to be free of the dead, and that the ceremony served, in part, to bring lurking spirits into the open, and, in dramatic fashion, to rid the earth of them by banning them again in the physical form of the costumes worn by the impersonators" [9, page 161].

The cremation ritual dealt mainly with the disposal of the body and with helping the bereaved over the initial shock. At the subsequent mourning ceremony, the focus was more on religious and social integration than on the personal adjustment of the bereaved. Yet this very strengthening of social integration doomed the Cocopa to a relatively sparse level of subsistence. Because funeral rites were the main expression of Cocopa tribal enterprise and because the destruction and lavish consumption of wealth were integral parts of the funeral complex, the Cocopa "were forever barred from the accumulation of capital goods, the development of complex tools and equipment, and the building of elaborate houses, temples or monuments. They were, in effect, held to a hand-to-mouth existence which was more efficiently pursued by independent families and small political units" [9, page 163].

The old tradition of death practices continued in force when Kelly worked among the Cocopa between 1940 and 1947. At that time, not one of the tribe had acquired and kept more wealth than a bare minimum of household goods and a secondhand automobile. No Cocopa had dared to inherit anything, money or property, from a dead relative. The one change in this, perhaps indicative of changes to come, was that in a few families a dead relative's automobile was not burned but was traded in for another model.

3

At the other end of the state of Arizona and at a vastly different level of culture, live the Hopi. They are one of the Pueblo tribes—agriculturalists who follow a highly ritualized, complex way of life. In recent years, automobiles and other appurtenances of Western material culture have become familiar sights in the eleven Hopi villages. Yet the traditional ways of religion, of ceremonialism, of social organization are still followed by many Hopi. Funeral rites continue to be held in the old tradition, and that tradition is one which minimizes the whole event of death and funerals.

The Hopi do not like the idea of death and they are afraid of the newly dead. Their funeral rites are small, private affairs, quickly over and best forgotten. Those who are bereaved may well feel the pain of loss as deeply as do mourners in any society, but they give themselves over to no overt transport of grief of the kind expected of mourners among the Cocopa, Kotas, and in many another society. The Hopi cherish the middle way: they seek to avoid excess of any kind; their most desirable universe is one in which all is measured, deliberate, and under control. Weeping may be unavoidable, but it is not encouraged, for any cause. If one must weep—Hopi parents have told their children—it is best to weep alone, outside the village, where no one can see [3, page 221].

As soon as a death occurs in a family, the women of the household do lament; they cry a bit and speak of their loss. But there is no formal wailing nor is there a public gathering. The body is quickly prepared for burial and put into its grave as soon as possible. A woman relative washes the head; prayer feathers and a cotton mask are put on the corpse; it is wrapped and carried off straightway by the men of the household.

As with the Kotas and many other peoples of the world, con-

tact with death brings pollution. Before persons who are thus
polluted can resume normal relations with men and with the gods,
they must divest themselves of the taint. Hence, on their return
from the burying ground, the members of the household purify
themselves ritually. The next morning a male relative of the deceased puts meal and prayer sticks on the new grave, prays for
rain—a central good of Hopi life—and asks the spirit not to
return to the village. To ensure the departure of the deceased, the
relative symbolically closes the trail back to the village by drawing
charcoal lines across it. When he comes back to the bereaved household, all wash their hair and purify themselves in piñon smoke.
"They should then try to forget the deceased and continue with life
as usual" [4, pages 57–58].

The spirit is believed to rise from the grave on the fourth morning and to follow the path to the land of the dead, somewhere in
the general area of the Grand Canyon. It then becomes one of the
great assembly of supernaturals. With these the Hopi are greatly
concerned. The supernatural spirits are continually invoked; they
are frequently asked for blessings; they come to the villages on
ceremonial occasions. But the spirits are not Hopi; they are a
different class of being and Hopi culture provides rules and means
for dealing with them. The spirits are depersonalized entities; they
do not have the characteristics of deceased friends and relatives.
The Hopi go to great lengths to make sure that the dichotomy of
quick and dead is sharp and clear. Many rites having to do with
spirits conclude with a ritual device which breaks off contact
between mortals and spirits [10, pages 491–492].

The Hopi are one people who express no desire whatsoever to
recall the memory of their deceased, whether for good or ill. Some
years ago a visitor to one of the Hopi villages took a picture of a
young woman. On a later visit to the village, he learned that the
young woman had died, so he presented the enlarged photograph
which he had with him to her mother. The next day the mother
begged him to take the picture back, saying that it reminded her

too vividly of her bereavement. The anthropologist's footnote to this account adds that "no Pueblo Indian of the older generation wants a picture of a deceased relative" [17, page 21]. Among the Hopi and other Pueblo peoples, "Fear of the dead and the will to forget them as individuals are extreme, but the dead have to remove from the living, not the living from the dead" [15, page 1150]. That is, the mourners do not have to destroy all mementos and property of the deceased; that would be quite contrary to Hopi precepts of balance, moderation, and thrift. Property is inherited and distributed in prescribed ways among various classes of heirs.

The emphasis in the funeral ceremony is quite different from other motifs in Hopi practice. Most life-cycle and calendrical rites are conducted with very elaborate ceremony, in contrast to the quick and meager ritual of the funeral occasion. Hopi society is an elaborate structure of interlocking organizations. In most cere-monies, members of different socioreligious organizations take part or attend at some stage. But the funeral ceremony is restricted mainly to the immediate household; there is little provision to show the multiple roles which the deceased may have occupied in the social network. The sovereign desire is to dismiss the body and the event. The urge is to dispatch the spirit to another realm where it will not challenge the Hopi ideals of good, harmonious, happy existence in *this* world and where, as a being of another and well-known kind, it can be methodically controlled by the ritual apparatus of Hopi culture.

4

Quite a different outlook on death and on life is shown in the funeral rites of the Roman Catholic people of Barra, the southern-most island group in Scotland's Outer Hebrides. Burial rites there, as F. G. Vallee describes them [18], take place in five stages. Only the close relatives are involved in the first; the total community is included in the last stage. When the final funeral bell tolls, every islander participates, in some degree, in the obser'ances of the occasion.

The first act of the sequence begins when it becomes clear that a person is approaching his end. The close relatives rally around to help. It is important to make sure that a priest will be present at the proper time to bestow the last rites—these rites are a most essential element in the "happy death" which the Barra Catholic asks for in his prayers.

Death is not a tabooed subject for conversation. A failing person may well discuss with his friends and relatives the likelihood of his being alive, say, next autumn. Nor is there in this culture any great dread of the departed spirit. "In no case that I knew of was it assumed that the soul of a particular individual went to hell after death, no matter how evil his life in terms of the community *mores*" [18, page 121].

When death occurs, the next stage of the ceremony is set in train. The news is spread throughout the community of some two thousand people. No group recreation takes place until after the burial; those in the neighborhood abstain from their regular work.

The chief mourner—the man most closely related to the deceased—goes to the public house to buy whiskey and beer for those who will assemble and to arrange for coffin and shroud. This is the first public act in the ritual sequence; the chief mourner receives condolences from the men at the bar.

As the news spreads, those who have had close social ties with the deceased gather to pay their respects. Cousins, in-laws, and close friends come. They bring supplementary food and refreshments; some of them stay through night, which is the night of the wake. The "watchers" during the night are mostly men. They talk through the night about seamanship, fishing, sheep, and similar subjects of male interest. Drinking whiskey and beer is part of the ritual idiom but there is no immoderation in drinking. A few women, mainly those of the household, are present and busy themselves about the kitchen. The men take turns through the night in keeping vigil beside the body. Several times during the night the whole company goes into the death room and all pray.

From Vallee's account of these formalities, it seems reasonable to infer that the wake serves both psychological and social purposes. The assembled kinsmen and friends are solicitous and helpful, giving psychic support to the bereaved. In their presence the mourners can give necessary vent to their grief but are constrained from intense and incapacitating brooding about their loss. The participants at the wake, by their presence, also assure the mourners (and themselves as well) that the bonds of kinship and friendship continue, that the death has not irreparably ruptured the web of social life.

In the afternoon on the day after the wake, the coffin is carried in procession to the chapel. In the funeral procession are the deceased's relatives, friends, and neighbors. Every man is given a turn at helping to bear the coffin, no matter how short the distance it is carried.

The final stage of the ceremony begins with a Requiem Mass on the following morning. Then the coffin is carried, again in procession, to the cemetery. This is a larger procession than on the previous day; people from a wide area attend. At the grave the priest conducts the burial service. After the interment, mourners disperse to kneel and pray at graves of other deceased relatives. Members of the bereaved household return home and are visited by their kinsmen.

The name of the dead person is recalled at High Mass each Sunday for a year in every Catholic congregation on the island. In the dead person's home church his name is formally mentioned in this way for two years after his death.

The people of Barra seem to have a smooth and easy set of patterns for dealing with the event of death. There appears, at least overtly, to be no great fear of the dead, no anxiety about speeding on the departed spirit, and no avoidance of the topic or of the memory of the deceased. Most men and women participate in some ten to fifteen funerals in their neighborhood every year; death ceremonies for them are normal events. Vallee notes how the sacred and secular elements are blended in the funeral. The occasion is a religious one complete with priest, prayers, and holy services. "Yet in the midst of these forms and acts of sanctity, mourners chat easily of ships and sheep, are concerned with ensuring that there is no shortage of liquor and food. Frequent attendance at these rites does more than breed familiarity with death; it intensifies the awareness of belonging to a community" [18, page 128].

The ritual sequence is complex; only the bare outline has been sketched here. It is a clearly known, frequently repeated sequence; hence hundreds can smoothly and spontaneously participate in a funeral. Even the few Protestants on the island know precisely when to take part and when to withdraw from the rites.

Funerals on Barra differ from those of our previous examples in that they are regulated and led by priests of the Roman Catholic Church—an institution which extends far beyond the given community in space, time, and authority. Catholic ritual prescribes certain funeral rites and Catholic dogma provides certain beliefs about death. But there is also a great deal in any Catholic funeral which is not laid down in the canons of the Church. In Barra, for example, the wake, the whiskey, and the procession are important elements of the ceremony, but are not prescribed by the Church.

Among other peoples who are Roman Catholic in religion, a funeral ceremony includes the same prescribed rites, but it may also include many different elements of social participation, cultural practice, and emotional emphasis. The Church does decree certain requirements for funerals and will not countenance practices which run counter to its theological precepts. But the limits of these requirements are quite broad; within them there is notable variation between, say, a Catholic funeral on Barra and one in Bavaria or in the Philippines. Hence, while funeral rites on

Barra appear to be smoothly attuned to social and personal needs, among another people of the same religion the funeral may not allay personal tensions or promote social concord in the same manner as on Barra.

5

Sometimes the very form of the funeral reflects personal ambivalences which arise from conflicting social and cultural conditions. Thus the Chiricahua and Mescalero Apache Indians of the American Southwest show two kinds of formal response to bereavement. Both are broadly similar to those previously mentioned for another southwestern tribe, the Cocopa. On the one side there is vigorous and public expression of grief by the relatives of a deceased; on the other side there is rigorous effort to banish all trace of the death and all memory of the deceased. There is a period when it is proper for mourners to give vent to their grief, and then they do so in quite violent fashion. At other times, the name and memory of a dead person must be expunged from recall and remembrance.

In his analysis of Apache death customs, M. E. Opler notes that "there is the tendency to publicly signify grief and attest to the loss, and an elaborately socialized machinery for banishing that grief and the objects and words which might awake it" [14, page 92].

These apparently contradictory practices, Opler suggests, are one manifestation of the ambivalence an Apache feels toward his relatives. Throughout his life an Apache is taught to assist and support his relatives, to avenge their wrongs at any cost. He in turn depends on them and under the economic and social conditions of aboriginal Apache life could not survive without them. But he was also taught to be independent and self-reliant, and this quality too was necessary for successful living in his natural and social environment.

The two demands, for group solidarity and for individual independence, often created conflict within the Apache individual. He generally acceded to the demands of his family group, but there was left in him a residue of resentment and hostility toward them. This hostility was shown in various ways. One was the belief that every Apache who received supernatural power was obliged to pay for this power with the life of a close relative, perhaps one of his children. Since "practically every Apache realized a supernatural experience," a person commonly feared those of his close relatives who were known to have particularly powerful supernatural helpers [14, page 100].

Hence the two kinds of bereavement reaction, Opler suggests, reflect the personal ambivalence which an Apache felt about his relatives—including his parents, his siblings, and his wife's parents and siblings. The permitted, florid mourning behavior expressed the emotional loss of a loved person on whom one was greatly dependent. The strong cultural directives to obliterate all trace of a deceased may be "the result of repressed and unconscious resentment and dislike of relatives which have their roots in the actual circumstances and events of Apache life" [14, page 107].

The cultural fiat to mourn and then to dismiss the memory of a dead relative evidently made it easier for an Apache to dismiss the fear he had of the relative when he was alive and of his ghost after he was dead. Such overt fear of one's close kin is not commonly manifested among the various peoples of the world.

More usual in human societies is another sort of ambivalence about death and funeral rites. Bronislaw Malinowski depicted the feelings of bereaved survivors in these words: "The emotions are extremely complex and even contradictory; the dominant elements, love of the dead and loathing of the corpse, passionate attachment to the personality still lingering about the body and a shuddering fear of the gruesome thing that has been left over, these two elements seem to mingle and play into each other" [11, page 30]. In the Melanesian funeral rites which he had observed, Malinowski commented, there was shown a desire to maintain the tie with the deceased and the parallel tendency to break the bond. By performing the prescribed religious acts, men can resolve this conflict, counteract "the centrifugal forces of fear, dismay, demoralization," and can reintegrate themselves as a group and reestablish their morale [11, pages 32 to 35].

6

Yet traditional rites are not always sufficient for the occasion and its stress. An illuminating analysis of a funeral in a small town in Java shows how, in that case, the use of the customary funeral ceremony brought on social discord rather than integration and brought more trouble than solace to the bereaved [7]. The principal difficulty lay in the fact that the traditional rites, which were suited to the needs of the occasion in an agricultural, village, folk milieu, are not as appropriate to the needs of the villagers who are transplanted to town life, where economic and political orientations differ from those of the village.

The episode occurred in 1954 when a ten-year-old boy, who was living with his uncle and aunt in one of the crowded neighborhoods of a town in east-central Java, suddenly died. The uncle dispatched a telegram to the boy's parents and then sent for a Modin, a Moslem religious official, to conduct the funeral in the customary, traditional manner.

In form, the traditional Javanese funeral is a combination of Islamic precept and indigenous practice, of scriptural dogma and local belief. As in the Roman Catholic rites on Barra, the requirements of the universalistic, scriptural religion are met in the idiom of native tradition. In Javanese village tradition, the funeral ceremony is one variety of a generic ceremony, called slametan, which is given at crucial points, not only of the life cycle, but of the agricultural and ceremonial cycle as well.

The slametan is mainly a communal feast, performed under religious auspices, for a group of neighbors. "The demands of the labor—intensive rice and dry-crop agricultural process require the perpetuation of specific modes of technical cooperation and enforce a sense of community in the otherwise rather self-contained families—a sense of community which the slametan clearly reinforces" [7, page 36]. The traditional funeral slametan is directed by an Islamic official, the Modin, who supervises the preparation of the body for burial, leads in the chanting of Arabic prayers, and reads a graveside speech to the deceased, reminding him of his duties as a believing Moslem.

This ritual form is carried through quickly and in a mood reminiscent of that described for Hopi funerals. The mourners are supposed to be relatively calm and undemonstrative. "Tears are not approved of and certainly not encouraged; the effort is to get the job done, not to linger over the pleasures of grief . . . the whole momentum of the Javanese ritual system is supposed to carry one through grief without severe emotional disturbance" [7, page 40]. Such was the expectation of the dead boy's uncle when he began funeral preparations and sent for the Modin.

But when the Modin came, the uncle's expectation was not realized and, to the great chagrin of the body's family and their friends, the Modin refused to lead the funeral rites. This untoward, discomfiting and exceptional refusal came about for these reasons.

There was in 1954 a great cultural-political split in this town, and elsewhere in Java. Those on one side were Islamic purists who wanted to emphasize the scriptural sanctions and diminish the indigenous practices. Those of the other side wanted to stress the indigenous practices and mute the Islamic elements. Allegiance to one or another side was expressed through political affiliation. In this town, the Islamic patriots belonged to the country's largest Moslem party, *Masjumi,* which supported an "Islamic State" for Indonesia rather than a secular republic. Those townsmen who advocated the indigenous tradition belonged to another political party, *Permai,* which was smaller nationally but locally strong. Its platform was a fusion of Marxist politics, anti-Islamic ideas, and nativist religion.

Worried about controlling the conflict between the two parties, the local administrative officer had called together the religious officials, the Modins, most of whom were *Masjumi* leaders. He instructed them not to participate in funeral rites for supporters of the *Permai* party.

Hence, on the morning of July 17, 1954, when a Modin arrived at the house where the boy had died, he saw a *Permai* poster displayed there and refused to perform the ceremony. He rubbed in his refusal by saying piously that since the *Permai* people belonged to another religion, he did not know the correct burial rituals for it. All he knew was Islam.

Though the *Permai* people are anti-Islam, they still had no other funeral rite than that traditionally performed and led by a Modin. The dead boy's uncle had never thought that his political allegiance would present such a distressing problem. The funeral preparations were halted, the people of the bereaved household were distraught, and the uncle exploded in rage—rather uncharacteristic behavior for a Javanese. Friends of the family gathered, but no one knew what to do.

When the dead boy's father and mother arrived, the aunt—who had earlier given vent to loud, unrestrained wailing—now rushed to her sister and the two women "dissolved into wild hysterics." These unusual and shocking outbursts made the assembled people all the more nervous and uneasy.

At last, through the good offices of a go-between, the dead boy's father requested an Islamic funeral, implying that he was not of the *Permai* party. The Modin then carried through the usual burial rites. But three days later, at the first commemorative feast, the usual slametan procedure—which includes an Islamic chant for the dead—was not followed. Instead there was a political speech and philosophical discussion, together with a strange and atypical talk by the dead boy's father expressing his feelings and his confusion.

His confusion arose because the traditional ceremony had become unsuited to his social circumstances. The ceremony functioned well when the group to be consolidated was a set of village neighbors who shared many close ties—economic, religious, personal, social. But in the town neighborhood, such village bonds are not as relevant; the important bonds are based on ideology, class, occupation, and politics rather than on local proximity. Hence the traditional funeral ceremony, when held now in an urban setting, "increasingly served to remind people that the neighborhood bonds they are strengthening through a dramatic enactment are no longer the bonds which emphatically hold them together" [7, page 52]. The boy's funeral provides an example of the incongruity between the old ceremonial form and the new social conditions. It is likely that this incongruity will not long exist. Ceremonial forms can be changed. In future years these funeral rites may be altered and may then accord better with the broad purposes of personal and social integration for which men, in Java as elsewhere, commonly perform the last rites.

7

"A funeral rite," Raymond Firth observes, "is a social rite *par excellence*. Its ostensible object is the dead person, but it benefits not the dead, but the living" [5, page 63]. This comment occurs in the course of an analysis of an incident involving a clash of interests in a chief's family in Tikopia. A grandson of the old chief has been lost at sea. The boy's father wants to prepare a suitably elaborate funeral ceremony; his brothers—the other sons of the chief—want to postpone the funeral lest it detract from a festival for the clan gods which the family should soon give in properly lavish style. There is a flare-up of temper; there is mollification by neutral people; finally the funeral is given precedence and familial solidarity is, at least overtly, reestablished.

For the very reason that funerals so often are occasions when social solidarity ought to be displayed in a society, they can also present situations where the lack of solidarity is dramatically highlighted. In the Kota Dry Funeral, there is a juncture when all Kotas who are present at the ceremony come forward, one by one, to give a parting bow of respect to the relic of each deceased.

Around this gesture of social unity, violent quarrels often rage [13, pages 226 to 229]. When kinsmen of a deceased Kota are fervent supporters of one of the two opposing factions in Kota society, they may try to prevent a person of the other faction from making this gesture of respect and solidarity. This is tantamount to declaring that those of the other faction are not Kotas at all—a declaration which neither side will quietly accept. Thus a ritual action which symbolized concord has frequently triggered a good deal of discord. Yet among the Kotas, as in other societies, neutral people try to bring about a compromise; the ceremony is somehow completed with as much show of social unity as can be managed—especially for funerals of the great men of the tribe.

Such show of unity is graphically depicted, on the grand scene of European history, by photographs of some memorable funeral corteges. If we turn to the picture of the glittering array of monarchs in the procession behind the coffin of Edward VII or the picture of the more somberly clad pallbearers carrying the coffin of Josef Stalin, we can appreciate that differences may be sunk, if only temporarily, on the occasion of a funeral.

In earlier European history, the State funeral was an important symbol of the continuity of monarchical power. In medieval France, for example, the death of a king might be followed by great disorder, because his successor was not sovereign until his coronation. By the sixteenth century, however, a new king in France exercised full powers from the moment of his predecessor's death. The royal funeral became not only a symbol of proper succession but also one of the agencies for the smooth transfer of power [8].

Funeral monuments like the Pyramids and the Taj Mahal attest to the political aspects which have long been entailed in state funerals. Codes of testamentary law reflect the economic aspects of death rites. The rites, the codes, the monuments—whether for a great personage or for an ordinary person—have often expressed religious ideas of immortality as well as those societal concepts which we have here discussed [cf. 2, 6, 1, 16].

In some societies, the belief in immortality is considered to be most important for the consolation of the bereaved; in other societies, as among the Kotas, the concept of the afterworld is not of any great interest. At funerals, social forces may be effectively rallied to solace the mourners or there may be special social conditions which hamper their readjustment.

In modern American society, E. H. Volkart suggests, such great attachment to the particular members of one's family is built up that readjustment becomes very difficult after their death. "Thus whereas we stress the sense of loss and recognize the need for replacement, basically the culture creates conditions in which the deceased is irreplaceable because he cannot ever really be duplicated. . . . In this way the bereaved person has no automatic cultural solution to the problem of replacement" [19, pages 299 and 300].

American culture has, in certain respects, and for some Americans, become deritualized. Persons bereaved by a death sometimes find that they have no clear prescription as to what to do next. In such cases, each has to work out a solution for himself. After the typical period of shock and disorganization, these mourners can receive little help toward personal reorganization. When individual solutions to such recurrent and poignant problems are repeatedly made, they may tend to coalesce and to become institutionalized. Hence it may be that the people who have reacted strongly against the older rituals—because they were rituals—may institute some new version of the old ritual forms.

Death ceremonies, like other cultural forms, are changed in time by those who use them as a result of changes in their social, cultural, and psychological environments. Yet the fundamental psychological and social purposes which are accomplished by funeral rites remain quite similar. These purposes, illustrated in the Kota example, can be met in many different ways. One way is the extravagant mourning ceremony of the Cocopa; another is the sparse, hurried ceremony of the Hopi. The death rites may be taken in the community's normal stride, as in Barra, or may touch on especially conflicting feelings among the survivors, as with the Apache. A funeral may rouse social conflict, as in the example from Java, but funeral rites are generally intended to be a means of strengthening group solidarity.

Rituals for death can have many uses for life. And the study of these rites can illuminate much about a culture and a society. Thus the Kotas' certainty about the effectiveness of their Dry Funeral provides a clue to their general certainty about dealings with the supernatural. The violent quarrels which have taken place at Kota funerals direct our attention to certain values which they hold most dear [13]. Once we have suitable analyses, from a number of peoples, of the ways in which death ceremonies (and other biologically based universals) fit into, reflect, and reinforce cultural themes, it will be possible to go on to some really interesting problems. For example, the Hopi funeral rites and those in the Javanese town are very dissimilar in specific detail but seem quite alike in mood. Is the similarity only a superficially apparent one, is it an epiphenomenon of little consequence, or does it give evidence of structural similarity of some kind between two societies widely different in the content of their cultures? In this and in other ways, the melancholy subject of funerals may provide one good entryway to the analysis of cultures and to the understanding of peoples.

REFERENCES

1. Ashley-Montagu, M. F.: *Immortality,* Grove Press, Inc., New York, 1955.

2. Bendann, E.: *Death Customs: An Analytical Study of Burial Rites,* Alfred A. Knopf, Inc., New York, 1930.

3. Brandt, R. B.: *Hopi Ethics,* University of Chicago Press, Chicago, 1954.

4. Eggan, F.: *Social Organization of the Western Pueblos,* University of Chicago Press, Chicago, 1950.

5. Firth, R.: *Elements of Social Organization,* Henry E. Walter, Ltd., London, 1951.

6. Frazer, J. G.: *The Belief in Immortality and the Worship of the Dead* (3 vols.) Macmillan & Co., Ltd., London, 1913–1922.

7. Geertz, C.: "Ritual and social change: Javanese example," *Am. Anthropologist,* **59:** 32–54, 1957.

8. Giesey, R. E.: "The Royal Funeral Ceremony in Renaissance France," unpublished doctoral dissertation, University of California, Berkeley, 1954.

9. Kelly, W. H.: "Cocopa attitudes and practices with respect to death and mourning," *Southwestern J. Anthropology,* **5:** 151–164, 1949.

10. Kennard, E. A.: "Hopi reactions to death," *Am. Anthropologist,* **29:** 491–494, 1937.

11. Malinowski, B.: *Magic, Science, and Religion and Other Essays,* Free Press, Glencoe, Ill., 1948.

12. Mandelbaum, D. G.: "Form, Variation, and Meaning of a Ceremony," in R. F. Spencer (ed.), *Method and Perspective in Anthropology,* University of Minnesota Press, Minneapolis, 1954, pp. 60–102.

13. Mandelbaum, D. G.: "The world and the world view of the Kota," in M. Marriott (ed.), *Village India,* University of Chicago Press, Chicago, 1955.

14. Opler, M. E.: "An interpretation of ambivalence of two American Indian tribes," *J. Social Psychol.,* **7:** 82–116, 1936.

15. Parsons, E. C.: *Pueblo Indian Religion* (2 vols.), University of Chicago Press, Chicago, 1939.
16. Puckle, B. S.: *Funeral Customs,* London, 1926.
17. Titiev, M.: "Old Oraibi," *Papers of the Peabody Museum, Harvard University,* vol. 22, no. 1, Cambridge, Mass., 1944.
18. Vallee, F. G.: "Burial and mourning customs in a Hebridian community," *J. Roy. Anthropological Inst.,* **85:** 119–130, 1955.
19. Volkart, E. H. (in collaboration with S. T. Michael): "Bereavement and Mental Health," in A. H. Leighton, J. A. Clausen, and R. N. Wilson (eds.), *Explorations in Social Psychiatry,* Basic Books, Inc., New York, 1957.

12

EDGAR N. JACKSON

Grief and Religion

In dealing with the problem of Being, the meaning of life and the experience of death of the self or of another, some approach must be made to the problem of Nonbeing. Often it is assumed that the only answer is that of two mutually exclusive conditions, "to be or not to be." The religious answer to the problem of Being seeks to remove the element of mutual exclusiveness and point the way toward a larger meaning for what we usually think of as "Nonbeing," namely, "to be AND not to be" [6, 10, 12].

This is made more acceptable by the tentative approach of modern science to a concept of exclusion, for the further we penetrate into our knowledge of the universe the more we are aware of the fact that the meanings of life are too large to be exclusive and that we must employ multiple explanations to begin to adequately interpret the phenomena that are experienced in existence [3]. The "both-ands" have acquired a new level of scientific respectability through efforts to deal with the quanta and ideas of freedom and responsibility.

As light can extend beyond both ends of the visible spectrum so mental activity can extend beyond the conscious. Comparable to the infrared would be the unconscious, and the superconscious might be compared to the ultraviolet, cosmic, and other fast wavelength radiation.

Only with special aids can the vision be extended beyond the white light or its components. Similarly it is only with special means that the boundaries of consciousness are extended. The function of religion is to extend the boundaries of consciousness relatively to the problem of Being and Nonbeing so that the personality can meet the fact of death at the physical level with a firm sense of reality, a healthful expression of feelings, and a capacity to reinvest emotional capital where it will produce the best fruits in life; but most of all its function is to furnish the basis for a philosophy of life and death that can sustain the highest spiritual aspirations of the individual [14].

Modern psychological understanding verifies the value of religious rites, rituals, and practices which, anthropological study has found, were long practical in fortifying the individual against the stress of grief and during the work of mourning. These group practices have developed out of the need to serve the full spectrum of mental life, and what is interpreted as irrational and superstitious at the conscious level is often satisfying a deeper need of the being beyond the normal bounds of conscious mental activity. So it is that the religious approach to the personality during the time of stress due to bereavement is concerned with depth and height as well as a breadth of understanding in dealing with the feelings of the individual [7].

The innate wisdom of religious practices seems to be not so much a matter of conscious design as of unconscious evolution. The benefits of these practices are not determined adequately by rational judgments alone, but demand rather an understanding of the response of the emotions and spiritual sensitivities of the whole being. The ancient wisdom of life is reflected in many of those forms that are employed to minister to the grief-stricken, such as the preparatory aspects of the initiation rites of primitive peoples, which recognize that adulthood involves a contemplation of both life and death and those contemporary religious practices that engage the total being, such as the Passover among Jews, the Passion Drama among Christians, and the idea of Nirvana among Buddhists [9].

REALITY MAINTENANCE

Because the grief experience reaches deeply into the emotional structure of the individual, it is important that the activities that engage him at the time of his bereavement encourage a firm grip on reality rather than a flight into fantasy. For some, the escapes into the unreal with narcotics for the body, sedation for the emotions, and fanciful philosophy for the mind, are already too much of a possibility. So the religious practices that are employed should fortify reality rather than deny it.

Some persons contend that there is a pagan or barbaric element in the body-centered type of activity that engages the family and friends during the period preceding burial or cremation. But for most persons an entirely spiritual approach is difficult and does not prepare the individual for the departure of the body of the loved one.

When a family has spent three days, as is the case in most Christian communities, or seven days as is the general Jewish practice, in accepted mourning procedures, the reality of the death of the body is impressed on the mind and emotions in a way that cannot be easily denied. The "viewing of the remains," the visits of friends and family, the rituals of the community and religious institutions that confront the mourner day after day in the presence of the motionless body, gradually bring the consciousness of death to all levels of being, and make it difficult for fantasies or illusions to develop in the thoughts or feelings of the individual [8].

This sense of the reality of death and the finality of physical separation is a painful process, and there is no known way of escaping the pain within a clear reality framework. Sometimes the rather tortuous process of talking to many people who try to say consoling words reinforces the consciousness that death is universal and separation a permanent though painful fact.

These conditions that are forced on the conscious mind suddenly are apt to penetrate the lower levels of consciousness more slowly. The experience of loss may well trigger a variety of feelings related to a long range of previous experience, and the working-through of these effects is a more complicated process. But the surrounding of death with rituals and practices that fortify the reality of death make it easier for time to saturate the unconscious with the awareness of emotional amputation and the need for the adjustments that relate it to reality.

However, the effort to become conscious of the finality of physical separation does not destroy the chance for a response at the superconscious level of being, for it is here that the religious faith projects itself in "that invincible surmise" that physical death does not destroy all of the qualities of personality. Perhaps one of the valid functions of religion is to engage those spiritual, psychic, and paranormal powers within the personality that may be the best bridge between the mind of the living and the mind of the deceased.

The persistent effort in our science-conscious culture to measure all experience within the bounds of space and time prejudices us against that type of experience that is not so limited. The emotions of the grief-stricken are too profound to be bound by limiting measurements, and the unbounded quality of the religious response serves an important emotional need in justifying such feelings at the time that it is directing them.

At this point there rises the danger of a religious attitude that regards personal immortality in terms of cosmic geography and physical abodes for the dead. Such wishful thinking projects a desire for measurement into the very realm where it is most incongruous, the boundlessness of the superconscious. This danger is one of the most inexcusable hazards that traditional religions have

placed before the individual who seeks to deal with the problem
of life and death in a realistic way.

HEALTHFUL EXPRESSION OF FEELINGS

The religious rites and practices surrounding the process of
mourning can help the bereft individual to engage all his feelings
in a framework that makes them not only acceptable but also easily
expressible. It is unfortunate when false values lead a person to
assume a pose of bravery. The deep feelings are not deceived by
a surface pose. The group practices that make a person feel comfortable with his own deep feelings speed the normal work of mourning and help to prevent those delayed reactions that are the product
of unresolved grief feelings.

The emotions of the grieving tend to cluster about three main
psychological processes: incorporation, substitution, and feelings of
guilt. Within bounds, each is normal and a valid expression of the
deep feelings of the individual which may be worked through and
resolved. When the expression is delayed or repressed, it tends to
find its outlet in less desirable forms.

In incorporation, the individual turns his feelings in upon
himself and in effect becomes in part the deceased person. It is
a psychological device for handling the deep emotional stress. In
a temporary and superficial incorporation or identification with
the deceased, the bereaved would say, "Mother would want me
to be brave and so I will be brave." The emotions or physical
characteristics of the deceased take the place of the feelings of the
mourning individual. More distressing is the condition in which
the bereaved acquires the symptoms of the illness of the deceased.
There are cases where the identity becomes permanent and damage
is done to the personality of the mourner. Because of the danger of
loss of his own identity, the person involved in incorporation needs
to move beyond it in order that the forward motion of his own life
may begin again [17].

A comparable psychological device is employed in substitution. Here the grief-stricken individual, in order to protect himself from the intolerable stress of his emotion, attaches it to somebody or something outside himself and resolves his feeling by such an external attachment. Some of this is involved in the working through of normal grief situations, where the old room, the clothes, the plot in the cemetery become more than the physical symbols of the person. In a sense they become part of the person for the bereaved as they are invested with more than normal emotional meaning. On a temporary basis this can serve a useful purpose while the bereaved is withdrawing his emotional investment from the past and is preparing to reinvest it in the future. College presidents have learned how to put such emotions to creative use through endowments and memorials. But if the attachment becomes so strong that the mourner is enslaved by the substitution, the forward motion of his life is impaired [13].

In acute grief, the element of guilt is invariably present. This is probably due to the ambivalent quality in the love relationship where there is self-giving and self-satisfying, a craving for mutuality between loved and lover, as well as the resentment of loss of freedom. When the love object dies, the feelings are set free and there is guilt. The guilt may be expressed in excessive idealizing of the deceased, or in such feelings as are expressed in phrases like, "If I had only known . . . ," "If I had it to do over again . . . ," or "Why did I fail to do . . ." Such self-condemnation is a normal part of the process of emotional withdrawal. However, if it is more an expression of low self-esteem than of normal grief, it may precipitate a period of depression and melancholia with all of the irrational and excessive feelings that accompany it [1].

In dealing with the normal feelings of identity or incorporation, substitution, and guilt, a ritual like that of the Mass or the Lord's Supper can serve a useful purpose not only in preparing for but also in working through the feelings. In the ritualized memorial service the person identifies himself with Jesus, a deceased individual of religious importance, in such a way that his whole being, conscious, unconscious, and superconscious, is engaged in a rite that involves both thought and action along with other persons. So it has social and religious acceptance at the same time that it has personal efficacy. It can help satisfy the need of the person for incorporation without placing damaging demands upon the personality. The bread and wine is ingested in a symbolic act that fulfills a need to take something into the self while it does it in such an abstract and symbolic fashion that it does not overinvolve the emotions of the individual performing the act. Thus it tends to become a safe channel for the deep feelings. Perhaps the historical explanation of such a sacrament is that it gives vent to feelings too deep to be understood or expressed and yet does it without a demand for interpretation or justification.

A similar process takes place in the symbolic and ritualized substitution, for the feelings of the bereft are attached to a historical religious figure in an acceptable memorial act at the same time that the values and ideals are accepted as a pattern of action. The pattern calls for a new life and a new dedication in such a way that the person can be freed of his past involvement at the same time that he is engaged in a socially approved emotional act.

This is probably most explicit in dealing with guilt feelings. The ritualized expression of unworthiness and the asking for forgiveness and a chance for a new beginning fulfill the deep inner needs of the individual struggling with ambivalence and self-judgment, but it does it in an abstract form that tends to keep it safe from emotional overinvolvement. This is not always the case, however, and one has to be alert to those situations where the deeply disturbed person experiences a chain reaction of emotions set off by a ritualized service.

It is important that the bereaved person have a safe framework within which he can express all the feelings that are set in motion by the loss of the beloved. It is also important that the means of expression meet the needs of the psyche at all three levels. The ritualized religious expression does this by releasing the emotional responses that grow from group need and group support, that justify and accept deep feelings of pain without requiring explanation, all at a level below the threshold of consciousness. But it does this in such a way that any conscious need for understanding and interpretation can be accomplished in a historical and theological frame of reference. However, neither the unconscious nor conscious response prejudices the higher needs of the person to fulfill the aspirations of the superconscious element of his nature. The very rituals that satisfy the basic needs can gently lead him toward those attitudes and insights that are achieved through the leap of faith. For the ritualized act may become a source of the feelings that are rooted in a mystical experience, a psychic response of what is called in religious terminology, a "revelation." While such phenomena cannot be reduced to the terminology of the other levels of consciousness, they are a reality to the person who experiences them, and that experience is its own justification [2].

REINVESTING EMOTIONAL CAPITAL

An important part of the process of working through the grief is that of withdrawing the emotional capital invested in the deceased and reinvesting it in the relationships that can continue to produce fruit in life. The religious institution serves two functions during this process. First, it gives security to the emotions when they engage themselves in the process, and second, it gives a framework within which the emotions can be reinvested.

The first is done both implicitly and explicitly. The religious institution in our society continues to be the custodian of the bold, frank look at the facts of Being and Nonbeing, the facts of life and death. Much of the rest of our cultural orientation is away from unpleasant reality. Most dying is done in hospitals with professional attendants. The military makes death impersonal and the prevalent entertainment makes death not so much a tragedy as a dramatic illusion. The religious institution, through its basic philosophy, its hymnody, its scriptures, and its acts of worship, thinks of life and death as ultimately real concerns that must be dealt with by each individual, and on individual terms. This prepares the person continually in the depths of Being for the inevitable event of his expiration or that of those close to him. From the early efforts of the dramatist in the book of Job to the latest existential interpretation of Biblical theology, the problem of Being and Nonbeing is made dramatically real. But the problem of Being and Nonbeing is not the problem of life and death. Rather, it is that deeper problem which seeks in the face of the inevitable fact of ultimate physical death to deal with a concept of life and a mass of anguished feelings so that from them can emerge a value structure that is not destroyed by that which is so incidental to the flesh. It persistently projects the most daring interpretation of the spiritual nature of life itself and the integral relevance of a view of life large enough to cope with the process of death without destroying the ultimate values of life. An adventurous and daring projection of meaning into the spiritual nature of life becomes a sustaining fact emotionally in the presence of physical dissolution and gives the firm base from which the process of reinvesting emotional capital can proceed.

Explicitly, the religious institution furnishes the social and personal framework within which free-floating emotions can be attached. While it uses the language that indicates the structure of a cosmic family with a direction in which father-, mother-, brother-, and sister-feelings can be engaged, it does something more practical. It furnishes a variety of small groups through which feelings can be expressed. A pastoral counseling relationship where feelings are accepted and worked through with safety and understanding, a sewing circle where a group of widows share their common feelings, a study group that parallels in method the group-therapy techniques of inner exploration and external relationship, a service of worship where the process of being alone and together at the same time is achieved, all in their own way become channels through which the unattached or free-floating feelings can be constructively related to the needs of life and its ongoing process.

Another significant factor is that the religious view of life not only deals with conscious and unconscious needs, but at the same time does not interfere with the superconscious needs for spiritual affirmation. It also encourages a type of hope that cannot be dissected in the laboratory but which sustains the spirit and ultimately gives validity to those phenomena that indicate this higher level of activity at the core of being.

LIFE AND DEATH

Liberal religion has looked upon the phenomena of the occult with suspicion and a general mood of rejection. Even in the face of recent theories of consciousness and experimental studies of these phenomena, a large degree of skepticism still persists. However, no contemplation of the philosophy of life and death from the point of view of the spiritual nature of man can be approached without a serious evaluation of the relationship between traditional religious assumptions and modern scientific verifications.

Parapsychology laboratories verify under carefully controlled conditions a mental capacity that functions beyond the measurements of space and time [15, 16]. A researcher at the RCA laboratories has devised an electronic device to measure the change in radiation of the body of a trance medium in the process of communication with an alleged discarnate spirit entity [11]. The Chief of Psychiatry of a large New York hospital has described his experience in communication through a medium and asserts to a group of his professional colleagues that he felt he was in contact with a discarnate spirit entity of unusual medical knowledge and that he had no other reasonable explanation for the phenomena observed [11]. Careful studies by the British and American Societies for Psychical Research produce a considerable volume of carefully validated material of psychic significance. These phenomena and the indicated judgments concerning them do not fit into any well-established and prevalent psychological system, but they cannot be ignored [14]. An editor of the *Scientific American* observed the conditions and has signed the affidavit now deposited in the Library of Congress which attests to the breaking of the Houdini code [5]. Some concept of life and the nature of the spirit large enough to accommodate such phenomena must be projected in order to deal with this level of mental activity.

The religious view of life has always projected this idea of the spiritual nature of man and the type of activity of the psyche that in some unexplainable manner persists. Without any attempt at scientific justification, the religious mind has sought to be guided by those spiritually disciplined and responsive souls whose mystical experiences and revelations have permitted superconscious material to be translated into the language if not the feelings of the conscious mind. While the religious view of life has never claimed that this type of experience is normal for all adherents, or that it is essential to the satisfaction of the needs of all persons, it has still recognized the possibility of such a response of the soul and has felt that for those who shared it, it represented the highest form of spiritual development and the final level of self-realization.

A wise agnosticism should chasten our efforts to define or describe the nature of the spiritual existence of discarnate beings. Such existence is well beyond any known frame of reference by which it could be made reasonable or logical. However, the intimations of immortality are a sufficiently valid part of the psychical nature of man to demand inclusion in any philosophy which purports to deal with the meaning of life and death. As this is usually well beyond the range of formal scientific thought, it remains for the religious consciousness to try to deal with it.

This sort of a religious consciousness cannot begin to satisfy the mental and emotional needs of modern man unless and until it makes a valid effort to relate its observations to the best scientific judgments of the day. This is not because the ideas need scientific verification to be valid but because man with his modern background and training requires scientific verification to make the ideas acceptable to him.

This is not to equate consciousness with electricity as Freud has suggested, but rather to feel that there are valid functions of Being that are not subject to analogy. We are enough at home in a physics that does not feel obliged to make a choice between waves or particles, and a biology that refuses to draw too sharp a line between the animate and inanimate, and a psychology that is not bound by a distinction between freedom and determinism not to feel that ideas are unacceptable unless they can be driven into a small corner.

In ministering to the emotional needs of the bereft it is important to be able to move toward a philosophy of life that makes valid what Santayana called "the soul's invincible surmise." It is at this point that the philosophical relevance of the ideas of a scientist like Whitehead have significance for us. His idea of a "prehension," a basic knowledge of relationship that is not dependent upon space and time, has meaning here. Beyond apprehension or comprehension, it denotes a basic fact of relationship not dependent upon conscious knowledge to fulfill itself. The mind steeped in the apprehension of grief and struggling with the comprehension that is the fruit of the work of mourning is sustained by a view of life that is rooted in something more basic, a prehension that does not violate a religious faith but rather gives it another dimension. At this point the mysticism of the philosopher of science who sees behind all of the dualisms of distinction a unifying force that reveals an ever-larger truth verifies the right of the soul to surmise and the consciousness to project a daring faith.

The fruitful study of the behavior of man can never be allowed to divert us into thinking that man is only behavior. An intensive study of the levels of consciousness of man can hardly be employed to limit the nature of being to consciousness as we have grown to conceive of it. The religious consciousness as an essential art form is concerned within the limits of disciplined thought with moving beyond concepts that constrain in order to achieve the largest conceivable view of life and of death. It is continually saying that biology while it describes life does not define it and that psychology though it illuminates the life of the psyche does not confine it.

The religious concern for measuring life in terms of values rather than in terms of space and time is the source of its ultimate meaning. Frankl puts it thus:

Man's existence is a responsibility springing from man's finiteness. This finiteness of life, the limited time man has upon the earth, does make life meaningless. On the contrary, death itself is what makes life meaningful . . . Temporality is therefore not only an essential characteristic of human life, but also a real factor in its meaningfulness. [6, page 85.]

The religious concern continually moves man more in the direction of contemplation and the creation of spiritual values rather than toward a concern for things and the convenient measurement of things.

Being is always larger than the bounds of consciousness-of-being. The struggle for a meaningful handling of self-consciousness not only compels a facing of the larger dimension of Being but also that which threatens Being. But the threats to Being do not deny Being, which is an achievement of fact, of existence, of personal history. Nor does it relieve the Being from building a meaning large enough to handle the threats to that Being. This inner need projected outward in its largest conceivable dimensions is the basic stuff of religion, and it is not bound by any partial concept of Being but rather has as its function the challenge to all partial concepts of Being. When dealing with death the religious view of life stands unchallenged by the partial views of life; for when the ultimates are faced, the ultimates are needed to contend with them.

SUMMARY

There is no place where the mind of man is compelled to deal with the unpenetrated boundaries of life as it is in the building of a psychology of death and dying. No small or partial view of life satisfies the needs of this basic act of reorientation. For most persons this involves a practical approach to the anguished emotions at times of stress. For others it demands a basic philosophy large enough to sustain such a practical approach.

Practically, the religious function within the community is to protect the bereft individual against destructive fantasy and illusion by surrounding the fact of physical death by a framework of reality that is accepted by both the grieving individual and the supporting community. This framework of reality is conceived to stimulate and make valid the expression of all the emotion that is a part of the process of mourning in a way that is acceptable to the community at the same time that it satisfies the deep inner needs of the personality. This expression of feeling is not designed to lead to despair and separation from the community but rather to make legitimate and more easily possible a reinvestment of emotional capital in the next chapters of life.

Philosophically, this practical expression of the religious approach to death and dying also tends to determine the attitude of the individual toward his own death and the process of his dying. And this approach views his life and the lives of others not as valueless and extinguishable, but rather as value-filled and thus measured by a standard different from that used on all material things. Beyond space and time it has the quality of the eternal, however daringly that may be conceived by the individual, and thus gives even to physical death a dimension of spiritual possibility that sustains the soul. The religious view of life always tends to do this because of its rejection of partial views of Being and its acceptance of a basic mysticism of existence that unifies all in a prehension that brings essence and existence into working unity.

References

1. Allport, Gordon W.: *The Individual and His Religion,* The Macmillan Company, New York, 1950.
2. Baillie, J.: *Idea of Revelation in Recent Thought,* Columbia University Press, New York, 1956.
3. Bohr, N.: *Atomic Physics and Human Knowledge,* John Wiley & Sons, Inc., New York, 1958.
4. Devereux, G.: *Psychoanalysis and the Occult,* International Universities Press, Inc., New York, 1953.
5. Ford, A.: *Nothing So Strange,* Harper & Brothers, New York, 1958.
6. Frankl, V. E.: *The Doctor and the Soul,* R. Winston and C. Winston (trs.), Alfred A. Knopf, Inc., New York, 1955.
7. Frazer, J. G.: *The Golden Bough,* The Macmillan Company, New York, 1950.
8. Irion, P. E.: *The Funeral and the Mourners,* Abingdon Press, Nashville, Tenn., 1954.
9. Jackson, E. N.: *Understanding Grief, Its Roots, Dynamics and Treatment,* Abingdon Press, Nashville, Tenn., 1957.
10. Kierkegaard, S.: *Concluding Unscientific Postscript,* Princeton University Press, Princeton, N.J., 1941.
11. Laidlow, R.: *Report,* Wainwright House Publications, 1956.
12. May, R., E. Angel, and H. F. Ellenberger: *Existence: A New Dimension in Psychiatry and Psychology,* Basic Books, Inc., New York, 1958.
13. Menninger, K.: *Man Against Himself,* Harcourt, Brace and Company, Inc., New York. 1938.

14. Myers, F. W. F.: *Human Personality and Its Survival of Bodily Death,* Longmans, Green, & Co., Inc., New York, 1903.

15. Rhine, J. B.: *The Reach of the Mind,* William Sloane Associates, New York, 1947.

16. Schmeidler, G. and R. A. McConnell: *Extra Sensory Perception and Personality Patterns,* Yale University Press, New Haven, Conn., 1958.

17. Weiss, E.: *Principles of Psychodynamics,* Grune & Stratton, Inc., New York, 1950.

PART 4

Clinical and Experimental Studies

13 ARNOLD A. HUTSCHNECKER

Personality Factors in Dying Patients

The physician, because he sees a human life when it begins and when it ends, is in a unique position to make many observations on life and death and their relation to behavior. Concerning the psychological aspects of the dying patient, two seem of special significance. One is that the dying patient, even in the face of death, remains more or less true to his basic personality (the term "basic personality" is used here to describe an individual's total responsive attitude to his environment and his habitual behavior patterns regarding his physical and mental activities irrespective of the picture he presents to the outside world); the other is the tragic realization of how many people enter their terminal disease with a sense of defeat, failure, and unfulfillment. When we find in the behavior of the dying patient surprising differences from his earlier behavior, we must bear in mind that a break-down of conscious controls reveals an individual in his basic unrestrained structure.

Over three decades ago, Alfred Goldscheider, one of my medical teachers at the University of Berlin, coined the term, "autoplastic disease picture." This means that each patient forms his own opinion of his illness, inde-pendent of clinical data or any objective judgment of the circumstances. The physician must understand this if he is to know his patient and what goes on in his mind. The

237

subjective idea of what is wrong with him is, however, only part of an individual's transitory state of mind. When a patient is alone in a noncritical physical illness, he retreats temporarily from reality into his own inner world. Here he weighs his position, seeking some clarity or decision as to his life and future. In the dying patient, standards and values of self-judgment and self-evaluation are different. He knows there will be no return. This may explain why most dying patients appear calm and reposed, while others show intense excitement and paroxysms of rage before they sink into the merciful state of unconsciousness and then die peacefully. If we discount accidents and homicide, it seems to me almost certain that deep within themselves most patients know when they are going to die and most of them are ready. A similar view was expressed to me by Dr. Frank Adair, noted New York surgeon, who stated his experience that, "The dying patient usually knows his condition and at the end is glad to go. This seems to be especially true of those patients who have deep religious convictions."

Clinically, a correlation seems to exist between the disease picture and the basic personality. That is to say there is a difference in behavior in different personalities suffering and eventually dying from different somatic diseases. The dynamic psychologist explains that specific emotional-structural conditions lead to somatic changes and eventually to circumscript morbid pictures; many conservative clinicians still contend that it is the somatic disease that brings a change in a patient's psychic behavior.

In an attempt to explore whether a common rule of behavior can be established, let us consider the two diseases which have become the two great killers in our society today: heart disease and cancer and its allied diseases. Let us examine whether a difference in behavior can be found in patients dying from one or the other disease. Also, let us raise the question whether it is accidental that these two diseases make such devastating and increasing claims. The 1956 report of the National Office of Vital Statistics lists as first, deaths from diseases of the heart, and second, deaths from cancer. The 1955 figure supplied by the American Heart Association states that deaths from heart and vascular diseases constitute 53.1 per cent of all deaths; the American Cancer Society reports cancer to be responsible for 16 per cent of all deaths. Since 1900, deaths from heart disease have almost tripled; deaths from cancer have more than doubled. Heller, Cutler, and Haenzel [4] estimate that 32 out of every 100 newborn children in the United States may be expected to develop cancer at some time during their lives and will eventually die from this disease. This would be about one-third of the total population.

Let us first consider cancer patients. The most arresting characteristic of these patients appears to lie in their attitude toward their illness. With the exception of a comparatively few personalities who exhibit an enlightened, scientific, and sometimes martyr-like attitude, most cancer patients are evasive and rejecting of their illness. This can be observed in their interest concerning symptoms, clinical findings, therapy, and marked attention to details. However, most of them avoid the direct question, "Do I have cancer?" Neither do they appreciate the honesty of the physician who volunteers this diagnosis to them. From a medical viewpoint, most of these patients in their outward behavior are "good patients," if we consider as "good" a submissive, cooperative attitude, and one which does not give the doctors and nurses any trouble. They can become, nevertheless, rebellious and hostile if they feel themselves rejected or slighted. Some, having come to the end of their trail, may now dare to release pent-up hostility against members of their family or friends in a desire to retaliate for previously suffered hurts and rejections; others, freed from lifelong conflicts and self-centeredness because they already live on another plane, are now capable of displaying touching courage and unselfishness. From a point of psychological evaluation, these patients appear to be immature, dependent, and often regressive personalities.

A brief case history may illustrate this type of patient: A 59-

year-old male patient came to see me because of his "neurosis," as he put it. His case history revealed that nine months prior to this first consultation, he had suffered a terrific pain in his chest and back. He had seen a local doctor who treated him for anemia and a spasm of the esophagus. He was unable to swallow food, even cereal because of "the nervous bubble in my upper chest." Since the start of his illness, the patient had lost twelve pounds, but added quickly that this was natural since he was unable to eat properly. The question as to whether he had received a radiological examination was answered affirmatively. An X ray taken two months earlier, apparently only a flat film, had not shown any organic disease. He concluded that the stabbing pains across his chest and stomach were new symptoms of his neurosis.

The family history disclosed that both parents had died at the age of 58; his father from a cerebral hemorrhage and his mother from cancer. One sister had also died from cancer. The patient himself was a shy, soft-spoken, melancholic man. He had never married. He had no relatives or close friends and lived by himself, pretty much withdrawn from the rest of the world. His emaciated body and history aroused my suspicion of a neoplastic involvement. A radiological examination revealed, indeed, a malignant growth in the esophagus with perforation into the bronchial tree. This diagnosis was confirmed a few days later at the New York Memorial Center. There the patient received a course of supervoltage X-ray therapy.

About two months later the patient returned to my office stating there had been some initial improvement but that now he had a constant pain in his back and across the gastric region. He was losing weight rapidly. It was apparent that metastases had invaded all his vital organs and that he could live only a few more weeks. Throughout the illness his behavior, outwardly at least, remained gentle, friendly, and cooperative. He was anxious to win approval and to relate to the physician as if he were the authority in whose hands his future fate rested. Though the New

York Memorial Center is known to be a cancer hospital, this patient, when he inquired about the duration of his hospital stay and his type of treatment, did not once ask about the nature of his illness.

In summary, we see the patient as a passive, dependent personality whose predominant attitude was a deep sense of futility and hopelessness. He was a lonely and pessimistic individual who, apparently, had been unable to establish any meaningful relationship and who had no purpose or ambition in life, nor any significant work that could serve as a sublimation for his creative being. Consequently, there was no reason for this man to continue an existence which had become intolerable. He may have unconsciously longed to be reunited with his mother, the one and only symbol of protection this man apparently had known. One may speculate, therefore, whether it was just an accident that this patient's illness began at about the same age at which his mother had died.

If we wish to assume any relationship between his emotional life and his illness, we must attempt to answer two questions: one with regard to the time of illness; the other, as to the nature of the illness. Let us first consider the question of the time of illness. In my own practice, I have long since learned to take into consideration and even, to some degree, to correlate somatic crises with a psychic trauma due to the loss of a parent. Depending on what the relationship with the parent had been and on the patient's personality (degree of integration or maturity), one patient will live through the critical period of a serious illness and another may become the victim of his own fear, love, or guilt, which are causing states of stress, somatic symptoms or illness, and, eventually self-destruction. The contributing role of genetic and psychodynamic environmental factors in repeating a family disease as a cause of death is far from clear at this time. It may be assumed, however, that both exercise influence in a continuous interplay. This is in accordance with present concepts of psychosomatic thinking. In a preliminary report Leshan and Worthington [5] found three factors which differentiated the protocols of cancer patients from control subjects: (1) the loss of an important relationship before the diagnosis; (2) an inability to express hostile feelings; and (3) tension over the death of a parent, usually an event which had occurred many years previously. While no position can be taken here as to the validity of the method applied in this study, the third factor, "tension over the death of a parent," appears to be of pointed significance.

As to the second question of the nature of the illness—in view of the growing evidence that continuous emotional stress can cause changes in human biochemistry, a correlation between psychogenic factors and malignancies cannot be simply dismissed. This important problem needs further intensive study and more attention than it has received during the past few years. Writing on the phenomena of carcinogenesis, Szasz [10] states that frustration of instinct leads either to a progressive or regressive adaptation and that while primitive systems tend to adapt progressively, complex organizations tend toward earlier, more archaic patterns of behavior. He assumes, therefore, that the development of malignant growth is due to complex systems living under stress and to the regressive tendency in highly developed organisms. Karl Menninger, referring to the above-mentioned Leshan and Worthington report, stated, ". . . one of these days the cancer research people who have had such enormous financial support and who have worked so frantically and intensively on the problem for the past 30 years will wake up to the fact that *psychology has an influence on tissue cells,* a proposition which they have consistently regarded even until now as a preposterous heresy" [6, page 15].

In classifying the cancer patient as an emotionally passive, dependent, or regressive individual, we must not be deceived by his occasional protective, aggressive facade. We deal with a behavior similarly evidenced by peptic ulcer patients, in whom outward aggression serves so often as a cover-up for dependency needs. In contrast, there is the cardiac patient, who is often an overwhelmingly aggressive personality. Flanders Dunbar [3] described these cardiac patients as persons striving for success, capable of postponing actions to achieve long-term goals. Such people often have difficulty in concealing their hostility to authority and cannot easily tolerate discipline. Most patients I have seen who suffer from an acute coronary thrombosis are rebellious; they frequently refuse to accept the diagnosis, minimize their condition, and say it is probably nothing but a state of indigestion. Others are defiant and mock at the warnings of the physician to remain quiet. They climb out of bed, are restless, and almost seem to provoke another attack at a time when the heart has difficulty in repairing the fresh damage. Some, however, and these are mostly those who eventually succumb to their attack, will calmly state, "I have a heart attack . . . do something about the pain." A case in point is that of a colleague who recently collapsed at the wheel of his automobile and mumbled, "This is it," as if he had expected his attack for a long time.

It is said that a first heart attack often comes on suddenly, without forewarning. This belief, held by a majority of cardiologists, is open to debate. It can be questioned whether a preoccupation with death or an unconscious death wish had not existed for some time in these individuals.

In an examination of a will before the Surrogate's Court in New York, the strange circumstances connected with the making of that particular will were under cross-examination. A woman, the heiress to a great fortune, had seen her lawyer one afternoon, asking him to change a previous will. Although her lawyer tried to persuade her to give him some time for the execution of the will, she insisted on having it signed that same afternoon. This was done. That same night this apparently healthy woman suffered a heart attack and died. For reasons unknown, the new will got lost. The court had to decide whether an unsigned copy represented the true last will of the deceased. Some members of the family of the deceased objected to the changes, while two children who benefited by this new will defended it. Their attorney asked this question of the lawyer who executed the new will at the court session: "Tell me, did the deceased express to you any reason why she was so insistent upon signing a will that afternoon?" The reply was, "Well, yes. She stated that she was a lady given to intuitions, that she followed her intuitions, and that she felt something unhappy was about to happen, so she wished to execute her will." The Court decided to accept the new will as a true expression of the deceased's last wish. What had prompted the woman to insist on the hurried execution of a new will is unknown, as is the explanation of the woman's intuition—other than perhaps as an unconscious death wish. Most cardiac patients that I have seen have struck me as reckless gamblers with life; when they reach an impasse, they think in terms of dying rather than accepting humiliation or defeat.

An example of this type of cardiac patient is the case of a 45-year-old man who came to see me because of frequent dizzy spells. Four years earlier he had suffered his first coronary thrombosis at the relatively early age of forty-one. He boasted of having shortened his prescribed bed rest to only one week. He was proud of not giving in to self-indulgence or self-pity. Against the doctor's advice, he continued to smoke excessively. As an explanation of his pain, he stated that his job as rent-collecting agent had put him under heavy strain because of continuous aggravation from belligerent and demanding tenants. Unaware of his own hostility, he always carried a loaded revolver to protect himself "just in case." He minimized the fact that his wife had left him for another man. He ignored the suggestion that his hypertension could be the result of his unresolved hostility. After his heart attack, he had remarried his first wife for the sake of the children "but it didn't work out."

His former wife, on the other hand, rejected his aggressive attitude, his continuous display of masculine strength, his childish pride, and his authoritative way of demanding that she accept more responsibilities. She was a romanticist, a passive, evasive, daydreaming individual, who summed up her problems with "I was born in the wrong century." During his sporadic treatments, the patient repeated his pattern of cutting short prescribed rest periods. He disregarded many warning signals such as pain in his chest and left arm. He lived, nevertheless, for nine more years, racing toward some insatiable goal of economic security. He married again at the age of fifty-three and died a year later, within twenty minutes, after a second coronary occlusion.

We have seen different personality syndromes in patients dying from different diseases. To relate disease to basic personality patterns is acceptable if we stress that while a human personality may retain its basic characteristics it is, nevertheless, open to dynamic changes. Hand in hand with such changes we may observe a change in somatic symptoms. We see passive, dependent personalities who have always reacted symptomatically with disturbances in the alimentary tract, suddenly develop diseases of the cardiovascular system. They may suffer threatening or fatal incidents of coronary attacks or cerebral hemorrhages as they now attempt to resolve life situations aggressively by either fight or flight, and their systems mobilize accordingly.

Observations indicate that symptomatic reversals probably occur when individuals become overwhelmed by a sudden realization that their hopes will never be fulfilled, or that their goals had been nothing but cobwebs of fantasy. Such a realization will cause some to fight and force others into escape. Most patients in these instances eventually become victims of their own self-destruction.

The liver and gallbladder seem to be organs that after a long period of stress show the effect of such stress either by developing functional disorders or by producing chemical substances in higher concentrations than their normal level. An example of this is a patient of mine whose outward, aggressive facade had served as a shield for great emotional needs which remained unfulfilled by an unsympathetic wife. He suffered from a cirrhosis of the liver, experienced two hematemeses, and died about one year later. His feelings and preoccupations with death are stated in a poem, "The Last Wish," which was found with his will. The thirteen verses began:

> When I'm all fixed up for my final ride,
> With my silver handles, three on a side,
> And scattered around me in heaps, pell-mell,
> Are fragrant flowers I cannot smell.

> When the few to whom I was really dear
> Have stifled a sob that I cannot hear,
> I shall not know and I shall not care
> What is happening around me there . . .

and ended:

> If one of these can truly say,
> As in my coffin still I lay,
> "That chap was sure a regular guy
> It's sort of hard to say, Good by."

> Then not in vain I'll reach my end,
> For I'll at least have made a friend.

The pioneering work of Walter Cannon [2], followed by the studies of the Franz Alexander group [1] and by Hans Selye's [9] theory of the general adaptation syndrome have helped to broaden our understanding of how the body responds to stress features. The idea that continuous states of stress may cause premature death was expressed by the German pathologist Rössle [8] in his thoughts about growth and aging. He held the view that normal death is physiological death, the wearing out of all tissues and organs at a harmonious rate. Normal death is death from old age, going to sleep and simply not awakening. From that point of view death is no struggle, nor is it a state of indecision or fear. Instead, it seems a desired state at a time when life with all its complexities becomes too burdensome to cope with. When a person of advanced age dies, we must keep in mind the lowered resistance resulting from the wear and tear of aging, regardless of the clinical diagnosis we physicians write on the death certificate. If we accept this concept of longevity, then most cases now being classified as "death from natural causes," such as cancer or heart attack, are really not natural but must rather be considered death from unnatural causes.

In line with this concept, that normal death is physiological death, are the thoughts and feelings of the late George Bernard Shaw. Only the morning before the accident which led to his death at the age of ninety-four, he wrote in longhand the following remarks on a pad, a copy of which was later handed to me by a mutual friend. It expresses his intense preoccupation with death but also his readiness to accept the end of his life without fear or regret. It reads as follows:

The will to live is wholly inexplicable. Rationally, I ought to blow my brains out, but I don't and I won't. Haydon cut his throat when his eyesight had failed. He lived only for painting. Edmund Gurney did himself in because his neuralgias were unbearable. These were cases of voluntary euthanasia, quite justifiable. Cancer cases die of morphia poisoning 'to control the pain.' This also is euthanasia. But most people hold on to the last moment and die a "Natural Death" as I mean to, though at 94 I ought to clear out, my bolt being shot and overshot. (G.B.S.)

Whatever the cause of death in a patient may have been we can say that, by and large, the man or woman who is about to die has made peace with himself. He has fought out his battle with life in his own specific way before he is overcome by, or submits to, his fatal illness. The one who has dreamed of being taken care of may wish to return to mother earth as a symbolic substitute for an earlier symbiotic existence in the womb. The other who thought in terms of conquest may wish to die as a hero with his boots on so that his environment should not see him as weak or a failure. The physician, while appreciating his patient's acceptance of death, is struck time and again by the far-reaching effect the basic personality has on an individual's life-death problem. It is disturbing to observe how few men and women have lived rich, full lives because of their emotional confusion and their difficulty in dealing effectively with the complexities of modern life. On the other hand, the person who is able to balance his life by integrating his primitive instincts with his moral, religious, and other demands can, as a rule, use his energies to work toward some meaningful goal.

Francis Bacon said that "Men fear death as children fear to go in the dark; and as that natural fear in children is increased with tales, so is the other." A man who called himself a "student for many years of the art and act of dying," Sir William Osler, the great clinician and teacher, stated in his memorable letter [7] to the editor of the *Spectator* in Oxford his strong protest against the pictures of tortures and torments of the dying painted by a church magazine, calling the grim warnings "the mould above the rose." "A few, very few," he said, "suffer severely in the body and fewer still in the mind."

In acceptance of this observation we can say that the fear of death is present far more often with the living than with the dying. At a time when a man is strong and mighty, and by the law of averages, still far from his estimated end, he seems to fear death most. The fear of death that often afflicts man in his middle years is obviously the fear that his own impotence or frustrations may prevent him from making the mark he considers necessary to satisfy his own standards. The wear and tear of his struggle with life takes too heavy a toll long before the normal time. And it is this ambivalence about life with its destructive repercussions which lead to the previously indicated conclusion that most people die prematurely.

The physician who, in the course of his professional life, is almost daily confronted with this tragedy of wasted human existence and premature death is—consistent with his belief in preventive medicine—searching for a deeper understanding of this problem. To recognize its origin the physician is grateful for the promise dynamic psychology holds out. In his attempt to help his patient, he will be most desirous of integrating into his clinical thinking the findings and concepts of this branch of science. The observing physician learns that the patient with insight into himself tends to accept life with all its responsibilities, and consequently suffers less from doubts, feelings of futility, and hopelessness. Only when people are able to live out their years maturely and unharassed by continuous fear, anger, and frustration, will they die when their time comes, peacefully and with a sense of accomplishment and satisfaction.

REFERENCES

1. Alexander, F.: *Psychosomatic Medicine,* W. W. Norton & Company, Inc., New York, 1950.
2. Cannon, W. B.: *Bodily Changes in Pain, Hunger, Fear, and Rage,* 2d ed., Appleton-Century-Crofts, Inc., New York, 1920.
3. Dunbar, F.: *Emotions and Bodily Changes,* 3d ed., Columbia University Press, New York, 1947.
4. Heller, J. R., S. J. Cutler, and W. M. Haenzel: "Some observations on the epidemiology of cancer in the United States," *J. Am. Med. Assoc.,* **159:** 1628–1634, 1955.
5. Leshan, L., and R. E. Worthington: "Some psychological correlates of neoplastic disease: a preliminary report," *J. Clin and Exptl. Psychopathol. & Quart. Rev. Psychiat. Neurol.,* **16:** 281–288, 1955.
6. Menninger, K.: "Dr. Karl's reading notes," *Menninger Library J.,* **1:** 15, 1956.
7. Osler, W.: "To the Editor of the *Spectator"* (Christ Church, Oxford, Nov. 4, 1911), in L. Farmer, *Doctor's Legacy,* Harper & Brothers, New York, 1955.

8. Rössle, R.: *Wachstum und Altern: Zur Physiologie und Pathologie der Postfötalen Entwicklung.* Verlag J. F. Bergmann, Munich, 1923.
9. Selye, H.: *Stress: The Physiology and Pathology of Exposure to Stress,* Acta, Inc., Montreal, 1950.
10. Szasz, T. S.: "On the psychoanalytic theory of instincts," *Psychoanal. Quart.,* **16:** 25–48, 1952.

14 GERALD J. ARONSON

Treatment of the Dying Person

In her remarkable novel, *Memoirs of Hadrian,* Marguerite Yourcenar has the Emperor say:

It is difficult to remain an emperor in presence of a physician, and difficult even to keep one's essential quality as man. The professional eye saw in me only a mass of humors, a sorry mixture of blood and lymph. This morning it occurred to me for the first time that my body, my faithful companion and friend, truer and better known to me than my own soul, may be after all only a sly beast who will end by devouring his master. [4, page 1]

Fortunately few of us immediately are in the situation of the Emperor—but we are often in the place of his physician. The Emperor (as does every man gravely ill) poses a threefold challenge: (1) How do we help him to retain his essential quality as man at the same time that (2) we are looking past the man into his "sorry mixture of blood and lymph," and (3) while we are doing both of these, are we not also obliged to counter the drift, however feeble or subtle, toward depression, suicide, or psychosis within the dying man as he experiences his body to be the "sly beast who will end by devouring his master?"

How to help the patient be an individual human being even though gravely ill and dying? We know how dehumanizing illness is, even where death is not a probable outcome. The doctors, hospital, and relatives set the stage for regression and dependency in a fashion, sometimes so

251

tempting, sometimes so forceful, that the ill patient is bothered far more by his guilt and shame in yielding to the regressive temptations than he is by pain or illness. A related difficulty suffered by the patient has to do with his attitude toward those who are well and who will remain alive. We talk often of the ambivalent feeling in the relatives of the dying patient; how guilty they feel about their wish that the dying one tarry no longer and be on his way. What of the ill one's horror at his dim awareness of his envy that others will remain alive, and of the wish that rarely enters consciousness that his spouse, parent, or child should die in his stead? It's like the story of the sick man who tells his wife: "If one of us dies, my dear, I'll spend the rest of my life in Paris." Can we suspect that it is this wish, in part, that breaks into action in those cases of seriously ill people who kill not only themselves but neighbors and family as well?

We know from our experiences in helping at the bedsides of the dying or in prowling our ghoulish vigil in hospital corridors trying to get autopsy permissions, how often the patient murmurs even toward the end, "I don't want to make a fuss." He wants to be a human, to play a role consistent with his identity, his individuality. I think no man is different from the martyrs who died according to a code of ethics, with an inbuilt script still rolling out. The last words of A. E. Housman, the poet, after being told by his doctor a thoroughly naughty story were: "Yes, that's a good one, and tomorrow I shall be telling it again on the Golden Floor." Or Henry James in his dying gasp, literary to the end: "So here it is at last, the Distinguished Thing."

How then as doctors and healers should we help to arrange matters so that the patient retains his sense of individuality and identity to the end? At this point the vexing question arises: Do we tell the patient? What? How? Who is to tell him? When is he to be told of his serious illness and impending death? Glib answers no one has. But I think we must be guided by the principle of permitting and helping the patient to keep up as much as possible the role that is important to him.

In order to do this I would suggest four rules:

1. Do not tell the patient anything which might induce psychopathology. Here your only guide is your clinical feel and the response of the patient to your comments and manner as you have been slowly going along with him in the course of his illness.

2. Hope must never die too far ahead of the patient; either hope of getting better, or hope of enjoyment of conversations tomorrow, etc. As an intern I attended a Hungarian artist who was dying of a vascular disease. He knew he was dying, I knew he was dying, and we were very uneasy and embarrassed with each other because of this mutual unspoken knowledge. Soon, however, we discovered another piece of knowledge swiftly made mutual—we played chess. And so we did every morning for two weeks. Gradually he could make allusions to his own fate by way of the chessmen. On the morning he died he beat me roundly, which tells you of his pride in his role as chesser—and also how badly I play. I believe it is entirely necessary to subtly support denial in such a way, by keeping some libidinal ties going, or fending off bad, terrifying, internal objects in some manner—however we wish to conceive of it, it is necessary to do so.

3. The gravity of the situation should not be minimized. Is this inconsistent with rules 1 and 2? The patient will not fail to understand from your demeanor that his situation is serious. If you are Pollyannish, he will become suspicious, press hard for an answer, feel cheated and lose trust. But if you are serious between the Scylla of his potential psychopathology and hopelessness and the Charybdis of arousing his mistrust in you as a physician, he will feel grateful, informed within the limits of his toleration, and human—not a vegetable. Goethe once said: "If we take people as they are, we make them worse. If we treat them as if they were what they ought to be, we help them to become what they are

capable of becoming." More good deaths are spoiled because the physician tries to jolly the patient or neglect him as a sentient being!

4. The fourth rule requires great tact and finesse. It is something I've aspired to but never quite managed. Eissler [1], in his valuable book *The Psychiatrist and the Dying Patient,* makes much of the structure of time. The fourth rule has to do with the management of telling the patient about his impending death in such a way as to avoid just idly sitting around, awaiting death. When do you tell a man he is to die? You must try to estimate the duration of a man's psychological present. The present to a child is an hour or half a day. To the pregnant woman the future begins when the baby comes. To the analytic candidate the present lasts ten years. If, to a dying patient, the psychological present stretches three months long, arrange to tell him in such a way and at such a time so that this time may be purified of the idea of death and hence still a field of activity. Either tell him at the beginning of the three months that he may live three years or 10 months or wait till the three months have passed. We must enable him to be in the position of the old horseplayer whose prayer is: "Lord, let me break even. I need the money."

These four rules have to do with our first goal: to keep Hadrian a man even as we look at him as a mass of humors, blood, and lymph. Terrible though it is to die, it doesn't have to be ignominious. Writes the poet Rilke of Paris' oldest hospital:

This excellent hotel is very ancient. Even in King Clovis' time people died in it in a number of beds. Now they are dying there in 559 beds. Factory-like, of course. Where production is so enormous an individual death is not so nicely carried out; but then that doesn't matter. It is quantity that counts. Who cares anything today for a finely-finished death? No one. Even the rich, who could after all afford this luxury of dying in full detail, are beginning to be careless and indifferent; the wish to have a death of one's own is growing ever rarer. A while yet, and it will be just as rare as a life of one's own. Heavens, it's all there. One arrives, one finds a life, ready made, one has only to put it on. One wants to leave or one is compelled to: anyway, no effort: Voilà, votre mort, monsieur. One dies just as it comes; one dies the death that belongs to the disease one has (for since one has come to know all diseases, one knows, too, that the different lethal terminations belong to the diseases and not to the people; and the sick person has so to speak nothing to do). [3, pages 17–18]

The second goal is to look steadfastly at the patient as a failing machine, at the same time as we psychotherapeutically, or with common sense, try to persuade ourselves and him that he is still a human, with a role and an identity. Nonetheless we owe it to him to know as thoroughly as we can, without doing harm to him or causing him unnecessary pain, the disease he suffers, its progress, and what measures can be undertaken to slow it or speed it. It is important for our own sanity that with dying patients we act as physicians—i.e., we entitle ourselves, by virtue of our professional role, our countertransference, and our fellow feeling, to that measure of denial and hope necessary to convert our despair and grief into sorrow and pity.

With respect to our last goal—in our medical ministry to Hadrian we must anticipate his feeling that "his body is a sly beast who will end by devouring his master." Should this fantasy grow into a stronger cathexis than a mere figure of speech, it warns us—of impending madness. Is there any patient suffering from cancer who does not toy with the lurking fantasy of an internal enemy that gradually takes possession of his body? In ordinary medical practice few cases of psychosis or suicide result because the doctor, the family, and the patient intuitively do what is necessary to stave off psychic catastrophe. But minor paranoias and major depressions are still evident to all internists and surgeons, hand in hand with apparent resignation to illness and death.

Freud [2] has told us: "No one believes in his own death. In the unconscious everyone is convinced of his own immortality." If this is true, then what are we afraid of? No, I don't think Freud is wrong. I think matters are more dreadful, because my logical question is right and because he is right: we are convinced of our immortality but who is there with us to share that immortality? We are alone, without libidinal ties, and in dread of that regressive tête-à-tête with our bad internal objects which always occurs when we are alone or when our hostile feelings are unsoftened by our tender ones. I don't want to make much of the psychodynamics but only of the clinical states of massive depression or paranoid decompensation sometimes seen in people after they are convinced they are going to die. How to counter this? The Egyptians took beloved objects with them into the tomb. Medieval man saw the moment of his death as his rebirth into a far better world, well populated. We try to maintain close family ties which, because of ambivalent feelings on both sides, occasionally cause harm. What is the physician to do to supplement intuitive social supports or to supplant these supports when they are absent or harmful? Again, we are indebted to Eissler's vigorous prescription of "the gift situation" as a means to reduce death's sting.

In brief, the physician should try to bring about a situation where he gives, unsolicited and anticipating the patient's need before the patient himself may recognize it, a gift—a piece of tender interest and affection exacting no counterservice from the patient. We may view the gift from the physician as an evidence of sublimated love, reinforcing the waning testimony of the internal good object against the isolating agony of death.

The psychotherapy of a woman patient in an Army Mental Hygiene Clinic was cut short by the administrative necessity to devote all treatment time to men. The patient, wife of an enlisted man, had been under treatment for chronic alcoholism. Over the course of several months no improvement in the alcoholism had occurred despite the detrimental effect of the drinking on the patient's long-term asthma and congenital heart disease. To her family's plea that she stop drinking, she would reply that it was too late. To the psychotherapist's bland assertion that it is never too late, her response would be: "Then I can quit some other time." Some months after the administratively forced interruption of treatment, the therapist learned indirectly of the worsening of the patient's organic diseases and her steady march toward death. Drinking had not stopped; blackest despair gripped her. The therapist, contrary to Clinic policy and social protocol, called the patient to come to his office in the late afternoon. There, for several hours, patient and doctor sat hunched over mildly watered bourbon provided by the doctor. Neither drank and both talked. The patient experienced the doctor's call, the late hour, the bourbon, and the opportunity to talk as an unambivalent tender gift from the doctor which staved off the lonely and forlorn agony of death's desolation. The depression lifted and, in the several weeks before her death, she carried herself with relative sobriety and dignity.

The following two deaths were not so successfully managed and illustrate how malice and ignorance on the therapist's part contribute to this lack of success.

A woman was dying in the Army hospital from frontotemporal astrocytoma. Because of her depression the neurosurgeon requested that the psychiatrist see and treat the patient. In the course of the first few talks at the patient's bedside, the psychotherapist noted a deepening of the depression, increase in hypochondriacal complaints, and a querulous, paranoid whining about the food, medications, and nursing care. The therapist, puzzled at the rapid development of these symptoms, was not content to ascribe them to the brain tumor or solely to the patient's awareness of her impending death. For he came to realize his sharp dislike for the patient, her saccharine mannerisms, and her affected Southern speech. He then perceived that, in her great need for some good, sustaining object that would stand against the attack from within, she had acutely sensed his hostility. Dependent upon him, she had to deny what she felt only too keenly. She projected her perception elsewhere—"The nurses don't like me" —but, as this device failed, her sense of being attacked from within grew into hypochondriasis, and her feeling of being entirely alone with the bad objects inside her was expressed as despair. The therapist arranged that a local, Southern psychiatrist take over her care. Within days, paranoid plaintiveness stopped, hypochondriasis lessened, and despair was replaced by appropriate depression.

The intern was called by an amused yet troubled nurse to see a patient who claimed to be dead. Several days previously, the patient had undergone bilateral frontal leukotomy for chronic schizophrenia. Now, her face was turned resolutely away from the door and, to all who drew her into contact, she alleged that it was no use, she was already dead. To the persistent and puzzled intern she would say only that she was dead and that "It is better to be dead." To his question "Better than what?", she replied haltingly, "Christ . . . Christ." The intern, no more enlightened than he had been, continued his rounds. When he suddenly realized that Easter Sunday was only a few days past, he returned to talk with this eerie patient: "You know, this is Easter time. Does your talking about death and Christ have something to do with the Resurrection?" The patient looked at him sharply and then mumbled something about "yes . . . yes . . . Christ and no one . . . no one there." A few days later the patient did die. One cannot lay aside conjecture: perhaps the patient sensed the imminence of death and the continuation of madness after she had hoped for resurrection from the surgery or from a change in her family's attitude. Perhaps the outer world, as well as the inner world, no longer contained good objects; the resurrection of Christ, the epitome of the good object, could not fill the void of "no one there." One can only speculate further about the impact of correct understanding and action by the doctor upon the affect of this patient aware of her impending death.

To counter the drift toward madness and despair—which is our third goal in the care of Hadrian—requires of the physician that he mobilize whatever resources he can to outweigh and neutralize his patient's grim awareness of "the sly beast who will end by devouring his master."

REFERENCES

1. Eissler, K. R.: *The Psychiatrist and the Dying Patient,* International Universities Press, Inc., New York, 1955.

2. Freud, S.: "Thoughts for the Times on War and Death," *Collected Papers,* Hogarth Press, Ltd., London, 1948, vol. 4.

3. Rilke, R. M.: *The Notebooks of Malte Laurids Brigge,* M. D. Herter (tr.), W. W. Norton & Company, Inc., New York, 1949.

4. Yourcenar, M.: *Memoirs of Hadrian,* Grace Frick in collaboration with the author (tr.), Farrar, Strauss, and Cudahy, Inc., New York, 1954.

15 AUGUST M. KASPER

The Doctor and Death

The average American's outlook on death seems to have changed sometime during the first quarter of the twentieth century. With great optimism we embraced science and reason. Sin went out the window, and with it, its wages—death. Sickness became preventable and curable, and its companion, death, seemed equally vulnerable to our attack, an attack which was largely an elaborate denial of death. The funeral parlor bloomed as a place to which the whole nasty business of death and departure could be removed so that the loved one's late home was not sullied. Out went the external reminders—sitting shivah, wakes, fancy funerals, ornate tombstones, crape on the door, mourning clothes, and annual remembrances. Condolences became awkward duties, as if one were expressing regret that a respected man had been imprisoned for molesting children. The departed was to be hastened away as speedily and unostentatiously as possible—no lying in state, no dreadful tears, no cold kisses, no embarrassing eulogies, no slow processions, no endless lowerings and fillings—the simpler and cleaner, the better—ashes to the winds as if the dead were victims of a plague—the plague of finitude. *De mortuis nil.*

A concomitant of this trend was a diminished dependency on the physician, as well as a general lessening of the blind respect for him. This does not mean that

259

Americans avoid medical care, or visit the doctor any less frequently than heretofore. Rather, they seem to go more as they do to the barber or tennis instructor. The doctor is no longer seen so strikingly as a protector against death; he has in some ways become a high priest in the cult of "health and beauty forever." His true mission has become socially awkward, if not shameful. He himself is permitted to avoid the thought of death if he wishes; patients are rarely rude enough to ask about it. So it is that society's partly real and partly magical dependency on the doctor's lack of fearful involvement permits and encourages his own denial of death. Moreover, in a culture where men are asked not to be fearful or emotional about death, the doctor is requested to be less fearful and emotional than other men. He is not even given much right to be sick—as a recent article in a magazine for doctors puts it, "Never Admit You're Sick" [3]. It may appear that the doctor is above personal sickness and fear, and a part of my thesis avers that this appearance, useful as it is in reality, is something he unconsciously desires to believe in.

There used to be a grim little verse intoned by children in obsessive play:

> "Doctor, Doctor, will I die?
> Yes, my child, and so will I."

It is somehow an improbable notion that a doctor should die. He is alleged to be an expert in matters of life and death and if a doctor cannot offer protection against death, who can? To a security-hungry culture, full of rage at saviors who won't save, a doctor's death offers the same horror and fascination as a rumor of the bankruptcy of AT&T. The challenge, "Physician, heal thyself!" is also a hint at what is possible for a physician. Here we glimpse part of the psychological motivation of the doctor: to cure himself, to live forever. We all work to live, but the doctor has a bonus incentive: he works directly against man's adversary, Death.

The doctor should know more about dying and death than any other man. The greater part of his life is spent with people who consider death, or its herald, pain, pressing enough to seek the doctor's help. Yet, I am not impressed with either the volume or profundity of medical thought concerning death or dying people. It is as if this one certainty of life were to be avoided not only by vigorous positive thought and action, but also by giving it, as an event, no more attention than one gives to a period at the end of a moving, impressive novel. I make no plea for the physician's becoming a metaphysician, but his attitude toward death and his patient's feelings about death are not mystical, but psychological existents, to be used or misused therapeutically. Doctors might be presumed to have shown more interest in the event which they labor to forestall, or, in their hearts, to prevent. Such a presumption is not warranted by any obvious evidence in medical literature.

In medicine, death is certainly present and seems to be dealt with directly, yet it is absent when we seek it as the conventional threatening skeleton. Early in his training, the premedical student has learned to feel, see, probe, and even kill living things; by the time he is in medical school, he is ready to call human skeletons "Max" or "Agnes"; and he can slap a cadaver on the backside as if it were a window-display dummy. With pride, he will go with his fellows, reeking of death, to dine in public places where his conversation will horrify the squeamish, hurt the mourner, titillate the silly, and annoy almost everyone. Does it need to be said that this bravado is largely counterphobic? Can one argue that a calvarium makes a superior ashtray? But this is the doctor's first contact with a dead human and the defenses he uses, while counterphobic and intellectual, are effective. This is why death is omnipresent in medicine, but the conventional symbols don't seem to apply; the doctor is desensitized, not to death, but to the symbols of death such as blood, bones, corpses, and stench which disturb most people. It is as if medical men had overcome a phobia and had then convinced others, and themselves, that they had no basic, inner fear. This desensitization is something that I think draws men into medicine, something laymen envy, but something which is more wishful illusion than enduring fact. Later, in the clinical years, the student will learn that the living are more difficult, disturbing, and insistent than the dead; but his first patient, the cadaver, has given him closeness to death, and he has survived, his magic permanently enhanced.

The physician's training stresses "scientific objectivity," and physicians are often fond of mistaking themselves for scientists. There are some very useful similarities between science and medicine, but whereas a scientist is interested in death, a doctor is against it. It is indeed possible to be a physician and a scientist, but it is a rare combination in practice. The physician qua physician is committed to a credo which is far different from that of the scientist, even if we insist that such tenets as knowability, order, and inductive method are articles of faith. Medical practitioners have the wistful audacity, thank God, to blindly insist that pain is bad and life is to be preserved. This patent value judgment is the basis of medicine, and only coincidentally has it anything to do with knowledge of observable reality. Some doctors wish to be scientists in order to gain mastery over life by treating people as interesting things. It is this orientation which permits a doctor to speak of a "good" case of leukemia; that is, the case in question corresponds closely to the standard description of a certain disease entity, so that the adjective "good" is correctly, if disturbingly, used. This oddly inhuman perspective makes it possible for the doctor to observe, codify, diagnose, and treat, free from interfering preoccupations with horrors of disease and fear of death. The layman, hearing the doctor so speak and act, often gets the idea that the physician is cold and is treating the patient as a "thing," but the layman doesn't recognize that all such talk and activity is premised on the idea that life should be maintained and pain avoided. I cannot be sure whether it is a good thing or not, but the doctor will often conceal his own fear of pain and death behind his prerogative to be "objective" or "scientific."

Subscribing to the notion that one's life plan reflects early efforts to master anxiety, we search for fear of death in the early histories of physicians. Somewhat disappointingly, we do not find it. As a rule, people with conscious death anxiety or overt somatic preoccupation stay away from medicine, although the ambition to become a doctor frequently crystallizes during an illness attended by an admired physician. But such foci of crystallization are largely fortuitous. They include illnesses, doctor relatives, threatened induction into the Armed Forces, and Mama's desires. These become determining, however, only in the presence of certain preexisting factors. What we do find with considerable consistency is a strong bond with an encouraging, even seductive, mother, and an ambivalent relationship with a father, seen as aloof, distant, but masculine and strong. There are more than ordinary doubts about sexual role, and womanly aspirations to feed, care for, and make happy are frequent. We find indications of not feeling equal to other boys, not wanting to be like father, being bookish and curious about nature. Conscious fear of competition and feelings of physical inadequacy are also more common in future doctors than in other children. Such circumstances, feelings and fantasies always involve worry and puzzlement about the *state and fate of one's own body*. (Psychoanalysts generally equate fear of death with childhood fear of castration.) This formulation barely approaches the complexities of any man—physician or not —but it suggests the possible source and course of the doctor's connection with death. He takes his own fears, puts them as intellectual questions, and tries to answer them for other people. This in no way implies that we can surge ahead in medical education merely by giving little boys a hard time of it in their oedipal relationship; the fortuitous events mentioned above are also necessary. And, in addition, that poorly defined but all-important quality of ego-strength is indispensible for the sublimation, integration, and partial resolution of essential infantile conflicts. It makes for the difference between disaster and success. Ego-strength, in such a situation, seems to depend on a father, who, at least in fantasy, represents masculine reality, and a mother who, despite seduction, basically desires the emancipation and success of her child.

I have noted some possible psychic determinants in the physician and some of his early training; one might well expect that his later medical training would undertake to illuminate his attitudes toward death. It does not. The only medical school discussion I remember concerning the feelings of the dying, or rather their relatives, had to do with a brief exposition on some impromptu motivational research anent the ways one might circumvent, or even exploit grief, guilt, and confusion, in order to get an autopsy consent. There are ways to get autopsy permits, and empathically identifying oneself with the mourner is not one of them, unless the doctor "uses" his rapport to press his worthy request.

There is the illustration of the young doctor's orientation toward the hopelessly ill, toward those whom he knows can respond only with gratitude, and often not even that. These are the people in dreary wards and cheerless rooms. They lie quietly, dreaming perhaps, but looking for all the world like the doctor's "first patient." They need to have certain things done: indolent ulcers must be cleaned, draining wounds dressed, fetid mouths tended, fecal impactions removed, and very often, because no other way will do, they must be sustained by fluids dripped into failing, clogging veins. And this last tenderness gives a name to the whole tour of mercy: "watering the vegetables." The dying are thus not neglected, but they are very rarely approached with hope or even interest, because, I suppose, they simply will not feed the doctor's narcissism by responding and getting well. Their care is demanding, frustrating, and far from helpful to the medical magician's self-esteem.

Later, in the hospital years, one again sees clearly the formal, if unwritten, code: doctors should never become personally "involved" while working at their profession. This is sometimes carried to the extreme I witnessed while an intern. A very competent and kindly surgeon was performing an operation on a nine-year-old boy which could only extend the youngster's life a few weeks longer at the most. During surgery, the doctor remarked that it was a shame that this boy would not live to marry and have sons of his own. The interns, residents, and nurses who heard this remark later speculated about why it had been made. The consensus seemed to be that it was, at least, in bad taste and might even be explained by assuming that the surgeon had been drinking before surgery. They were wrong, I believe; but this very excellent doctor did often drink heavily *after* the day's work. He seemed to have reached the necessary truth, but like the fabled neurotic, he was unhappy about it.

Wheelis [4] offers a vivid and literate picture of the professional man's final but necessary disillusionment. He writes of what happens when a man travels a long road to salvation and, until he is too far along to go back, doesn't realize that he is headed for the abyss. Nor could anyone have told him earlier. His hope then lies in finding that it would have been the same no matter which route he had chosen, and that he can help himself and others along the way. A mature resolution, but a poor one when compared with early dreams of ultimate conquest. For the man who cannot mature in his profession, every subsequent day of his life challenges his magic and with it his identity. He has staked his life, like Faust, on learning the secret and he cannot turn back admitting failure. He knows well enough that he cannot win—that he will die, as will all his patients. He knows this not with equanimity but with the cynicism of the frustrated idealist. He less than other men is suited to face the dying; they are a personal affront, a symbol of his human helplessness, and an end to his life. He whose marriage is shaken because he cannot bear his wife's small complaints, whose children cry in their

nights of illness for a father who *has* to be at an induced de-
livery—this man must often help a stranger to die, and what can
he do? He can be tough about it, maybe breezy, or maudlin—or
maybe he can get an intern or nurse to drink the dregs of his
heady wine while he is called to more positive and hopeful cases.

This brings us to what may loosely be called the countertransference problem of the physician under such circumstances.
I will only mention the ungrateful affrontery of one who dies despite our most skillful ministrations, the narcissistic damage to
a vaunted intellect proved ignorant, the deep wounds to omnipotence when we are shown to be quite impotent. In addition, we
are busily denying death, and here is a person doing his level
best to demonstrate its reality. I submit that it is no wonder
psychiatrists say little can be done with dying patients; it is true,
but I suspect it is not the fault of the dying patient. The countertransference expectation, that all patients get well under our care,
is in opposition to the sympathetic and realistic words of Trudeau
in delineating the physician's function—"to cure sometimes, to
relieve often, to comfort always."

We suggested earlier that the doctor continues his maternal
identification and vicarious dependency by caring for others. This
ordinarily works very well because he helps people, and they are
grateful and "like" him. But everyone knows how fickle is the
affection of the "helped" person, how his dependency is felt as
a weakness in which he has submitted to the helper, the physician;
the doctor fears and the patient broods on the turning of the
tables. The doctor works hard to keep the relationship from
changing; traditionally, this omnipotent help is not even contami-
nated (made realistic) by talk of money for services rendered—
as if both parties preferred the God-supplicant arrangement. Besides this, or as part of it, the doctor often is pretty unpleasant
about people who don't understand how wonderful he is; on this
point, one might consult nurses, curious patients, and Armed
Forces personnel who had to command doctors. All this then to

indicate that the doctor keeps his power, his patients' love, and his invulnerability by fending off death and illness. And when the magic doesn't work, the doctor who still believes the myth is in serious danger of disillusionment and disgrace. Such a doctor has often treated his patients so highhandedly that the latter will actually sense the situation and find some small comfort in the spiteful revenge of dying. We talk about positive and negative transference, but most doctors accept the first as their normal, just due, and any other reaction as recalcitrance or ingratitude. A convenient notion, an enviable viewpoint, but the doctor who subscribes to it simply cannot face the anger and rejection of the hurt and disappointed patient. Most doctors would rather not ever have to, but it is necessary at times—if only for the reason given by Hippocrates: "And by seeing and announcing beforehand those who will live and those who will die, he will thus escape censure." [2]. If we could, without censure, maintain our reputation for omnipotence, I wonder how often we would admit our inadequate skills.

If a doctor's death is dismayingly incredible to the dreamer in everyone, it is even more poignantly noted when a medical man hears of a psychiatrist's suicide, a surgeon's pancreatic cancer, or an internist's coronary occlusion. Here even the initiated are awed by the surrender of the specialist to his intimately familiar foe. Specialization would seem to offer some fascinating opportunities for more specific resolution of the search that leads men into the "noble art." I am not in a position to compare one specialty with another in this regard, but I would like to say a word about my own. Psychiatrists, often thought to be so far from organic disease, pain and death, hear a lot about how these things affect people. But if a surgeon hides behind his mask, a psychiatrist has an even more effective shield. I do not mean the couch, which is good in its way, but rather that wonderful step in intellectualization whereby we alter the quality of reality through nomenclature. This allows us to treat a man's fear of death as we would a fear of things in the dark. In practice, this is a good idea, i.e., it works because phobias are irrational fears. But where there isn't anything in the dark, there is death, and the man who doesn't recognize death is unlikely to preserve his life effectively. So it happens that the psychiatrist can deny death as he denies the apparent source of any other phobia, and some seem to take advantage of this possibility, although Freud wrote, "If you would endure life, be prepared for death" [1]. An even more elaborate formulation is often interpreted as meaning that we die because we "wish" it or are psychically impelled toward it. Again this may be, but I imagine we would die whether or not it were so. It is the oversimplification and misunderstanding of such concepts that make the playwright and novelist depict us as unctious, smug possessors of secrets that would give man complete freedom from anxiety, guilt, and death. It seems to me however, that psychiatrists are less likely to give this impression now than previously, perhaps because we are understood better and understand more.

Almost all doctors are reluctant to make and reveal serious diagnoses. While touched by pain and saddened by each patient's death, they often contrive to show their feelings in devious and distorted ways. I recently saw a woman in consultation who gave a perceptive picture of the two types of doctors she had encountered during some twenty years of being treated for pulmonary tuberculosis. Doctors had assumed a God-like stature in her mind because her life literally depended on their judgment and treatment. Because of this she was unable to express any resentment directly to them. She said that at one extreme was the doctor who was solicitous, overly kind, protective, but afraid of her illness and its possible consequences. He seemed uncomfortable in touching her and took elaborate, sometimes extreme, precautions against becoming infected by her. He was so concerned and fearful that on many occasions he behaved too conservatively in his treatment and was reluctant to do anything that inconvenienced or hurt her. At the other pole, there was the doctor who was rough, brusque, and practically manhandled her. She liked being so treated to some extent because at least it made her feel respected as a person of some strength. However, this type of man told her very little about her progress, minimized her symptoms, and laughed at her complaints. Once when a chest X ray was made, he only told her that if anything was wrong, he would call her. He then let her worry for several weeks until she finally called him—only to be told that the chest plate was negative, and what the devil did she expect him to do: call every patient who had a negative X ray? The patient said she felt most doctors were probably inclined toward one or the other extreme, and that they were able to be pleasant, warm, and personable only as long as there was nothing seriously wrong with the patient, that is, so far as their own specialty was concerned. It is painfully evident to this woman that technical excellence cannot substitute for personal courage and warmth in the doctor's task to help his patient. She would be happy if she could deceive herself about her doctor, but her sensitivity to his feelings prevents it.

It is often unfortunately true that the seriously or hopelessly ill patient senses the doctor's emotions clearly. The doctor's disillusionment, depending on his maturity, will show as sympathy, anger, disgust, indifference, interest, disappointment, or embarrassment. Though not exhaustive, this list suggests the many ways a patient may perceive how his doom affects his physician. The hardest to bear is indifference because it is so defensive, so weak, that the patient cannot believe that which such a man tells him. I have sometimes seen attitudes closer to anger rouse a man from guilt and dread and keep him emotionally with his family until the real death. Those feelings at the opposite pole—true grief, sympathy—are most supportive for the dying one, not only because he feels loved, but because he then sees that the living need his help. He feels called upon to soothe the physician's hurt, to comfort those who will mourn, to assure men of their dignity. Such a man will live his life to the end, as well and as productively as he ever was able.

And the doctor will help to this end if he can know his own fear and weakness and hope. Realizing the human condition, he will not be too disturbed by his failure and disillusionment. He can function as comforter and, while not promising life, can offer hope.

REFERENCES

1. Freud, S.: "Thoughts for the Times on War and Death," *Collected Papers*, Hogarth Press, Ltd., London, 1948, vol. 4.
2. Hippocrates: "The Book of Prognostics," in R. M. Hutchins (ed.), *Great Books of the Western World*, Encyclopaedia Britannica, Inc., Chicago, 1955, vol. 10.
3. Price, C.: "Never admit you're sick," *Med. Econ.*, 36, 166–172, 1959.
4. Wheelis, A.: *The Quest for Identity*, W. W. Norton & Company, Inc., New York, 1958.

16 IRVING E. ALEXANDER AND ARTHUR M. ADLERSTEIN

Death and Religion

We live today in an era in which the problem of death is part of the *Zeitgeist*. The discovery of tremendous sources of power which, if used destructively, could obliterate nations and perhaps our entire planet has placed death in the focus of human consciousness. In the case of the individual it is as though that which was thought of as a natural process with an indefinite time referent has increased in immediate probability value.

One of the consequences of these troubled times has been a trend toward religion. Churches and synagogues report higher present membership and better attendance than at any other time in recent history. These are the times when revivalists preach to capacity audiences in large sophisticated cities in Europe and America and when Orthodox Jewish groups are expanding religious school facilities.

What is the increased attraction of religion in times of distress? To this question countless people, professional and lay alike, have directed their attention. No simple answer has emerged; yet it seems reasonably safe to propose that any answer will have to consider as a possibility the reduction of uncertainty and its somatic counterpart—the reduction of anxiety.

Although it has often been assumed by theologians and philosophers alike that religious belief is effective in

271

reducing death anxiety, there is no direct experimental evidence to support such a contention. In fact there is all too little reliable information about any aspect of the death problem as it concerns man. Only in the most recent past, and perhaps as a further indication of the *Zeitgeist,* has such information appeared [1–3; 6–8; 12].

It will be the purpose of this paper to report the results of a study in which a variety of reactions to the concept of death were measured in a population that differed in one parameter, "religiosity." Specifically we were concerned with eliciting information as to how the concept of death affects a population of young people and also how critical a variable religion is in attitudes and feelings about death.

To pose such a set of broad questions immediately suggests difficulties. Is there enough uniformity within the categories, religious and nonreligious, to make an inquiry worth while? To what extent will the results depend on whether the subjects are men or women; children or adults; Catholics, Protestants, or Jews; rich or poor; sick or healthy; and so on. To design and carry out a study that could account for all these possible variables would be the effort of many years or considerable expense. Our approach to the problem was that of the laboratory: to take a limited, but carefully selected, sample and to extract from this sample a great deal of information.

The subjects, male college students, were selected with specific criteria in mind. In the religious group we wanted people with strong religious beliefs whose participation in religious practices had been a continuous part of their way of life since childhood. In the nonreligious group we sought people whose way of life had not included membership in religious groups or sustained personal contact with formal religious systems, beliefs, and practices. The nonreligious group was not negatively disposed toward religion. They were rather neutral, or indifferent, or not clearly decided.

The selection procedure was rigorous and included objective test scores, background questionnaire information, and interview data. As a check on this procedure the results of a paper-and-pencil scale for selecting dominant life values were also used. Fifty subjects, equally divided into two groups, constituted our final population.

The experimental procedure was designed to elicit responses on several levels of functioning. A word-association task was employed to measure the change in somatic response (galvanic skin response, GSR) when death words are used as stimuli. Osgood's Semantic Differential technique [10] was employed to extract the "meaning" of a group of death words. A questionnaire similar to ones used earlier by other investigators [5, 9] was administered to determine conscious attitudes toward death. In addition, a structured, open-end interview with each subject was conducted. Included in the interview were such topics as the subject's beliefs concerning an afterlife, life's purpose, the effects of early experiences with death, family attitudes toward death, thoughts and feelings about his own death and those of loved ones, and conjecture concerning the time and circumstances of his own death. The effects of conscious deliberations about death were assessed by measuring the differences in scores on split halves of a manifest-anxiety scale. The first part of the scale was filled out immediately after the word-association task, the second part following the interview.

In reporting the results we shall deal first with whether religious belief is a critical variable in reducing anxiety about death. Here a word of caution is in order. It must be remembered that our evidence pertains to a clearly specified segment of the population, namely, male college students, Protestants, middle- and upper-class, high intellectual potential, and so forth. It is not known to what extent these results would generalize to other religious and nonreligious populations with different background characteristics.

We found that our religious and nonreligious groups exhibited

similar patterns in most of the aspects of behavior concerning death
that we measured. Both groups showed an increased galvanic skin
response (GSR) to death words. Both groups assigned the "meaning" of "bad" and "potent" to death words on the Semantic Differential and both groups were much alike in their consciously
expressed attitudes toward death.

A way in which they differed is in the change in manifest
anxiety as a result of the experimental procedure. Although the
two groups ended up with comparable anxiety levels (the nonreligious group was slightly higher), the religious subjects increased significantly from the first to the second test, while the
nonreligious subjects remained relatively the same. Had the groups
shown comparable anxiety levels at the initial testing, the interpretation of this finding would have been straightforward. This, however, was not the case. The nonreligious subjects had a significantly
higher manifest-anxiety level than did the religious subjects when
they were measured immediately after the word-association task.
One could argue cogently that the fact that the nonreligious group
showed a higher level of manifest anxiety to begin with pre-
cluded the possibility of a consequent rise as a function of discussing death.

To assess the potency of this argument the data were analyzed
in another way. The groups were split on the basis of responses to
the Rotter Incomplete Sentence Blank which was one of the instruments used in the selection procedure. "High-neurotic" and "low-
neurotic" groups were constituted, with an equal number of
religious and nonreligious subjects in each group. In this case the
high-neurotic group was reliably higher in manifest anxiety immediately following the word-association task. We now had the
parallel for our religious–nonreligious difference. The consequent
procedure affected the high- and low-neurotic groups differently
than it did the religious and nonreligious groups. The high-neurotic group increased further in manifest anxiety while the low-
neurotic group remained roughly the same; the group mean

dropped slightly. There is therefore no reason to believe that the manifest-anxiety level of the nonreligious group prior to the face-to-face discussion of death was so high that a further increase was not possible.

Since, in our selection of religious and nonreligious groups, we had controlled for factors which are known to be correlated with manifest anxiety (i.e., neuroticism) and in addition the GSR levels of the two groups after the various parts of the word-association task were not reliably different, we were puzzled to explain both the initial difference in the groups when manifest anxiety was measured and the consequent finding that the rate of increase for the religious subjects was reliably greater than that for the nonreligious subjects. The most plausible explanation, assuming that manifest-anxiety level was equivalent for the two groups prior to the experimental session, is that death anxiety is aroused much more rapidly and with less direct stimuli in the nonreligious group. A word-association task that has death words embedded in the word list is enough to raise the manifest-anxiety level of our nonreligious subjects, while face-to-face discussion about personal death is needed to set off this response in those of the religious group.

Let us turn now to the major expressions of conscious attitude toward death in our population. For this we shall examine the responses to the prepared questionnaire and open-end interview.

Again we must stress the over-all similarity between the two groups in their responses. The two items in the questionnaire upon which the groups differed reliably were concerned with feelings related to visiting a cemetery and the duration of depression after attending a funeral. In both instances the pattern is clear. *The nonreligious subjects were less likely to either have, recognize, or report feelings connected with death or burial.* The nonreligious group reported mainly "indifference" in feelings after visiting a cemetery while the religious group reported "peaceful" feelings. The religious group reported feelings of depression after a funeral lasting for a longer period of time than did those of the non-religious group. In view of the fact that from the indirect measures we have evidence that death is an anxiety-provoking concept for both groups, it is very likely that these differences in questionnaire responses are manifestations of basic defenses against death anxiety. With regard to feelings about death, it is as though, in the language of William James, our religious subjects were "tender minded," our nonreligious subjects "tough minded."

Other instances of this difference in the expression of feelings about death are found in the following questionnaire responses. When reading about death in either fiction or poetry the religious subjects more often reported a feeling of depression while the nonreligious subjects reported indifference. When asked to gauge the strength of fear of death the distributions for the two groups showed interesting trends. The nonreligious group distributed itself in the following manner: seven reported no fear; eight, very weak fear; five, weak fear; four, moderate fear; and one, strong fear. In the religious group we saw more of a trend toward bi-modality. Ten of the subjects reported no fear; four, very weak fear; two, weak fear; eight, moderate fear; and one, strong fear. More of the religious subjects were at extreme ends of the scale, indicating less uniformity of opinion in the group.

A considerable part of the questionnaire was taken up with the frequency of thoughts and wishes about death. It is clear from the results that our groups did not differ greatly in their reports of conscious concern with death or dying as it pertains to the self or to others. Yet even when slight differences appeared they usually followed the direction indicated above. The great majority of subjects used the categories "never" or "very rarely" in answer to such questions as frequency of nocturnal dreams of dying or being dead, frequency of wishing for death, and frequency of thoughts of suicide.

The categories "occasionally" or "frequently" were most often used by both groups when responding to the following questions:

frequency of reading newspaper stories about death, frequency of thoughts about the death of others, and frequency of thoughts of death of loved ones.

Some slight indications of difference were found in responses to the following items: the religious-group members reported having thought of their own death more frequently within the last year; this group also reported more frequent conscious thoughts about personal death and more frequent thoughts of death when ill; the nonreligious group thought more frequently of personal death as a result of accident and also thought of death as being painful more frequently.

The interview material is more difficult to summarize. Most of the early questions were concerned with probing the nature of the religious belief and its effect on daily living. The concept of the afterlife and its influence was discussed. The answers to this portion of the interview were used as a final check point in the selection procedure. The belief in an afterlife concept was employed as an absolute point of differentiation between the groups. All of the religious subjects had a strong belief in heaven while the nonreligious people expressed clear disbelief. When asked to describe heaven, the religious subjects spoke in terms of communion with God. The nonreligious people spoke either in terms of the "golden streets" stereotype or vague, intellectualized descriptions. With regard to hell as a region of the afterlife, the religious group saw it primarily as the absence of God while the nonreligious group reported mainly in terms of the mythical "fire and brimstone" description. In answer to a question concerning the purpose of life, the religious group spoke of fulfilling God's plan, whereas the nonreligious group decided either against a definite universal purpose for life or for the fulfillment of individual life goals.

When asked to describe the effects of their belief or disbelief on daily living, the religious subjects mentioned prominently the reduction of fear about death. The nonreligious subjects were most likely to attribute no relationship between their lack of belief and everyday existence. In those instances, when a connection was made, the emphasis was put on the importance of life and a lessening of the importance of death.

Inquiry was made directly about the effect of religious conviction on feelings toward death. It is important here to note that in both groups the most frequent response was that their convictions make death less fearful. For the one group there was the assurance that death is not the end; for the other, the acceptance of death as the end removed the cloud of uncertainty and doubt. We shall discuss this finding further in a later section.

Early thoughts about death were quite similar for both groups. The typical themes reported by Schilder [11] and Anthony [4] we found in our subjects' responses. Sleep and death were frequently equated. Fear of going to sleep was reported. Concern about the death of the parents was frequent. One's own death as an instrument of punishment also appeared often.

A sharp difference between the groups was found in the age at which one first became aware of the fact that people die. Eighty per cent of the religious subjects reported this experience to occur before the age of six. Fewer than thirty per cent of the nonreligious subjects reported similar experiences. Despite the fact that specific memories about death occurred earlier in the religious group they tended to have clearer recollections about these events.

There was little difference in response when the subjects were asked how they feel about the fact that they must die. The typical response was the philosophical shrug followed by a justification in terms either of God's will and the afterlife or the natural order of things.

Typical times and circumstances for thoughts about death were in cars or airplanes. While both groups gave this as a preferred response it was given with greater frequency in the nonreligious group. Other times and circumstances for the religious group included in church, when contemplating life goals, when death comes to a friend or relative, when the close kinship with a girl friend or family is brought into awareness, and when death is the focus of something they are reading. For the nonreligious group three additional circumstances pretty well cover the major reasons given: when they are sick, when they are reading about death, and when they are alone at night.

Both groups expressed little concern about death. When asked how they feel when they think about death, a frequent response was a denial that any feelings are involved at all. In some instances a feeling of sadness or depression was reported and in others a fear of dying or that death will be painful. The groups were distinguishable in response to this question in terms of their major solution. In the responses of the religious subjects there was a frequent impression of security in the knowledge that there is an afterlife. In the responses of the nonreligious subjects there was an expressed feeling that death is natural and will come in its time.

The aspects of death that bothered our subjects are the same for both groups. The fear of a painful death was most prevalent. This was followed in importance by the thought of a separation from loved ones, the problem of facing death properly, and the thought of being buried in the ground. The major difference between the groups in their replies to this question again related to their principal conscious attitude. The religious subjects were troubled about the possibility that an afterlife may not exist or that they will not be able to attain it. The nonreligious subjects expressed concern that their lives might end without their having accomplished anything of importance.

Toward the end of the interview the subjects were asked to speculate about the age at which death will come. Although both groups estimated life expectancy a little beyond that of the actuarial tables, the religious group expected life to go on for a slightly longer period of time. Both the median and mode for the religious group fell between 75 and 79 years of age. For the nonreligious group the corresponding figure was between 70 and

74 years. This small difference was also evident in the range of estimates. The extreme estimates for the religious group started at a slightly higher age (55–59 vs. under 54) and ended at a slightly higher age (90 vs. 85–89) than those of the nonreligious group.

A final question dealt with the manner in which death will come. There were no group differences in the response patterns to this question. Roughly half of the subjects chose heart attack as the expected cause of death. Another 25 per cent chose "natural causes." The remainder were split up among various choices including accident, violence, war casualty, cancer, and so forth.

What is it that we can take away from this set of observations? What have we learned from the way human beings react to their inevitable fate?

We feel that the evidence from the indirect measures, both physiological and verbal, points to the fact that death is a negatively-toned affective concept for both of our groups. However, as soon as one begins to deal with the problem directly, on a conscious level, as in our interview, there is a tendency for subjects to act as though they are not at all concerned over the prospect of their own death. These findings seem to be the same for both our religious and our nonreligious subjects. If we were concerned solely with testing the contention that a "religious solution" to the problem of death is more effective in reducing anxiety than is a "nonreligious solution," we would have to conclude that, for our samples, there seems to be no real difference in anxiety levels. Both groups show anxiety concomitants on some levels, indifference on others. One group responds to less direct stimuli, the other to direct confrontation; yet one is struck by the apparent difference in the way the problem is handled in discussion by our respective groups.

The nonreligious subjects see death as the natural end of life. It is not the climax but rather the end in the sense that the rose fades away. The emphasis for these people is on life and the rewards of living. Two basic kinds of psychological reactions appear to prevail in this group: One we might term "masking," in which the individual plunges into the affairs of life and keeps himself wholly occupied without opportunity for reflection about death. This is essentially the phenomenon described by Schilder and Wechsler when dealing with reactions to death in children [11]. The second is repression, in which the threat to the ego is handled by banishing the problem of death from consciousness. In this case one could be a reflective person but simply never find that death is one of the topics upon which he reflects.

The religious subjects are much more likely to keep the problem of death a conscious matter. They have earlier and clearer memories about death. They express more feeling when confronted with death and they appear much more comfortable in discussions about the subject. It is only when one probes directly the personal aspects of dying that a change in the anxiety level is brought about. The typical response pattern might be described as one of displacement of focus. It is as though that which is negative in the field is made peripheral and that which is tolerable is made central. In this instance the elements of the figure-ground relationship that we refer to are the act of dying and the afterlife.

In reflecting on the generality of our findings we hold no strong brief for the possibility that the types of response patterns that we felt were indicative of our selected groups would in fact be duplicated in more diversely constituted religious and nonreligious groups. That death is a threat to the intact ego and as such must be handled by all humans no matter what their religious conviction is a statement that finds support in our results. That religious and nonreligious people solve this problem differently is, we think, an oversimplification, for it is clear that all religious systems do not embrace an afterlife concept.

Perhaps our suggestion—that two solutions for the reduction of death anxiety present themselves; one emphasizing the importance of life, the other the importance of afterlife—is a more general aspect of human functioning and as such crosscuts our original dichotomy. It is the "nothing but" versus "something more" controversy in a slightly different form. Certainly one can see both positions within religion itself, for example, the attitude toward death in Judaism as opposed to that of Christianity. For the Jew the crux of his being is the way life is lived—the ethics, morals, and values by which he lives. These in themselves are his reward. For the Christian, the "good life" is a preparation through sacrifice for salvation, the reward of the afterlife. We can see the essence of these two arguments presented over and over again in the history of ideas. Transcendentalism versus realism, mysticism versus orthodoxy, innate ideas versus a "tabula rasa," vitalism versus mechanism, tender minded versus tough minded—these are but a few more of the opposing positions that carry within them some flavor of this basic dichotomy.

What we should like to propose now is that in answer to the ever-present threat of its ultimate demise the ego is forced toward a position on one or the other side of this coin. When a position is taken, anxiety can be kept to a minimum except in extreme circumstances. If no clear stand is adopted, death anxiety may be very close to the surface and thus easily stimulated. Psychopathological groups and preschool-age children may be clear examples of those who fall in this latter category.

Such a proposal would allow us to comment rationally on our opening observations that in this era of greater awareness of death there is an increased trend toward religion. Our contention is that there is an increased trend toward any definite view. It could be one that includes an afterlife concept, as in many religions, or one that attempts to explain the meaning of existence, as in some modern philosophical views that have attracted the public eye. This appears to be an age in which those in doubt, the people who have not adopted a philosophy of death, are forced to act because of the tenuous balance of international relationships and the clear-cut consequences of the weapons that the prospective belligerents carry.

REFERENCES

1. Adlerstein, A. M.: "The Relationship Between Religious Belief and Death Affect," unpublished doctoral dissertation, Princeton University, Princeton, N.J., 1958.
2. Alexander, I. E., R. S. Colley, and A. M. Adlerstein: "Is death a matter of indifference?" *J. Psychol.*, **43**: 277–283, 1957.
3. Alexander, I. E., and A. M. Adlerstein: "Affective responses to the concept of death in a population of children and early adolescents," *J. Genet. Psychol.*, in press.
4. Anthony, S.: *The Child's Discovery of Death*, Harcourt, Brace and Company, Inc., New York, 1940.
5. Bromberg, W., and P. Schilder: "Death and dying," *Psychoanal. Rev.*, **20**: 133–185, 1933.
6. Feifel, H.: "Attitudes of mentally ill patients toward death," *J. Nervous Mental Disease,* **122**: 375–380, 1955.
7. Feifel, H.: "Older persons look at death," *Geriatrics,* **11**: 127–130, 1956.
8. Meissner, W. W.: "Affective response to psychoanalytic death symbols," *J. Abnormal Social Psychol.,* **56**: 295–299, 1958.
9. Middleton, W. C.: "Some reactions towards death among college students," *J. Abnormal Social Psychol.,* **31**: 165–173, 1936.
10. Osgood, C. E., G. J. Suci, and P. H. Tannenbaum: *The Measurement of Meaning,* University of Illinois Press, Urbana, Ill., 1957.
11. Schilder, P., and D. Wechsler: "The attitudes of children towards death," *J. Genet. Psychol.,* **45**: 406–451, 1934.
12. Shrut, S. D.: "Attitudes toward old age and death," *Mental Hyg.,* **42**: 259–266, 1958.

17

EDWIN S. SHNEIDMAN AND
NORMAN L. FARBEROW

Suicide and Death

The relationships between suicide and death are many and are more complicated than they would appear to be upon superficial contemplation. Paradoxically, although the commission of suicide always involves death, suicide itself is more a way of *living*—in which the distinguishing feature is that the termination of living is self-administered —than it is a way of dying. Suicide may involve many attitudes toward death, but it always incorporates this one attitude toward living. Further, it can be assumed that the suicidal act itself is probably consistent with the other patterns of living of the individual. The philosopher Paul-Louis Landsberg, in *The Moral Problem of Suicide* [4], stated: "Suicide is not just a type of death; it is a human act."

It is generally agreed that there is a paucity of systematic studies on the psychology of death—indeed, this volume is dedicated to help fill that lacuna. This particular chapter reports some findings from a systematic approach to some of the psychological problems of the self-administered termination of living (suicide) and thereby attempts to increase our total understanding of death.

Suicide in the United States ranks among the first ten in the morbid list of "killers." Thus, effective reduction of the suicide rate is one of the most pressing contemporary sociopsychological problems. Inasmuch as the act of suicide destroys the source of the data, the methodological issues involved in investigating the causes of suicide are among the most challenging in current research. This paper attempts to describe a series of experiments, employing both traditional and exploratory techniques, aimed at investigating the social and psychological nature of suicide and to present some tentative findings from the studies to date.

In the interest of clarity of exposition, the kinds of subjects and the types of materials used in the study will be indicated at the outset. The "experimental" subjects consist of individuals who have committed suicide; the "control" subjects consist of several sets of individuals: persons who have attempted suicide, threatened suicide, are nonsuicidal, etc. The data for the study (for subjects in all groups) consist of psychiatric and social case histories, psychotherapy materials, psychological test protocols, and (genuine and simulated) suicide notes. A graphic summary of the subjects and the types of data comprising the experimental design is presented in Table 1.

The study was primarily an empirical study, the major aim of which was to develop hypotheses based upon analysis of data about the sociopsychological nature of suicide, which might, in future studies, be tested and eventually used in aiding the more complete understanding (including recognition and treatment) of individuals who are suicidal risks.

The remainder of this paper will be devoted to a discussion of some of the outcomes of the studies to date [2, 3, 7, 8] and some implications of these findings. Each of the three general questions stated below will be discussed in terms of inquiry, relevant data, findings, and, where possible, inferred practical suggestions for suicide prevention.

1

The first general question was what hypotheses or clues could be obtained from comparisons of *psychiatric and social case his-*

Table 1

Design for Experimental Approach to Sociopsychological Aspects of Suicide

| | Experimental Group | Control Groups* | | | |
| | | Suicidal | | Nonsuicidal | |
	Completed Suicide	Attempted Suicide	Threatened Suicide	Psychiatric	Nonpsychiatric
Case Histories	150 case histories obtained by checking 8,000 suicide names against 150,000 local NP hospital names	32 case histories from NP hospital, plus 50 from general hospital	32 case histories obtained from NP hospital	32 case histories obtained from NP hospital	
Psychological Tests	50 sets of psychological tests obtained as indicated above	32 test batteries from NP hospital, plus 50 from general hospital	32 test batteries obtained from NP hospital	32 test batteries from NP hospital	25 test batteries of Buerger's disease patients in general hospital
Suicide Notes	700 genuine suicide notes obtained from Coroner's office	25 simulated suicide notes obtained from general hospital			50 simulated notes from labor unions and fraternal groups
Psychotherapy Notes	Psychotherapy notes from psychiatrists treating suicidal patients	25 sets of psychotherapy notes obtained from psychiatrists in the community	25 sets of therapy notes from psychiatrists in the community		
Miscellaneous	(The occasional diary, autobiography, etc. obtained from various sources)				

* Other proposed control groups will include individuals who have committed homicide, are in severe physical pain or severe psychological pain, etc.

tories among (matched) subjects of the following groups: individuals who had committed suicide, attempted suicide, threatened suicide, and are nonsuicidal. One may ask whether it is possible that such data, compared in as many aspects as are available, might yield any clues which would be useful in understanding, predicting, and preventing suicidal behavior.

Psychiatric and social case histories were obtained for 32 adult male subjects who had been hospitalized in a neuropsychiatric hospital and who, some time after discharge, had committed suicide. The controls were three other comparable groups of neuropsychiatric hospitalized males, each group consisting of 32 subjects: a group who had attempted suicide, a group who had threatened suicide, and a group who were nonsuicidal, i.e., who had no history of suicidal tendencies. The basic procedure in obtaining the group of completed suicides was to secure the weekly lists of all suicides in Los Angeles County from the Coroner's office for the past ten years, to check the hospital rosters for the names of any individuals who might have been in the hospital previously. These cases were then compared with an equal number of cases in the attempt, threat, and nonsuicidal categories. When 128 case histories of these individuals were analyzed in terms of more than one-hundred different social, economic, cultural, and psychological categories, the following results emerged: The age distribution of the four groups was found to be similar; the religious affiliations of the groups were remarkably similar; educationally 50 per cent of the men of each group had completed the tenth grade, with no differences among the groups; a survey of the occupational classifications indicated that all groups showed relatively poor work histories but there were no differences among the groups; familial histories, when checked for more than one-hundred psychiatric and sociological factors such as economic level, types of early environment, age at parents' death, parents' separation or divorce, number of parents' previous or subsequent marriages, by whom the patient was raised until adolescence, the number of siblings, and the presence of intrafamilial strife or conflict, showed no significant differences among the four groups. When family histories were checked for chronic illness, mental illness, or other psychiatric data, only one item emerged as distinctive. The family histories of the completed-suicide group showed that 33 per cent had had members of the family in mental hospitals, while none of the other groups showed more than 6 per cent.

An obvious but still very interesting conclusion emerges from the comparison of the methods used by the Completed group with those used by the Attempt group. A significant difference was found between them, with the Attempt group using sedation or wrist-slashing most often, while the Completed group used hanging or guns.

Diagnostically, the three suicidal groups showed a significantly higher number of reactive depressives in the neurotic categories, while the Control group seemed to tend more toward anxiety reactions. In the psychotic categories, the three suicidal groups were significantly higher in the number of paranoid schizophrenics than was the Control nonsuicidal group. There were no important differences in any of the other nosological categories.

An investigation of the relationship between suicide attempt or threat on the one hand and completion of suicide on the other hand revealed that 62 per cent of the completed-suicide group had histories of previous attempts at suicide. When those cases in which known threats of suicide had been made were added, it was found that 75 per cent of the cases had been suicidal at a previous time.

When the data for the 32 subjects who had completed suicide were analyzed with attention to the interval between release from hospital and suicide, it was discovered that 13 people or 41 per cent took the final step within three months of discharge, and 22 people or 69 per cent committed suicide within one year after discharge from the hospital. This figure of 41 per cent, or close to half of the patients, committing suicide within three months of leaving the hospital seemed so remarkable that a more detailed examination of this subgroup of 13 subjects was made. This perusal indicated that for almost all of these patients it had been decided that recovery from emotional stress and a stabilization of mental status had been effected. In other words, these patients had appeared to be sufficiently better, or getting better enough, to allow them to leave the protective confines of the hospital.

From this aspect of the study three implications can be drawn:

1. On the basis of the case-history data, little emerges as useful in differentiating suicidals from nonsuicidals except for the possibility that the diagnosis of reactive depression or paranoid schizophrenia along with the history of a previous attempt or threat at suicide seems significant. Also, a previous history of mental hospitalization among the members of the family seems to be important. On the whole, however, the similarity among all the groups points to the difficulty in judging a mental-hospital patient as suicidal on the basis of psychiatric or anamnestic data alone, however stressful or traumatic it has been.

2. A past history of suicidal attempt or threat stands out as a marked danger signal—should certainly not be taken lightly—and characterizes the Completed group particularly. People who commit suicide have, by and large, previously threatened or attempted it.

3. There appears to be approximately a three-month period following the emotional crisis of suicide (and after which the patient was adjudged by professional opinion to be on the way to recovery) in which he was indeed most dangerous to himself. A possible explanation for this is that at the depth of the crisis the patient lacks the psychomotor energy to commit the deed and that the appearance of recovery is simply a return of increased psychomotor pace rather than the dissipation of morbid ideation or the resolution of the affect of depression. At any rate, the find-

ings would seem to imply that physicians and relatives should be especially cautious and watchful for at least ninety days after a person who has been suicidal appears to be recovering.

2

The second general question was what hypotheses or clues could be obtained from comparisons of *psychological test protocols* of individuals who had attempted suicide with those of subjects who had threatened suicide. One might raise the specific question whether a suicide attempt serves any psychodynamic function (in the psychic economy of the individual), and one might propose the hypothesis that individuals who had attempted suicide would, by and large, be less disturbed emotionally than those who had made serious threats but who had not acted on their impulses.

Psychological test protocols were obtained for each of 96 subjects—32 each of hospitalized attempted, threatened, and nonsuicidal subjects. (The psychological test results of the subjects who committed suicide have not been analyzed as yet, but are being collected by "backtracking" from the coroner's list to the hospital files, as described above for the case histories). The psychological tests included such techniques as the Hildreth Feeling and Attitude Scale, the Thematic Apperception Test (TAT), the Make a Picture Story (MAPS) test, the Minnesota Multiphasic Personality Inventory (MMPI), etc. Sets of tests were obtained on groups of hospitalized individuals who had attempted suicide, threatened suicide, or were nonsuicidal, and comparisons of the test results were made among the three groups.

There are three findings to date from the analysis of the psychological tests. One finding was that there are psychological differences among individuals heretofore loosely classified as "suicidal." One must differentiate among people who attempt suicide or threaten suicide in terms of their immediate emotional disturbance. On the basis of psychologica¹ test scores and interpretations, one cannot speak of suicidals as a group unless a sharp definition is made of the types included.

Another finding, related to the first, was that the individuals who have threatened suicide show more guilt, aggression, irritability and agitation (in a word, more disturbance) than do the individuals who have attempted suicide. The people who have attempted suicide are more like the nonsuicidal mental hospital patients, except perhaps more withdrawn. It is almost as though the attempt itself may have operated in an abreactive and therapeutic manner to lessen the immediate seriousness of the personality disturbance. The data for the other tests independently corroborate these two findings.

The third finding had to do specifically with the thirteen individuals who committed suicide within three months of discharge from the hospital. Perusal of the available test data seems to indicate that, at the time of admission to the hospital, this type of patient will not admit to psychological test items which relate directly to suicidal intent, but is willing to indicate that he felt blue and unhappy, useless, that he brooded, had been disappointed in love, worked under tension, wished to be a child again, etc. The more general implication would seem to be that persons who later commit suicide may deny direct inquiry concerning suicidal intent but will reveal depressive and dysphoric feelings and ideation.

3

The third general question was what hypotheses or clues could be obtained from analyses of genuine *suicide notes* (of individuals who had killed themselves) as well as comparisons between genuine suicide notes and simulated suicide notes elicited from individuals who were nonsuicidal.

The Los Angeles County Coroner's office keeps files of suicides and copies of every suicide note written in Los Angeles County, where they become part of the public records. With the permission of the coroner, 717 genuine suicide notes of individuals who had killed themselves in Los Angeles County in the period from 1945 to 1954 were collected. These represented close to one-hundred per cent of all the notes written—although only about fifteen per cent of the people who kill themselves leave notes.[1] As will be discussed below, suicide notes are not only a one-way mirror to suicidal motivation, but they are also invaluable data and are relevant to the traditions of (and amenable to the techniques of) thematic analysis (Murray, Berelson, etc.), discomfort-relief concepts (Mowrer), personal documents (Allport), communication theory (Reusch), and the function of language (Whorf).

Table 2 presents some data about the individuals who wrote the 717 genuine suicide notes simply for purposes of information. No conclusions about suicidal individuals are intended to be conveyed from this description. It will be noted that there are approximately three times as many men as women (540 as compared with 177), that practically all of the individuals of this sample are Caucasian, that the great majority of them are native-born, that most of them are married, and that most men kill themselves by shooting whereas most women take their lives by sedation.

Certainly there are many theories (or hypotheses) about suicide: meteorological, ecological, economic, sociological, psychoanalytic, etc. One might ask the question whether or not any single current theoretical explanation would be sufficient to account for all the suicidal data which could be enumerated. One method of pursuing this question would be to inquire whether a large group of suicides—for example individuals of the various *age* groups who commit suicide—could be explained in terms of any single hypothesis. For the purpose of a first test of this notion, Karl

---

[1] The fact that the sample may be a selective one raises certain questions. However, analysis of the data has shown that individuals who leave notes are almost identical in economic, social, and cultural factors, as obtained from the death certificates, with those who do not leave notes. In addition it is hoped that the question of why people write personal documents can be investigated.

TABLE 2

RACE, NATIVITY, MARITAL STATUS, AND SUICIDE METHODS BY AGE AND SEX, OF 717 SUICIDE-NOTE WRITERS

Age	Total	Sex	Race White	Race Negro	Race Oriental	Nativity United States	Nativity Other	Marital Single	Marital Married	Marital Divorced	Marital Widowed	Method Shooting	Method Sedation	Method Hanging	Method Jumping	Method Cutting	Method Poisoning	Method Carbon Monoxide	Method Other
10–19	7	M	4			4		4				3							1
		F	3			2	1	3				2			1				
20–29	61	M	41	2	4	40	3	22	18	3		19	4	8	1	1	2	7	1
		F	17	1		18		6	10	1	1	8	5	1			2	1	1
30–39	119	M	74	5	4	80	3	8	71	4		30	14	7	3		3	18	8
		F	35	1		35	1	3	25	6	2	14	13	2			4	1	2
40–49	164	M	124	1	2	109	18	18	92	15	2	48	13	10	5	8	11	29	3
		F	37			33	4	2	21	8	6	5	17	3	2		5	4	1
50–59	150	M	107	1		81	27	22	52	26	8	37	22	12	8	5	3	17	4
		F	42		1	36	6	2	24	7	9	6	19	6	1	2	3	2	3
60–69	130	M	99	1	1	64	36	13	56	15	16	36	15	12	5	6	11	8	7
		F	30			22	8	3	9	2	16	4	12	5	1		3	2	3
70–79	63	M	50		2	36	16	4	24	6	18	25	5	10	2		3	3	4
		F	11			10	1	2	1	1	7		7	1	1				2
80–89	20	M	20			13	7	4	5		11	9	2	5			1	2	1
		F																	
90+	3	M	3			2	1	1		1	1	3							
		F																	
Totals		M	522	9	9	429	111	96	318	70	56	210	75	64	24	20	34	84	29
		F	175	2		156	21	21	90	25	41	39	73	18	6	2	17	10	12
Totals	717	717	697	11	9	585	132	117	408	95	97	249	148	82	30	22	51	94	41

293

Menninger's modification of the Freudian theory of suicide, as described in his book *Man Against Himself* [5] was selected. The materials used were 619 genuine suicide notes (selected from among the 717) consisting of all the notes written by individuals who were Caucasian, native-born, and over twenty years of age. The males (489 notes) ranged in age from 29 to 96, while the females (130 notes) ranged in age from 20 through 78. Menninger's theory, which categorizes the assumed psychodynamic motivations underlying the act of killing oneself, states that there are three components in the suicidal act: the wish to kill, the wish to be killed, and the wish to die. (In translating these three components operationally—prior to an analysis of the genuine suicide notes—considerable help was obtained from personal communication with Dr. Menninger.) All 619 notes were grouped, according to the age of the writer, into three age groups; 20 to 39 (137), 40 to 59 (267), and 60 and over (215); or into what might be broadly conceived as young, middle-aged, and older groups. The notes were then classified, independently, by two raters, under one of the above three categories, or in an unclassifiable category if the note did not give enough information to allow classification. A check of the reliability of the two raters by means of chi-square analysis indicated they agreed quite well in their classification. (The obtained chi square was 751.47 which for nine degrees of freedom is significant beyond the .001 level.) The notes where discrepancies in scoring had appeared were rescored and the differences were resolved, so that a single classification was obtained. The percentages of notes scored as wish to kill, wish to be killed, wish to die, and unclassifiable for each age group were then computed. The results are presented in Table 3.

The main conclusions to be drawn were that the wish to kill and wish to be killed decreased with age, whereas the wish to die increased with age. A more general and perhaps more significant inference in terms of the theory itself is that inasmuch as the patterns or constellations of the various psychodynamics motivating

TABLE 3.

NUMBERS AND PERCENTAGES OF 619 SUICIDE NOTES CLASSIFIED ACCORDING TO MENNINGER'S HYPOTHESIS

Ages	Sex	To Kill No.	%	To Be Killed No.	%	To Die No.	%	Unclassifiable No.	%
20–39	Male	31	31	27	27	23	23	18	18
	Female	12	32	8	21	8	21	10	26
40–59	Male	50	23	35	16	75	35	55	26
	Female	15	29	9	17	15	29	13	25
60+	Male	20	11	18	10	99	57	38	22
	Female	6	15	2	5	30	75	2	5
	Total Male	101	21	80	16	197	40	111	23
	Total Female	33	25	19	15	53	41	25	19
	Totals	134	22	99	16	250	40	136	22

the suicidal person tend to show marked shifts depending on age, perhaps the theory needs to be refined or elaborated to include this. This seems important enough to warrant further investigation. In addition this analysis points to some practical implications for treatment and management of suicidal persons, as follows.

In general, when persons between twenty and thirty-nine years of age come to the attention of a therapist because of suicidal urges or attempts, the therapist may expect to find the more intense interpersonal motives operating in over half of these patients while the chronic depressive feelings will be dominant in only about one-quarter of the cases. The method of choice for treatment, once the necessary medical procedures have been taken, seems to point to a type of dynamic psychotherapy. The aim would be to provide them with the opportunity for working out and gaining insight into the tensions and the intense feelings which had been operating in their interpersonal relationships. In the case of the older patient, both male and female, the therapist must be prepared to institute more environmental and milieu therapy and to treat with the purpose of offering a great deal of physical relief for pain and suffering. In addition to providing analgesics and sedatives, he must be prepared to offer much support aimed at relieving feelings of discouragement and uselessness, as well as feelings of being a burden. This means that he may have to take a much more active part than he might generally, by actually entering into the patient's environment and dealing with relatives and friends in helping to reestablish fading environmental bonds and lost feelings of usefulness and belonging.

The analysis of genuine suicide notes in terms of Menninger's hypothesis is of course only one of many possible approaches to these data. Another quite different approach is that which analyzes the *logical* or *semantic* qualities exhibited in the suicide notes, specifically the formal aspects of the logic involved.

On superficial thought, one of the outstanding characteristics of the suicidal act is that it is illogical. Yet one can take the position that there is an implicit syllogism or argument in the suicidal act. Although we cannot be sure that our logical reconstructions of suicidal logic are correct, it remains that the suicidal person behaves *as if* he had reasoned and had come to certain —albeit generally unacceptable—conclusions.

In formal or symbolic logic, there are a number of errors, called logical fallacies, which can be made. One of many types of fallacy is illustrated in the deductive logic implicit in schizophrenic thinking—first described by Storch [10] and then by von Domarus [11] and recently called paleologic by Arieti [1]. In normal logic, before identity can be made, certain conditions have to be satisfied. Paleologic sweeps aside these conditions and arrives at fallacious identities. Two examples of this type of reasoning, one from Arieti and one from Bleuler, can be given: (1) "Switzerland loves freedom, I love freedom, therefore I am Switzerland"; and (2)

"The Virgin Mary was a virgin, I am a virgin, therefore I am the Virgin Mary." [2]

Another type of logical fallacy, other than the deductive fallacy, wherein the error is dependent on the form of the argument, is the semantic fallacy, wherein the error is dependent on the meaning of the terms occurring in the premises or conclusion. Our examination of the suicide notes indicated that the fallacies of reasoning committed were primarily of this latter type. An example of a semantic fallacy is as follows: "Nothing is better than hard work, a small effort is better than nothing, therefore a small effort is better than hard work." Here the fallacy is not dependent upon the form of the argument but rather on the ambiguous meaning of a specific term, namely "nothing." Another example of a semantic fallacy, this time with suicidal content, is as follows: "If anybody kills himself then he will get attention, I will kill myself, therefore I will get attention." Deductively, this argument is sound, but the fallacy is concealed in the concepts contained in the word "I." Here the logical role of this pronoun is related to the psychology of the conception of the self.

We see then that in addition to what has been described as the logic of the normal and the paleologic of the schizophrenic, we have the reasoning of the suicidal. We call this type of thinking "destructive logic" or "catalogic." It is destructive not only in the sense that it disregards the classical rules for semantic clarity and formal reasoning but also in that it destroys the logician.

---

[2] These two syllogisms illustrate the process of identification in terms of the attributes of the predicate—as indicated by Arieti—but it can be pointed out that they can be seen in quite another way: that is, they also demonstrate straightforward Aristotelian reasoning if one only supplies the missing or suppressed premises. What these two syllogisms have in common is that the focus of attention is narrowed to only one attribute of class. Consider: If Switzerland were the *only* class that loved freedom, and if I loved freedom, then I would indeed have to be Switzerland. Psychologically, this narrowing of focus may reflect the difficulty that the emotionally disturbed person has in grasping other than what is immediately before his mind.

As a result of our analysis of the semantic qualities exhibited in the suicidal notes, it appeared that the logic could be understood best in terms of two implied components of the "I" or the self. The first we call I_s. This is the self as experienced by the individual himself. I_s refers to the person's own experiences, his pains and aches and sensations and feelings. He says in the note "I can see you crying" (and adds by implication from the tenor of the rest of the note, "I'll be glad this is going to trouble you"). The second aspect of the semantic self is called I_o. This is the individual as he feels himself thought of or experienced by others. This would be what he considers his reputation, based on other people's attitudes, other people's actions, ideas, and remarks; that is, what others think of him. This comes out in the notes in the extreme concern with practical and trivial details such as the repair of the automobile, the distribution of goods, the canceling of appointments, etc. The suicide says in effect, "I_o will get attention, that is, certain other people will cry, go to a funeral, sing hymns, relive memories, etc.," but he also implies or states that, even after death, I_s will go through these experiences, that is, "I will be cried over, I will be attended to," as though the individual would be able to experience these occurrences. This is the heart of the semantic fallacy or ambiguity.

More accurately, it is not a fallacy in the words of the reasoning, but rather it is a fallacious identification. Hence we call it a "psychosemantic fallacy." Parenthetically, we believe that this confusion or ambiguity might indeed occur whenever an individual thinks about his death, whether by suicide or otherwise. It may arise because an individual cannot imagine his own death, his own cessation of experience, a state where there is no more I_s after death.

Our perusal of the suicide notes in terms of logical analysis led to the tentative formulation of four types of logical processes. These, together with the personal characteristics of each type and the implications for the treatment, are indicated in Table 4.

TABLE 4

OUTLINE OF TYPES OF SUICIDE AND SUGGESTED TREATMENTS

Logical Type	Personal Characteristics	Psychological Label	Suggested Mode of Treatment
LOGICAL. The process of reasoning is acceptable according to Aristotelian standards.	Individuals who are typically older, widowed, and who are in physical pain.	*SURCEASE SUICIDE.* Person desires surcease from pain and reasons that his death will give him this.	Treatment is in terms of giving freedom from pain through use of analgesics and sedatives, and providing companionship by means of active milieu therapy such as clubs, activities, home placement, etc.
PALEOLOGICAL. Makes logical identifications in terms of attributes of the predicates rather than of the subjects.	Individuals who are delusional and/or hallucinatory.	*PSYCHOTIC SUICIDE.* Not all suicides are psychotic, but psychoses can be unpredictably suicidal.	Treatment has to do primarily with the psychosis and only subsequently with suicidal tendencies (if remaining). Treatment should include protecting the individual from his own impulses.
THANATOLOGICAL. The logical or semantic error is in the overemphasis on the self as experienced by others.	Individuals whose beliefs permit them to view suicide as a transition to another life or as a means of saving reputation.	*CULTURAL SUICIDE.* The belief concerning the concept of death in relation to the self plays a primary role in the suicide.	Treatment has to do with deeply entrenched religious and cultural beliefs and would have to deal with and clarify the semantic implications of the concept of death.
CATALOGICAL. The logic is destructive. It confuses the self as experienced by the self with the self as experienced by others.	Individuals who feel lonely, helpless, fearful, and pessimistic about making meaningful personal relationships.	*REFERRED SUICIDE.* The confusion in logic and in the psychological identification is "referred" (like referred pain from other root problems).	Treatment would consist of psychotherapy wherein the goal would be to have the patient establish a meaningful, rewarding relationship so that his search for identification would not be barren.

299

Some experimental support for our hypothesis about the special semantic and psychological confusions of the suicidal person— especially his confusions relating to his concept of the self revolving around the multiple logical components and meanings contained in the pronoun "I"—is indicated in a study reported elsewhere [9] which applied Mowrer's Discomfort-Relief Quotient [6] to thirty-three pairs of genuine suicide notes and elicited suicide notes, the latter obtained from matched nonsuicidal persons.

One may speculate about the psychological significance of the confused suicidal logic. It may well be that the confusion relating to the subject of the premise manifested by the suicidal subject reflects his problems which have to do primarily with identification. It is this fallacious identification between the self as experiences by the self (I_s) and the self as it feels itself experienced by others (I_o) which enables the suicide to accept erroneous premises and invalid conclusions and which accounts for his making his tragic deductive leap into oblivion.

References

1. Arieti, S.: *Interpretation of Schizophrenia,* New York, Robert Bruner, Inc., 1955.
2. Farberow, N. L.: "Personality patterns of suicidal mental hospital patients," *Genetic Psychol. Monographs,* **42:** 3–79, 1950.
3. Farberow, N. L., and E. S. Shneidman; "Attempted, thtreatened, and completed suicide," *J. Abnormal Social Psychol.,* **50:** 230, 1955.
4. Landsberg, P. L.: *The Moral Problem of Suicide,* Philosophical Library, Inc., New York, 1953.
5. Menninger, K. A.: *Man Against Himself,* Harcourt, Brace and Company, Inc., New York, 1938.
6. Mowrer, O. H.: *Psychotherapy: Theory and Research,* The Ronald Press Company, New York, 1953.

7. Shneidman, E. S., and N. L. Farberow: "Clues to suicide," *Public Health Repts.* (*U.S.*), **71:** 109–114, 1956.

8. Shneidman, E. S., and N. L. Farberow (eds.): *Clues to Suicide,* McGraw-Hill Book Company, Inc., New York, 1957.

9. Shneidman, E. S., and N. L. Farberow: "Some comparisons between genuine and simulated suicide notes." *J. Gen. Psychol.,* **56:** 251–256, 1956.

10. Storch, A.: *The Primitive Archaic Forms of Inner Experience and Thought in Schizophrenia,* Nervous and Mental Disease Monographs no. 36, Nervous and Mental Disease Publishing Company, Washington, 1924.

11. von Domarus, E.: "The Specific Laws of Logic in Schizophrenia," in J. S. Kasanin (ed.), *Language and Thought in Schizophrenia,* University of California Press, Berkeley, Calif., 1944.

18 CURT P. RICHTER

The Phenomenon of Unexplained
Sudden Death in Animals and Man*

My interest in the phenomenon of unexplained sudden death stems from a series of chance observations on the behavior of the common laboratory rat.[1]

In the summer of 1951, Dr. David Mosier and I had just completed some experiments which showed that rats will not only accept diets with a very high salt content (25% to 35%) but will thrive on them, providing they are able to drink 50 cc. to 60 cc. of water per gram of ingested salt [12]. When I mentioned these results to Dr. Gordon Kennedy, a visiting Englishman at the Hopkins, he decided to measure the sodium output of some of these rats on the very high salt diets. To collect urine we placed each rat in a small cage over a collecting funnel and gave it access to a food cup (filled with powdered food) and a graduated inverted water bottle. In order to prevent food spillage into the funnel, the food cup was placed in a narrow passageway well beyond the edge of the collecting funnel. Three rats were used for these pilot experiments.

---

* Reproduced by permission from a chapter in *Physiological Bases of Psychiatry,* compiled and edited by W. Horsley Gantt, 1958. Courtesy of Charles C Thomas, Publisher, Springfield, Ill.

[1] These studies are now being carried out under grants from the U.S. Public Health Service and the National Science Foundation.

Even though the food cups were further and further removed from the cages, we found food was still being spilled into the funnels. This, of course, obscured the urine-collecting records. It occurred to us that the rats must be carrying the food on their paws and whiskers. To minimize this, the hair and whiskers of each of the 3 rats were trimmed with electric clippers. Almost at once one of the 3 rats began to behave in a very peculiar way. It pushed its nose into the corners of the cage and into its food cup incessantly with a sort of cork-screwing motion. It was still doing this when we left the laboratory four hours later. The next morning it was dead and neither the cause nor the direct mechanism of death could be determined by careful autopsy. The others were alive, and from our experience with many other rats on these high salt diets we knew that this rat should have lived a long time. This observation was "salted away" so to speak, for later consideration.

Two years later, while studying the effects of swimming stress on rats, we had occasion to recall this observation. In these experiments we were swimming rats in glass jars while exposing them to a jet of water in the center of the jar.

Figure 1 shows a photograph of a battery of such jars. The jet served two separate purposes: (1) it kept the water in constant turmoil, thus precluding any floating rests for the swimming rats, and (2) it maintained a constant temperature, which could be adjusted within ±2° at any level between 60° and 115° F. The length of time the rats survived was a definite function of water temperature, as may be seen in the following graph which shows the average swimming time for 120 adult rats. At the lower temperatures, 60° to 75° F., the rats swam only 60 minutes or less. As the temperature increased, swimming time increased until at 95° F. it reached a peak average of 62 hours. As the temperature was increased above 95° F., the swimming time decreased at a rapid rate.

It occurred to me then to determine what effect, if any, trimming of the whiskers would have on the rat's swimming perform-

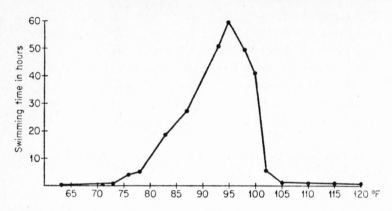

ance. Would the rat show the cork-screwing motion or any other unusual behavior?

These observations were started with 12 tame rats from our colony. They were swum at a water temperature of 95° F. at which our rats swim on the average 60 hours and some rats as long as 81 hours.

After its whiskers had been trimmed, each rat was placed in the turbulent bath. The first rat tested swam around excitedly on the surface for a few seconds, dove to the bottom, obviously searching for an avenue of escape, then continued to swim around below the surface until it suddenly stopped swimming and died. Autopsy revealed no signs of drowning. One other rat showed a very similar behavior and also died within minutes. The remaining rats were still swimming actively at the end of 6 hours when they were removed. They undoubtedly would have swum for many hours more. None of the 12 rats showed the peculiar cork-screwing motion noted in our original observation.

Wild rats were also being used in our stress experiments, and these were then tested in the same way. By wild rats I refer to rats that had been trapped from the streets and from alleys and cellars and kept in captivity for some time.

1

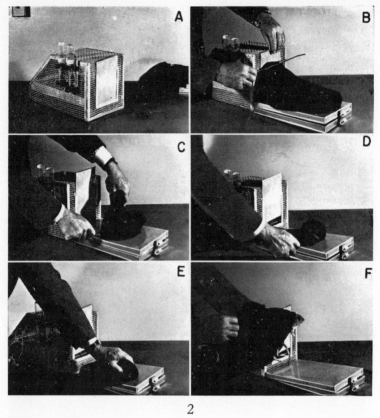

2

All 34 wild rats tested behaved in much the same way as did the two domesticated rats and died in 2 to 8 minutes, in most instances again without any detectable signs of having drowned.

It appeared then that the loss of the whiskers—and the resulting deprivation of one of the chief sources of sensory contact with the outside world—constitutes a great stress, enough to end the rat's life. However, when in further experiments it was found that some wild rats with intact whiskers died in the same mysterious manner, it became clear that we were dealing with a more general phenomenon of unexplained sudden death.

At about this stage in these observations my attention was called by Philip Bard to a paper by Walter Cannon on *Voodoo Death* [1] in which other instances of sudden unexplained death in man and animals were described. Cannon had observed that decorticated cats in a constant state of rage often died in a few hours. The results of studies made by himself and co-workers indicated that the cats died as a result of a combination of overstimulation of the sympathico-adrenal system and inhibition of outward expression of the emotions.

When Cannon learned about the phenomenon of "voodoo" death in man, well known to anthropologists, he decided that it bore a close resemblance to the rage death seen in his decorticated cats. Observations made on primitive peoples all over the world showed that under the influence of a "voodoo" or "hex," previously apparently entirely healthy individuals may die within less than 24 hours despite all efforts to save them. He suggested that these individuals might be dying from an excessive stimulation of the sympathico-adrenal system which was responsible for the death of his decorticated cats.

The reading of Cannon's paper stimulated me to start a search on a wider basis for an explanation of the sudden unexplained deaths of our rats. This search has led me to new and unexplored fields.

Since the laboratory phenomenon is so much more common in

the wild rat, it is necessary at this point to state more in detail what is meant by the wild rat.

This animal is the wild Norway ancestor of all of the ordinary tame domesticated rats seen in laboratories. It is the most common wild rat in the world. It is very fierce, aggressive, suspicious, and makes prompt use of every opportunity to escape. Its adrenals are much larger than those of the domesticated rat, and it differs in a number of other ways—anatomical, physiological, and behavioral—from its domesticated descendants. By means of specially designed traps it can readily be captured in the yards, alleys, and cellars in cities and in and around barns or farms [11].

Even after months in the laboratory the wild rat is ever ready to inflict serious bites and so cannot be handled without the use of special devices—that is, if anesthetics are to be avoided and it is not to be injured.

Thus, it becomes necessary to describe in some detail the various steps involved in transferring the wild rat from its cage to the swimming jars. Figure 2 shows the various steps involved in this process. To remove the rat from its cage (A), which has a sliding door at one end, the open end of a lightproof black bag is placed over this sliding door (B). When the slide is removed the rat sees the black hole—an avenue of escape—and quickly runs into the bag, where its escape is prevented by placing a rod over the open end of the bag (C). By means of the rod the rat is gradually forced to the bottom of the bag where a firm hold can be obtained on its head and body (D). It is held by placing the thumb and forefinger of one hand around the jaws, while the body is held by the other fingers and the entire palm (E). The bag can then safely be peeled back exposing the head for trimming the whiskers (F). After this, the rat can be directly released into the swimming jars. So far we have handled several thousand rats by means of this device and no rat has ever attempted to bite through the bag.

On the basis of Cannon's conclusions and under the influence of the current thinking about the importance of the part played by the adrenals and sympathetic nervous system in emotional states, we naturally looked first of all for signs of sympathetic stimulation—especially for tachycardia and death in systole.

Electrocardiographic records were taken of the heart rate from the time the rats were first restrained until they died. Sharpened copper wires dipped in electrode jelly served as electrodes. These were inserted under the skin of the two fore-legs and one hind leg and held in place with plastic elastic tape. The electrodes were connected with the electrocardiometer by fine insulated wires which still permitted the animal full freedom of movement in the water. Surprisingly, the records under water were identical with those in air. The preliminary observations indicated that the rats usually died as a result of a slowing of the heart rather than an acceleration, though in some instances the heart rate increased immediately after the rats were restrained, then decreased. In others it decreased at once. At autopsy the heart was found to be filled with blood.

The analysis of the various maneuvers seems to indicate that the three important steps are restraint, trimming of the whiskers, and confinement in the glass jar with exposure to the water jet.

A few of the possible effects of restraint which we are now working on are: (1) Vasodepressor reaction which could result from the rush of blood to the muscles—where it is needed for fight or flight—and then the blocking of any actual movement and of the possibility of getting the blood back into circulation [5]. This can result in a reduced cardiac output and cerebral hypoxia. None of our animals actually seemed to faint, but many of them became quite limp at one stage or another of the restraint. (2) A vasodepressor response to holding of the breath, a common occurrence. This could produce a great increase in the thoracic and intra-abdominal pressure, thus preventing the return of blood to the heart. This would be a Valsalva effect. (3) Vagal inhibition of the type first described by Gowers [6] and later by Lewis [8].

It is well known that fright, pain, and a great variety of disturbing stimuli may stop the heart through vagal inhibition.

Further, vagal stimulation may affect not only the heart but have a direct effect on other processes controlled in the brain—both in the cortex and in the lower centers, perhaps most likely in the hypothalamus or reticular formation.

Immersion of the rats in warm water may also be expected to produce vasodepressive effects. The warm water may induce a marked peripheral vasodilatation and so draw blood away from the head or brain.

It is well known that diving greatly reduces the heart and respiratory rate of many other swimming animals [7].

Thus, we recognized that many of the possible reactions to restraint or to immersion in warm water would produce effects opposite to those which would be expected to follow sympathico-adrenal stimulation.

So far, a few wild rats pretreated with atropine have not shown the death response.

Of interest here is that domesticated rats which only rarely show the death response can be made to show it quite regularly by injection of minute amounts of cholinergic drugs—Mecholyl, physostigmine, and morphine—which in general have a parasym-pathetico-mimetic effect. Thus, 1/30 of the LD50 of morphine suffices to bring out the death response of the domesticated rats. Their behavior then is the same as that of the wild rat.

That the wild rats may be more sensitive than the domesticated rats to vagal stimulation is possible since it is known that wild animals in general are more vagotonic than domesticated animals, that vigorous animals or persons are more vagotonic than less vigorous ones [2].

This sudden-death phenomenon may however be considered also as a reaction at a much higher level of integration. The situation of these rats is not one that can be resolved by either fight or flight—it is rather one of hopelessness: being restrained in the hand or in the swimming jar with no chance of escape is a situation against which the rat has no defense. Actually, such a reaction of apparent hopelessness is shown by some wild rats very soon after being grasped in the hand and prevented from moving. They seem literally to give up.

Interesting evidence showing that the phenomenon of sudden death may depend on emotional reactions to restraint or confinement in glass jars comes from the observation that after elimination of the hopelessness the rats do not die. On several occasions we have immersed rats in water and promptly removed them. The animals quickly learned that the situation was not actually hopeless and so became aggressive and tried to free themselves or escape and showed no signs of giving up. Such conditioned rats swam on the average 40 to 60 hours or more. Once freed from restraint in the hand or confinement in the glass jar, speed of recovery is remarkable. A rat that would quite certainly have died in another minute or two becomes normally active and aggressive in only a few minutes.

Still further evidence comes from the observation that so far Thorazine has prevented the appearance of the death response in a number of wild rats—about half of the rats tested with Thorazine survived; and removal of the amygdaloid complex which tames the wild rats has prevented the appearance of the death reaction in a few rats.

Restraint alone rarely kills a rat; immersion in the swimming jar and exposure to the jet rarely kills any rats nor does trimming of the whiskers. It seems to be the combination of the reactions to the various stresses in rapid succession that produces the phenomenon with regularity in all the wild rats.

Sudden-death reactions have been observed in a number of other species of animals—again almost without exception in the wild form.

It is well known that the European wild rabbit succumbs quite readily in captivity or when handled. Hares in this country also have been reported to show this phenomenon. Recently captured mice have been known to die in handling. It has been reported that shrews die in response to restraint or even sudden noises. Mink are known to die in response to a variety of disturbing stimuli.

There are many reports of sudden unexplained deaths of wild animals in zoos. In one of our large zoos a musk ox died in a few minutes after having been immobilized to have his hooves trimmed; a chimpanzee died under restraint, likewise a puma.

In another large zoo a variety of animals died as a result of being changed from one cage to another or being exposed to disturbances from building operations going on in adjoining cages —10 animals; 4 otters, 3 mink, 1 European lynx, 1 cheetah, 1 serval died within a few hours after having been transferred to new exhibition sites. Death of a caracal followed a fight with cage mates, although its injuries were limited to superficial scratches. An arctic fox died after having shown moderate excitement over repair of an adjoining cage. An otter and a raccoon were found dead in unaccustomed cages [3].

A similar phenomenon has also been described in a variety of birds. Oscar Riddle who has had much experience with pigeons told me about the following experience. It seems that for weighing pigeons he had used a special form of immobilization. None of the thousands of tame domesticated pigeons had ever shown any untoward effects as a result of the process. In contrast 3 out of 5 wild pigeons received from Peru died while being put on the scales. Wild pigeons die very readily when put under ether anesthesia [10].

I understand that it is a common experience among bird banders to have wild birds die in their hands during the banding.

I understand also that some species of fish are said to die sudden deaths when restrained.

Many instances of sudden death are known **in man—apart** from the observations reported by Cannon.

A parallel to the hexing or "conjuring" as it is called, has been reported among the Negro population in southern states in this country. Of interest here is that just as in the case of the rats the victims recover almost at once when rescued—even though in only a short time they would have died. Also as in the rat, it appears to be a one-time response—once a person survives he never again can become a victim of hexing.

Nor is sudden death limited to primitive, and thus presumably easily alarmed, populations: the medical literature is filled with reports of instances of sudden death, occurring under a great many different conditions and in individuals of all ages. Death as a result of fright, sight of blood, hypodermic injections is well known. It is true that in some instances autopsy has revealed previously unsuspected heart defects or other pathology. However, in some instances, no pathology was found on extensive and thorough post mortem examinations.

Reports of coroners always include a fair percentage of unaccountable sudden deaths. Dr. R. S. Fisher, coroner of the City of Baltimore, told me that every year men die after suicidal attempts when the skin has scarcely been scratched or only a few aspirin tablets have been ingested.

During the war a number of unaccountable deaths were reported among soldiers in the Armed Forces in this country. These men died at a time when they apparently were in good health; at autopsy no pathology could be uncovered [9].

Sudden unexplained deaths of asthmatics have also been reported [4].

In most of these instances it appears that the patients have died as a result of increased vagus activity rather than of sympathetic overactivity as was also true of our wild rats.

Some of these instances seem best described in terms of hopelessness—literally a giving up when all avenues of escape appeared to be closed and the future holds no hope.

I should also like to mention a number of instances that have been brought to my attention, in which individuals in a hopeless situation died a slower death—over a period of weeks or months. Whether these involve the same mechanisms as those present in the sudden death we do not know. We are now attempting to reproduce these deaths by prolonging the various maneuvers involved in the death response of the rat—restraining them over a longer period of time and confining them in the swimming jar with less-strong jet pressure.

In the patients just as in the rats we see the possibility that hopelessness or death may result from the effects of a combination of reactions—all of which may operate in the same direction.

Thus, in summary, attention has been drawn to the phenomenon of unexplained sudden death of animals and man. It was shown that this phenomenon can be studied under experimental conditions in the Norway rat, especially the wild form. At present it appears that death results from an excessive stimulation of the vagal system, but the results are still in a too preliminary stage to permit any definite conclusions to be drawn. The sympathico-adrenal system may also play a part; an excessive stimulation of both systems must be considered. From the psychological level some of the observations indicate that the rats as well as human beings die from a reaction of hopelessness.

REFERENCES

1. Cannon, W. B.: "Voodoo death," *Am. Anthropologist,* **44:** 169, 1942.
2. Clark, A. J.: *Comparative Physiology of the Heart,* Cambridge University Press, London, 1927.
3. Christian, J. J., and H. L. Ratcliffe: "Shock disease in captive wild mammals," *Am. J. Pathol.,* 1952, **28:** 725–737, 1952. (These authors believe that the deaths result from a hypoglycemia.)
4. Doust, J. W. L., and D. Leigh: "The interrelationships of emotions, life situations, and anoxemia in patients with bronchial asthma," *Psychosom. Med.,* **15:** 292–311, 1953.

5. Engel, G. L.: *Fainting: Physiological and Psychological Considerations,* Charles C Thomas, Publisher, Springfield, Ill., 1950.

6. Gowers, W. R.: *The Border-Land of Epilepsy,* The Blakiston Division, McGraw-Hill Book Company, Inc., New York, 1907.

7. Irving, L.: "The action of the heart and circulation during diving," *Trans. N.Y. Acad. Sci.,* [2], **5:** 11–16, 1942.

8. Lewis, T.: "Vagovagal syncope and carotid sinus mechanism, with comments on Gowers' and Nothnagel's syndrome," *Brit. Med. J.,* **1932, I:** 823–876.

9. Moritz, A. R., and N. Zamcheck: "Sudden and unexpected deaths of young soldiers," *A.M.A. Arch. Pathol.,* **42:** 459–494, 1946.

10. Personal communication.

11. Richter, C. P.: "Domestication of the Norway rat and its implication for the problem of stress," *Research Publs. Assoc. Research Nervous Mental Disease,* **29:** 19–47, 1949.

12. Richter, C. P., and H. D. Mosier, Jr.: "Maximum sodium chloride intake and thirst in domesticated and wild Norway rats," *Am. J. Physiol.,* **176:** 213–222, 1954.

PART 5

Discussion

19 GARDNER MURPHY

Discussion*

The organization of a symposium on the psychology of death and dying at the American Psychological Association Convention in 1956 was an event epitomizing a boldness, scope, and realism for which official American psychology may be grateful. The organizer of the symposium, Dr. Herman Feifel, who is likewise the editor of this book, has attempted to show in his own introduction the ambivalence and escapism of modern Western man regarding death and to show directions in which theoretical analysis and empirical material might help us to understand more fully those who are dying, those who, like ourselves, are more slowly approaching that inevitable moment; and those who, attempting to stand on an eternal pinnacle of timelessness, undertake to ask the meaning of death. Under this third caption, for example, should be included studies of the confrontation of death in literature and the arts, as well as in science and philosophy. Emphasis is rightly placed on the issue of gathering richer and fuller material from the individual's facing of death and the act of dying, as constituting central material without which all else is diluted and derivative.

Not all the present papers were actually presented at

---

* Chapter 15, The Doctor and Death, is not discussed because it was included after Dr. Murphy's discussion had been submitted.

the panel meeting mentioned above. The editor saw fit to cast his net more broadly for the sake of a more complete sampling of the range of realities. We have, therefore, more than the recognition of one physical meeting, rather, an attempt to get a broader view of what the psychological sciences can offer.

PART 1

It is interesting to see the patriarchal figure of C. G. Jung, the Nestor of analytical psychology, as the first voice in our symposium. Jung has always been a symbol of libido and of life and always a direct confronter of death symbolism and of death as reality. I was personally troubled that none of Jung's rich concreteness is given in his introductory words, which deal, rather, with generalizations about the first and last halves of life, which would, indeed, be difficult to verify in the experience of men and women carefully studied. Near the end, however, he begins to talk about those persons whose passage into the reality of death he has himself observed. Yet no confident conclusion is reached from the material which he presents, and we learn that the interpretation of the problem "exceeds the competence of empirical science," another of those generalizations which could best be tested by seeing what could actually be accomplished by empirical science. The courage, however, with which the facts of parapsychology are noted at the end and the directness of Jung's testimony to the reality of transspatial and transtemporal events, make one feel that there is youth here, despite the aforementioned patriarchal or Nestorian need for broad generalizations.

Dr. Wahl's testimony as a psychiatrist regarding the confrontation of death begins, as does Dr. Feifel in his introduction, with the helplessness of man who, otherwise glorying in his new knowledge and power, finds himself impotent in the face of ultimate reality. The issue is rapidly developed through a recognition of the fact that the effort to escape the facing of death may constitute a deep source of ill health—a generalization which, if true, might force not only upon patients, but upon their psychiatrists a more direct analysis of the pathology of such escape. The empirical material sought by Wahl lies primarily in the experience of the child. In terms, however, of the statement that "our magical feelings of omnipotence are our main defense against death anxiety," one would have preferred to see more specific research material offered. We are told of Freud's early discoveries and of the parallelism between the riddle of the Sphinx and the riddle of death, but one could wish that the material quoted from Sylvia Anthony and from the author's own observations in cases of suicide had been offered us here. Wahl concludes on the note, agreeing with Freud, that it would be well for us to be realistic and Spartan in the facing of death. This may seem like a self-evident truth in an era where escapism is damned and reality testing praised. One could hope, however, for a quiet little voice of empiricism which would attempt to find out under what specific conditions the facing of death can be constructed in mental health terms. Does Wahl mean that the fact has been established that *all* facing of death represents gains in mental health? Are there any examples where it has been constructive to belie, defy, evade, turn aside from, or just plain ignore death? Do we actually know enough about the psychology of death and its confrontation to know what is good mental health with reference to such issues?

As one passes here from *analytical* papers to *theological* papers, one passes from a deep labyrinth to a high mountain top; from the region of complex and intersecting pathways to a region of a driving wind. There may, indeed, be some opportunity to watch the surface guides upon which we rely for terrestrial navigation, but there is perhaps in places a degree of seeing too far and a bit unclearly. Dr. Tillich entitles his paper "The Eternal Now." In this we are immediately plunged into an act of prayer, defined as "elevating oneself to the eternal," and we learn, as if it were a Euclidian proposition, that "there is no other way of judging time than to see it in the light of the eternal." On the contrary, "as men, we are aware of the eternal to which we belong and from which we are estranged by the bondage of time." How does one know things like this? Indeed, how does one know the kinds of things the psychoanalysts have taught us? The conception of eternity is perhaps offered us as one by which we may lift ourselves out of time and therefore out of a universe in which death is real. But how this articulates with the need to understand death and its phenomena is not clear to this discussant.

As we come to Walter Kaufmann's chapter we enter expressly into the world of existentialism and death. If we are interested in existentialism, we find ourselves in the habit of beginning with Kierkegaard, digging beneath the level of philosophical abstraction and dealing empirically—James would say with *radical* empiricism —with the experiences of dying, of slaying, and being slain, as not only fundamental in an existentialist view of human life, but in a certain sense a quintessence of life itself, as if one had to say that life cannot be apprehended except in the act of participating in the death process.

This discussant would like to know why the existentialists cannot quite accept living itself, except as a preparation for or alternative expression to dying; why the John Donne and the Walt Whitman kinds of living reality cannot be accepted as real; and why it is that anxiety is regarded in some deep sense as a clue to reality or being, which joy or love cannot offer. This in itself is a cardinal problem for the psychology of attitudes toward death. I should like to see the screen turned around, so that instead of looking forever at the grim skeleton and crossbones and told that *this* is reality, I have a chance to look at the observer himself, regard him as the reality, and ask why skulls and crossbones are the chief realities *for him*. This would, for me, be the central psychological issue.

In this same context I am somewhat uneasy with the need of Kaufmann to set Heidegger in opposition to those who are simple, human, and reasonable. This implies value judgments rather than the effort to grasp what Heidegger seeks to express. The same holds for his comments on Camus. It may be true that Camus is less profound than John Donne, Walt Whitman, or Sigmund Freud, but the task, I think, should be to try to understand him.

For Herbert Marcuse, the primary fact in the experience of thoughtful men of the West relative to death seems to be the capacity to make death a fulfillment or consummation, a biological reality involving more than the sheer termination of life; the establishment of a dualism in which death both terminates and fulfills life. Conceptions of immortality, such as those derived from Plato, are, however, compared with more shadowy conceptions in which existence beyond death is left in uncertainty. It is doubtful whether death as an abstraction involving the negation of life can be equated in such fashion with death as a fulfillment of human existence through an eternity. This ambiguity of the concept of death, involving at the same time the negation of life and the eternal fulfillment of life, can only involve philosophical confusion and conceptions which simultaneously insist upon the end of life and upon the beginning of immortal reality. The psychologist may ask: What holds back the thinker, clogs the flow of thought, as such a dualism is confidently offered?

PART 2

One recovers the sense of reality in Maria H. Nagy's paper "The Child's View of Death." Here is the kind of rich psychological material which had been tentatively and sketchily hinted at in the early chapters and which bogged down in a series of conceptualizations in which it was not quite clear what material, in whose experience, was actually the basis for the generalizations.

It is unfortunately true that Nagy's material is limited in depth and in cultural perspective (Nagy does not seem to be aware that her data depend in any serious degree upon historical, sociocultural, or specific local conditions), but she does have her feet on the ground in dealing with real children and with real interpersonal communications—oral, pictorial, and verbal. The confusion between what happens to the body and what has happened to the soul or personality of the deceased person, conceived as continuing to exist, is clearly brought out in the excerpts from her material: "He cries because he is dead . . . he is afraid for himself." . . . "a dead person feels it if you put something on his grave . . . he feels that flowers are put on his grave. He hears everything. He would like to come out, but the coffin is nailed down." Nagy goes on to some sharply defined and limited generalizations. Children (of the latency or elementary school period) are clear about death, funerals, cemeteries, and coffins, but believe that the dead are "still capable of growth" and "they know what is happening on earth." Life for the dead is "limited, not so complete as our life." The child's literalism in understanding of religious instruction about death and heaven in conspicuous: "He lies for four days." "Why for four days?" "Because the angels don't yet know where he is. The angels dig him out, take him with them, they give him wings and fly away." "What stays in the cemetery?" "Only the coffin stays down there." At the same time there is magnificent elaboration, fantasy, and personal interpretation: "They take out the coffin for it to be there if somebody dies . . . they clean it up, good and bright . . . if it's a woman, she does the cleaning. If it's a man, then he'll be an angel. He brings the Christmas trees." There are interesting cross references here to concepts of death in other cultures.

Nagy goes on to a "stage 2: personification of death," which she regards as most characteristic in children between the ages of five and nine. Death is a separate person or is identified with the dead. Death "carries off bad children." He is "white as snow." "At night the real death came. It has a key to everywhere." The personification tendency seems similar to many primitive and literate personifications of benign and malignant forces. Some of the latency-age children have, in addition, clear conceptions of death as a kind of ghost; "death and ghosts go together, like fairies and angels."

In stage 3, beginning at age nine, death is viewed as the cessation of corporeal life: "it is like the withering of flowers," but with the recognition of a something beyond . . . "but the soul lives on." There is immense value in this direct introduction to children's ways of thinking and feeling about an experience which, at least for many of them at this age, is intensely real, and which however elaborated by fantasy, make-believe, play-acting, and sheer verbal dueling with the investigator, rings essentially true.

Nagy's chapter on the child is followed by Robert Kastenbaum's "Time and Death in Adolescence." He finds that the average adolescent's attitude toward death does not appear to belong to the structuring principle dominant at this point of his life, but to a second psychic organization. The adolescent seems to live in an intense present; past and future are relatively unreal. Not only death itself, but the remote future in general is devoid of significant positive values, and even the past is regarded as a vague and confusing place, where the adolescent is "none too sure of his personal identity." For a few, however, "the prospect of death is very much alive." Aging, it is held, will be a different process among such persons. There is likely to be less disorganization as the time between oneself and death is seen to diminish.

There follow some questions as to whether the vigorous association with the now, the good, and the self-fulfilling can be carried forward through life with an "anachronistic and inappropriate pattern of behavior," not adapted to the facing of death, or whether a "death-shaped time field produces a wise and valuable synthesis that could be achieved at no other time." The author concludes with emphasis on the likelihood of profound disturbances "as the reality of death increases through the years."

The chapter by Dr. Feifel, "Attitudes toward Death in Some Normal and Mentally Ill Populations," relates the denial of reality in some patients to a magical holding-back, if not "undo-ing," of the possibility of death, though pointing out that in broader perspective, existentialism and Christianity may find con-summation of the meaning of life in the fact of its termination. Research studies he is now carrying on reveal answers to the question "What does death mean to you?" which represent on the one hand the stoic acceptance of the inevitable, on the other, the "precondition for the true life of man." (The question itself aroused much anxiety, often being understood, especially among mentally ill patients, in terms of death by violence.)

To the question, "If you could do only one more thing before dying, what would you choose to do?", most of the mentally ill refer to social and religious activities; most of the others emphasize travel, new homes, etc. Regarding the age at which people think most persons least fear death, it is interesting to see that many name those who are over seventy, perhaps because fear of idle-ness and uselessness may be worse than fear of death. Most people hope that they can die peacefully, swiftly, with minimal suffering, and many hope to avoid the "fuss" which their own death would cause for others. Religious persons seem to be personally more afraid of death than those who are nonreligious. The penalties of dying, so to speak, are different for both groups. The belief that one will go to heaven does not necessarily entail absence of per-sonal fear of death.

The frequent need encountered among patients to talk about their feelings and thoughts about death makes Dr. Feifel wonder whether it is wise to close off the avenues which would permit this. There is much rational, as well as irrational, fear of loss of communication. One may, indeed, reactivate or intensify the dying person's fears, but one may do something worse by shutting off channels of personal communication. This is the entering wedge for a broad plea for readiness to communicate freely re-garding death.

Interviews with those facing death found that it was not *what* the patient was told, but *how* it was done that counted. Patients could face death if they were properly prepared for this. There are, however, definite individual differences related to psychological maturity, prevalent coping techniques, the nature of the organic process, and the attitudes of the physician and other significant persons. Death can mean different things to different persons. The paper concludes with an interesting series of suggestions for research on individual and situational factors responsible for the very wide qualitative differences in the attitudes of individuals.

PART 3

Among a group of chapters headed "Death Concept in Cultural and Religious Fields," Frederick J. Hoffman's chapter, "Mortality and Modern Literature," begins with the fact that the "disposition toward death is in twentieth century literature different from that of any other," because of impersonal killing and because the "balance of expectation" in the human physical and spiritual organization has been considerably changed: mysteries have tended to shrink. Death served a place in the moral economy, and the thought of death was less unpleasant, because it was the entrance into eternity. A moral and intellectual imbalance have resulted. As the belief in immortality becomes less certain, more attention must be paid to time, and "time achieves a spatial quality." Literature must begin to emphasize the spatial quality of time, rather than sheer succession.

In a chapter which is philosophically rich, verbally facile, and contentwise enormously demanding upon those not steeped in modern literature, emphasis is placed upon *grace, violence,* and *self.* Grace is a condition of assurance of immortality; personal immortality may be dissolved into social immortality. The past and present miseries point to future joys. The death died today symbolizes and introduces tomorrow's grace; death is, moreover, a means of purification. Immortality is gained at the expense of life.

But physical law, rather than grace, dominates the world, and the intuitive link between the need for felt violence and the observation of violent death is shattered by a sense of causelessness. One might well ask whether there has really been change since the Greek conception of "blind faith" or the irrationalities of both gods and men as pointed out by E. R. Dodds in *The Greeks and the Irrational;* but the canvas on which Hoffman is working is full of august and beautiful materials, and the critical task of evaluating it is beyond this discussant.

Emphasis then shifts to the role of the self in modern literature, with emphasis upon existentialism, the stream of thought, and the religious struggle to reconstitute the importance of selfhood— much too brief, and leaving us uncertain as to the manner in which the struggle for fulfillment of selfhood may be compensatory for a lost immortality.

Carla Gottlieb's chapter, "Modern Art and Death" compares the preoccupation with death in the epoch around A.D. 1400—the epoch of plague epidemics—with the period of the last hundred years. This modern period is said to reject the importance of death, reflecting a need to counteract the dejection caused by the dreadful events of recent years. A painter must soothe.

She goes on to a comparison of representations of death through symbolism and the representation of death in its concrete reality, noting that the former, more abstract portrayal is not characteristic of the last hundred years. She emphasizes the role of symbolism: the skeleton, the scythe, the leafless tree, the vulture, the weapon, the clock. The composite in which the most intensely real aspects of death are combined with symbolism is appropriately noted in reference to Picasso's *Guernica,* and in similar vein, the representation of death in relation to dying societies as a reflection of despair or compensatory renewal of hope. She discusses with profuse and excellent illustrations the content and style of dominant works of art. Indeed, the canvas is so encompassing and detailed that it is difficult to discover a broad movement, if there actually is such a movement, during the hundred years in question. One wishes that there were *more* attempts at a pageant of historical drama, as suggested in the following: "We saw the nineteenth century withdraw from emotions and pose for one transitional moment on the crest of a wave of pure spectatorship, with Manet's *Funeral*. In contrast, the twentieth century turns toward the 'externalization of the invisible,' and we note the emotions of premodern art which had been banished during the second half of the nineteenth century." These modern emotions are "joys without causes" and "fears without causes."

The last two sentences before her conclusion interest me especially, coming as they do near the keystone position in this book which emphasizes the *need to face death*: "I have postulated that modern art keeps away from the portrayal of death. Even where it does show death, modern art minimizes it. And why should it not do this? It is life that is important; not death."

Yes, there is a need to face death; also a need to face away from it.

David G. Mandelbaum introduces us to the sphere of cultural anthropology by a vivid and concrete discussion of social uses of funeral rites. People must find a way of coping with the fact of death, closing ranks, maintaining solidarity, commemorating events formerly of intense importance to them, finding external expression for deep needs and deep conflicts.

He begins with the funeral ceremonies of the Kotas of South India. Through it all is the feeling that one must get back somehow to life, which has been interrupted, and likewise the reaffirmation of the social order, notably the kin relationship, impressively rehearsing "the proper precedence among the constituent parts of society." Proper performance of the funeral assuages grief and gives reorientation.

Other societies are compared with the Kotas with emphasis

upon similarities, especially the assistance of the spirit in making its departure and helping the bereaved through the period of shock. The Hopi, however, are cited as an interesting contrast, minimizing the event of death, avoiding all excesses, including those associated with grief: "If one must weep—Hopi parents have told their children—it is best to weep alone, outside the village, where no one can see." The anthropologist reminds us of the differences between those who deeply need to maximize and those who deeply need to minimize the reality of death. The chapter goes on to compare the wide social and personal differences in the confrontation of death among peoples who all overtly subscribe to the same religious faith, for example, Roman Catholicism. Comparison is likewise made with non-Christian groups.

Edgar N. Jackson's chapter, "Grief and Religion," is essentially a plea for recognition that "the emotions of the grief-stricken are too profound to be bound by limiting measurements, and the unbounded quality of the religious response serves an important emotional need in justifying such feelings at the time that it is directing them." We are made aware of the deep feelings, the normal work of mourning, and protection against the delayed reactions that come from unresolved grief.

The emotions of the grieving are said to cluster about incorporation, substitution, and feelings of guilt. Incorporation is symbolized by "Mother would want me to be brave, and so I will be brave." The mourner may actually identify permanently with the deceased, and needs basically to work through the period of mourning while preparing for the gradual loss of the intense feeling invested in the deceased person. One's emotional investment is put into the possessions, the room, the physical symbols of the deceased. This, too, must be worked through. The universally experienced guilt related to the ambivalent love relationship may lead to excessive idealizing of the deceased and poignant regrets, "if I had it to do over again." A ritual like the Mass may make possible the symbolic act of taking something into the self at a sufficiently abstract level while carrying out memorial acts symbolizing the action patterns enjoined by the deceased. There must be a framework available for the expression of the various unresolved feelings. And finally there must be reinvestment of the emotional capital. There must be both turning away and a turning toward, a kind of rejection of death and reaffirmation of life.

The chapter continues on to refer to types of human experience which transcend time and space, making brief reference to psychical research. (One should not overlook the serious and credible work now being done in this area.) Emphasis is placed upon the basic knowledge of relationships "not dependent upon space or time" . . . "at this point the mysticism of the philosopher of science who sees behind all of the dualisms of distinction a unifying force that reveals an ever larger truth, verifies the right of the soul to surmise and the consciousness to project a daring faith."

PART 4

Arnold Hutschnecker's chapter, "Personality Factors in Dying Patients," begins by noting that the dying patient's basic personality appears essentially unchanged. Nevertheless, a sense of defeat often accompanies terminal disease, and the patient's own view of his illness may assert itself. Most patients appear ready for death. Some exhibit episodes of excitement and rage, but apparently most dying patients are "glad to go." Empirical material on deaths from heart and cancer causes are contrasted, with some mobilization of fragmentary evidence of psychogenic factors in cancer. There are, additionally, some suggestions of passivity as a common feature in the cancer group, agitation and aggression in the cardiac group, and some observations that attempts to resolve life situations aggressively may express themselves in coronary attacks or cerebral hemorrhages. Although provocative, the present exploratory nature of the material makes one wonder about generalizations as this: "Whatever the cause of death in the patient may have been, we can say that by and large the man or woman who is about to die has made peace with himself." And in contrast to the frequently heard statement that those who have the least to live for are the most afraid of death, we are here told that the man "strong and mighty" seems to fear death most.

Gerald J. Aronson's chapter, "Treatment of the Dying Person," shrewdly begins with the recognition of the special strengths and weaknesses of the physician's point of view: how to help the patient be an individual human, even though gravely ill and dying. We know how dehumanizing illness is, even where death is not a probable outcome. The dying, moreover, may be envious of the living, and the living may chafe at the procrastination of the dying.

What shall the doctor tell his patients? Don't let hope die, but don't minimize the gravity of the situation. Treat them as Goethe suggested, as if they were what they ought to be. While being genuine and realistic about death, face the "psychological present," whatever it is, of the individual patient, and don't let him "sit around awaiting death." Face the fact of his physical disintegration, while continuing to accept him as a human being with an identity. There is a possibility of "massive depression or paranoid decompensation." Remember the Egyptians who took beloved objects with them into the tomb; remember that many believe intently that they are passing to a better world; maintain affection both with the patient and with those closest to him; there is much in just plain spending time with the patient. The physician, in other words, must use every resource, personal and professional, in helping his patient to face, to work through, to control, to remain human to the end.

The chapter, "Death and Religion," by Irving E. Alexander and Arthur M. Adlerstein stresses a possible relation between the likelihood of sudden death in the modern era and the problem of generalized uncertainty and anxiety. This paper undertakes to determine how the concept of death may affect a population of young people, especially in the context of a religious outlook. Male college students with strong religious beliefs were contrasted with those who were religiously indifferent. In interpreting some rather complex quantitative relationships resulting from their work, the authors conclude that "death anxiety is aroused much more rapidly and with less-direct stimuli in the nonreligious group." Moreover, "a word-association task that has death words imbedded in the word list is enough to raise the manifest-anxiety level of our nonreligious subjects, while face-to-face discussion about personal death is needed to set off this response in those of the religious group." In general, the similarities between the two groups are much more striking than the differences. Except for some concern about accidents, both groups expect to live long lives, and both seem rather unconcerned about death and about what may follow it; except insofar as there is among the religious group some feeling of anxiety as to what the beyond-death experience may mean.

The paper on suicide and death by E. S. Shneidman and Norman L. Farberow involves a comparison of data on subjects who commit suicide with data on various control groups, i.e., those who attempt suicide, threaten suicide, and are nonsuicidal. Its major aim was to develop hypotheses which might be tested in future studies. One of the outcomes of the psychological testing was the implication that "persons who later commit suicide may deny direct inquiry concerning suicidal intent, but will reveal depressive and dysphoric feelings and ideation."

An interesting part of the material gathered was a collection of 717 suicide notes of individuals who had killed themselves in Los Angeles County between 1945 and 1954—almost all of the notes that had actually been written. Karl Menninger's conception expressed in *Man Against Himself* is quoted to the effect that there are three components in the act of suicide—the wish to kill, the wish to be killed, and the wish to die. The conclusion drawn was that the wish to kill and the wish to be killed decreased with age, whereas the wish to die increased with age. Conclusions are reached regarding psychotherapy based upon the study of the individual patients in terms of discouragement, uselessness, and feelings of being a burden and, in general, the need of the therapist to enter actively into the patient's environment in dealing with relatives and friends in reestablishment of environmental bonds and lost feelings of usefulness and belonging. The article concludes with an outline of modes of treatment, detailed in terms of the psychodynamics of the individual's suicidal tendency.

An interesting paper, "The Phenomenon of Unexplained Sudden Death in Animals and Man," by Curt Richter notes a variety of interrelated stress conditions by which unexplained death in the rat may occur. Some relatively simple interpretations are discussed tentatively, and then the statement suggested: "This sudden death phenomenon may, however, be considered also as a reaction at a much higher level of integration." The animal cannot escape the water bath or other difficult situation by either fighting or fleeing. The situation is rather one of hopelessness, being restrained in the hand or in the swimming jar, with no chance of escape. The wild rats seem literally to "give up." When once hopelessness is removed, rats do not die. Animals which have had a chance to escape from immersion may be put back and swim 40 to 60 hours more. It is not restraint, immersion, nor trimming of the whiskers, which in itself kills most of the animals. There are comparable observations on many other animals and birds. Wild birds, for example, may die while their legs are being banded. And some similar material for man is obtained by "hexing" or "conjuring." If a man survives, he will never again become a victim of hexing. Unexplained deaths among men in the Armed Forces and deaths of asthmatics may belong in these categories. Again, the combination of factors leading to hopelessness may be essential.

PART 5

I am sure you have all been impressed, as I have, with the tremendous richness of the material and the inherent confusions that lie so deep in our culture and probably in most cultures regarding attitudes to the essential reality of death. To my mind come back the phrases attributed to Woodrow Wilson in the last moments of consciousness, "I am a broken machine. I am ready to go." This curious double talk is interesting; the self is the physiological organism and also a conscious entity conceived to be separate from such a physiological machine and capable of "going." A broken machine ready to be interred does not *go* in the sense in which Wilson used the phrase.

And I have also been impressed, in reading these stimulating chapters, with the cultural contradictions that lie even in the deepest scientific thinking about this whole matter. It seems to be assumed in our tradition that man is both terminated by death and capable of continuing in some other sense beyond death. Practically all human beings, as far as we know, that ever have existed as human beings on the face of the earth (in terms of archeological data or studies of anthropology) have assumed continuity beyond death. Now within the last few decades that particular conception has become so anachronistic that we can't quite understand why the deep ambivalence still continues. We ask: why is it that people expect something more than sheer, simple physical termination?

Reading these papers, I kept finding common factors which perhaps were not evident as they were presented. It seems to me that there are *at least* seven different systems of attitudes toward death that have become patent as these studies have been presented:

1. "Death is the end"—this phrase has been used several times. This is not in itself, as far as one can ordinarily see, any-

thing to be afraid of. One takes a journey and it's a delightful thing; then vacation is over and we go back to our work and we are sorry that something interesting has come to an end, but this is not an occasion of panic, at least not ordinarily. Why should the end be frightening?

2. Then there is fear of losing consciousness, which probably points toward various psychoanalytic realities. This is noted in the fear of being hypnotized, taking hypnotic drugs, of sleep (it is not uncommon to have people fight against falling asleep—the ordinary problem of holding out, fidgeting around, and then going to sleep suddenly rather than fading slowly out), and of what one might call psychological mutilation: fear of becoming insane with loss of ego control in the broad sense. Death represents the most complete illustration of this kind of loss of mastery, if you like, or loss of consciousness in its full sense.

3. Certainly fear of loneliness came in—the word was not used but fear was evident of separation from those among us with whom we share life—and, of course, the sometimes balancing factor of hope of regaining those who have crossed over.

4. Fear of the unknown in the broad sense—not any specific thing that one fears, but the Hamlet soliloquy or "undiscovered country" kind of thing.

5. Fear of punishment—this came out very strikingly in Feifel's material. In addition, I thought it was backstage in some of the other presentations. Fear of an end is quite different from fear of either temporary or permanent punishment. Fear of hell-fire for an eternity as portrayed by Dante, for example, is either in the conscious or near-conscious structure of a great many people and deep in the culture. I think this ought to be considered more. Its relation to fears of mutilation was briefly mentioned in terms of psychoanalytic concepts.

6. Then perhaps at a more immediate, earthy level—fear of what may happen to one's dependents.

7. Finally the fear of failure—the end of life is the last opportunity to do things. This means there won't be any more chance to do the things you hoped to do, and it can become emotionally a pretty harrowing kind of business.

So why don't we raise some questions of an empirical sort, perhaps along the lines of Dr. Feifel's study and some of the others, as to the relative weight of these seven or maybe seventy-seven different components? It is apparent that fear of death is not psychologically homogeneous at all, even in a narrowly defined cultural group. It is a very complex thing with conscious, preconscious, and unconscious aspects and all sorts of predetermining cultural, historical, and religious factors. It seems to me that one of the things this book has done extraordinarily well is to open up, as by a few sharp strokes here and there, a fascinating area which will show us that we have much more than a single problem emerging here. Hutschnecker's material from a medical point of view would likewise seem to point not only to the possibility that different personalities have different kinds of unconscious attitudes and demands, but that maybe the seven and others that I have tried to stress may all be present but in different weights and in different interactions.

It may well be that a condition of fear is often less impressive than a state of hope. We see this in many people, if life is complete or if there is nothing more they expect to do in this life. They don't pretend *necessarily* to know what's beyond, but there may be people who *do* pretend to know what is beyond and are absolutely certain of the particular kind of bliss which will then begin for all eternity. At least in the Protestant Christian denominations that I have an association with, the desire for death is a very common thing, particularly among people who have no area of usefulness immediately before them and who very literally ask God to "take them," and thank God for taking other people who have completed their lives, who have been very ill, and what not.

I would think that in a total pattern the fear of death, indifference to death, and the desire for death would all be brought into the total pattern for investigation.

Then I wondered why there wasn't more stress put on the ordinary, everyday psychology of perception and attitudes, since we are perceiving death and have attitudes toward death, as general background material. There was a Vassar professor of other years who came gasping into his class, slumped into his seat, and asked the young ladies to forgive him for a moment. As he choked, he found it difficult to speak—he had just seen a man killed. He gradually got his breath together again and managed to stand. Actually it wasn't just at the moment—he had taken a plane and saw this at the airfield just before he left. He had flown in from California, and it had been about five hours since it happened. As a matter of fact, it was the previous evening. He had stayed over on the way. The thing got to the point where it had lost all its meaning as anything to arouse affect, because after all, although the man had been killed, this point was displaced 3,000 miles in space and nearly twenty-four hours in time. Now I think this is the clue to a lot of our paradoxes. What is close in time and space, as we know from study of World War II and Korean conflict combat troops, is entirely different from what might happen next year or might happen in different life situations. These normal young men were by no means putting off death, uncertain about it. They were just plain scared. The great bulk of normal men who face death are terrified, and they have all sorts of different ways of controlling it—not always successfully, but some kind of coping techniques. I think if we just brought in the motion-picture camera and studied the degree of *nearness* or the degree of displacement of death from ourselves in terms of time and space, it would clear up a lot of the apparent contradictions. The Augustine experience is a very clear illustration. It is commonplace to have people regard death as a thing old ladies talk about;

then they lose a son and the world is a different world, and it takes on aspects which have not been evident in the ordinary questionnaire or psychiatric techniques that are used.

Additionally, I think relevance depends on the frame of reference used. We have a frame of reference which comes from nineteenth-century concepts of evolutionary theory, the physiological laboratory (from which psychological laboratories arose), and modern medicine; so-called materialistic (at least diffuse and nondualistic, nonidealistic) philosophies, which have led to *the view that investigation of what happens after death becomes a silly thing to do*. Therefore, from this point of view, not only is death by definition a termination of human existence but investigation of the question whether there is an existence beyond death becomes a way to waste one's time. Now this is a system of assumptions [2] which is highly structured among scientists, to an extent somewhat more than among most other intellectuals and persons with intellectual pretensions.

You get an interesting contrast if you take religious bodies as they cope with the problem of what may happen after death and those who study the behavior of these religious bodies. Take the spiritualist group, for example, who not only profess the usual confident Christian belief in eternal existence but who make use, according to their scheme, of techniques of communication, as they understand them. Many of these are, from a psychological point of view, credulous people, that is to say they regard as evidence what would ordinarily not pass as evidence. But it is also very interesting that the conception that there *could not* be any evidence worthy of consideration becomes a major tenet in the scientific approach, and therefore there is no possibility that these people that we are investigating might be doing something more than hallucinating when they make contact, as they think, with evidence of continuation beyond death. I was interested when A. A. Roback, an exceptionally scholarly and systematic man, brought together some years ago a perfectly tremendous bibliography on personality and character [4]. Frederic Myers, who was one of the great founders of the modern theory of the subconscious and of the nature of genius as involving subconscious and creative powers, wrote a tremendous two-volume work with hundreds of pages of documentary material, entitled *Human Personality and Its Survival of Bodily Death* [3]. In his annotated bibliography Roback commented that this was a more profound book than you would expect from its title. That is, when you talk about the survival of bodily death you cease to be profound. This is the frame of reference within which scientific psychology is attempting to move. Now psychical research is a name for those investigations which do make scientific pretensions which are concerned not with a priori likelihood of paranormal events but with the question of evidence. I shall give an illustration of the sort of thing that a psychical research investigation would want to try to find out about.

There was a teacher of an amateur astronomy class in Dallas by the name of Hayworth [1] who came home at midnight, sat on the bed a little while, thinking, when to his amazement, as he looked up, there was his father. He got up to shake hands with his father, who he noticed was dressed in work clothes, a caliper ruler in his coat. His father disappeared. The doorbell rang a few minutes later and a Western Union boy brought a message saying that his father had died that afternoon. He had died in California, the young man being in Dallas, and at the time of his death had on heavy work clothes with a caliper ruler in the outer coat pocket.

These cases are numerous. They have been elaborately studied. My question now is why, by definition, these happenings are all put into a category. Just as a reminder of the frame of reference in which we work, this might be almost anything: an odd hallucination, a prepsychotic manifestation, a coincidence—there are lots of names. Could it be contact between the dying father and the boy? This is one thing we know it *could not* be because as scientists, this has been ruled out as a possibility!

Now the issue is this: why do we assume, as we investigate attitudes toward death, that we have the parameters, the frame of reference for the investigation of death, and that it can only be that which the wheel has turned our way in the last few decades? Is there a possibility that general psychology would say, "We don't yet have a time-space reference for the study of death any more than we have a time-space reference for the study of personality"? We have a pretty good medical frame of reference; we have a pretty good historical frame of reference, but as for a personalistic frame of reference, that is, a sophisticated system of pegs which we could put down to define what we know and what we don't know about personality, we don't have one. Therefore, we find ourselves in the odd position of trying to use the concepts of personal maladjustment—psychosis, psychosomatic medicine, and so on, and the general system of ideas which are useful in psychology, to confine and order the whole deep, complex system of human beliefs and attitudes, expectations and frustrations as they relate to the termination of our physiological existence.

I would think that we face a great big job, and I think Dr. Feifel in organizing this has started us on our way. I would think, however, that perhaps the next few jobs to be done would all involve, in various ways, the study of the enormous complexity of this attitude syndrome, the enormous undefined factors—psychological, biological, cultural, and so on—which are in the background of the system of ideas, including the limitations of each one of us, depending upon his own special bias to the subject. The things that I have brought away from this book that are most precious to me are the empirical materials yielding light on the richness of factors which I though were rather thin and the ease of getting data, which I had formerly thought to be pretty near unattainable, together with the honesty and charm of much of the material presented. I believe, in other words, that this is an area in which human beings can give testimony and that the testimony is going to be profoundly useful to us.

REFERENCES

1. Case: *J. Am. Soc. Psychical Research,* **39:** 113–125, 1945.
2. Leuba, J.: *The Belief in God and Immortality,* Sherman Publishing Co., Boston, 1916.
3. Myers, F. W. H.: *Human Personality and Its Survival of Bodily Death,* Longmans, Green & Co., Inc., New York, 1903.
4. Roback, A. A.: *Bibliography of Character and Personality,* Sci-Art Publishers, Cambridge, Mass., 1927.

Name Index

Subject Index

Catalog

If you are interested in a list of fine Paperback
books, covering a wide range of subjects
and interests, send your name and address,
requesting your free catalog, to:

McGraw-Hill Paperbacks
1221 Avenue of Americas
New York, N.Y. 10020